Terry Frost

TERRY FROST

A personal narrative by David Lewis

With contributions by David Archer
Ronnie Duncan
Adrian Heath
Linda Saunders

Edited by Elizabeth Knowles

Foreword by Sir Alan Bowness

Lund Humphries

This paperback edition first published
in 2000 by Lund Humphries
Gower House
Croft Road
Aldershot
Hants GU11 3HR

Lund Humphries is part of Ashgate Publishing

Ashgate US office:
131 Main Street
Burlington
Vermont
05401
USA

Distributed to the book trade in North America by
Antique Collectors' Club:
91 Market Street Industrial Park
Wappingers Falls
NY 12590
USA

A catalogue record for this book is available from
the British Library

ISBN 0-85331-793-3 (paperback edition)
ISBN 1-85928-041-2 (hardback edition)

The jacket illustration has been created by the artist for
this volume.

First edition produced for the publishers by
John Taylor Book Ventures, Hatfield, Herts

Designed by Peter Guy

Made and printed in China by
Midas Printing Ltd.

Acknowledgements

The publisher and the editor have many people to thank
for their kindness in helping with this book. Firstly there
is David Lewis and the other contributors, David Archer,
Ronnie Duncan and Linda Saunders. Then there is
Roger Mayne, who has contributed a photo-essay as well
as numerous documentary photographs.

Those who have kindly given permission for texts,
poems and extracts include:
Faber & Faber
Yan Kel Feather
Nessie Graham
Corinne Heath
Patrick Heron
Rose Hilton
Norbert Lynton

We are grateful to those who have supplied or given
permission for us to take photographs, and to those
owners whose works have been illustrated. There are one
or two we have not been able to trace, to whom thanks
are also addressed.

We have had a great deal of help at all stages in the
preparation of this book and would like particularly to
express our gratitude to:
Peter Adie
Ricky Atkinson
John Austin
Tom Barrett
Tom Cross
The late William Desmond
Sarah Fox-Pitt
Matthew Frost
Simon Frost
Peter Griffin
Irving Grose
Norman Levine
The Mayor Gallery
Newlyn Art Gallery
Sheelagh and Finian O'Donnell
Susan and Dan Owens
The Tate Gallery Library and Archive
Mike Tooby of the Tate St Ives
Alan Wood
Philip Wright

Photography credits

The photography for this book was undertaken
by Colin Mills and illustrations of Terry Frost's
work are all by him, with the exception of those
on the following pages:
Arts Council, 105
Bob Berry, 11, 20, 35, 77, 112, 124, 139, 144, 149,
189, 226, 227
Laura Castro Caldas/Paulo Cintra, 106
D. Chesterman, 26
Jim Gorman, 61
Lancaster University, 18
Jorge Lewinski, 17, 27, 42, 46, 53, 60, 63, 67, 98,
120, 122, 185, 197, 198, 200
Alistair Peebles, 62, 183
Studio St Ives, 93
Tate Gallery, 19, 43, 51, 86
Tate Gallery St Ives, 47, 50, 54, 58
John Webb, 162

Contents

To Kathleen, first and foremost.

To the University of Life, Stalag 383,

the Denis Mitchell School of how to be helpful to others,

the True and One Life,

the Hesitant Footstep and consequent results.

Foreword

One associates Terry Frost's painting with the imagery of light: the radiant sun filling the canvas with warm colours. Or its reverse: the changing phases of the moon, from full to crescent, the coldness of moonlight on water, of light on snow, the enveloping blanket of a snowstorm – the absence of colour, all grey and white and black. The paintings radiate energy, filling our world. They are the opposite of self-effacing.

Of course the pictures are the man, as anyone lucky enough to know the artist personally realises at once. Though he can talk eloquently about his work, Frost doesn't need words to explain his paintings. They are an extension of his personality, and something completely natural and alive. This is what art is for Frost: a part of everyday life, something that should be relevant to everyone because of the great gift it offers. And yet this is unfortunately not the case. Perhaps Frost appreciates this better than most of us because he knows how nearly he missed out on being a painter.

In the pages that follow the artist talks of his ordinary working-class background in the English Midlands. In many ways it was a warm and supportive society, and yet it was one with no place for art. Despite his interest in drawing there would have been no possibility of young Frost breaking away from his background had it not been for the accident of war. A 26-year-old prisoner of war has time on his hands, and so Frost began making portraits of his camp comrades, more than two hundred of them, trying to please as critical an audience as one could hope to find.

By great good fortune there was a young artist in the prison camp who had the perspicacity to recognise Frost's potential. Adrian Heath, five years younger than Frost, played a crucial role in his early career, helping him to get an ex-serviceman's grant, a place at Camberwell Art School, and encouraging him to make his home in St Ives, in Cornwall.

These were the right decisions. Frost, the late starter, got a good training in what was probably the best art school in post-war London. He made some important contacts, and learnt to study and love the painting of the past. And in St Ives Frost found a community of working artists and the invaluable experience of seeing everyone's work at close quarters.

Away from London, both anonymous and cliqueish, Frost found himself able to make an important contribution to the revival and expansion of abstract art that was taking place in St Ives in the late 1940s and early 1950s. It is difficult now to appreciate quite how hostile towards abstraction the artistic climate in Britain was at the time.

With the patronage of the pioneers, Pasmore and Nicholson, Frost found that it was the abstract language of form and colour and light that he could use to express himself most naturally. Though far from insensitive to the world about him, he has remained faithful to abstraction since 1949. This partly explains why collage and construction have been such a constant in his work: paper, canvas, wood are more real than paint, and thus more abstract.

By the time of his Gregory Fellowship at Leeds in 1954–56, Frost was established as a leading spirit of his generation, painting pictures that spoke directly to an international audience. There was freshness and a *joie de vivre* and a freedom about his best work that was irresistible. His handling of certain forms, mainly the parts of a circle, and of the picture's structure was masterly.

Both before and after going to Leeds, Frost was active as a teacher. He happens to be a born communicator who has learned from his teaching, using it as a way of creative discovery. The teaching has in fact sustained the painting, but there is a conflict, and perhaps in mid-career Frost's reputation as a painter suffered, unfairly but understandably.

Frost has been sustained throughout his career by his love of landscape and of painting, and by his devotion to modern poetry which culminated in, not the *illustrations to* but the *illuminations of* Lorca which he made in the 1980s. It is a final turning to the warm sun of the Mediterranean that characterises the late work, filling the pictures with light and colour.

This book is a labour of love on the part of everyone involved in it, and particularly Frost's old and faithful friend, David Lewis, whose documentation through conversation has had such splendid results. But it is the illustrations that carry the text, reminding us of how much the artistic life of the country in the last half century has been enriched by Terry Frost's presence and his painting.

Alan Bowness

Publisher's Note

On the pages which follow texts are distinguished typographically, as follows:

The linking personal narrative by David Lewis is set in Ehrhardt roman.

Writings by Terry Frost (other than short quotations in the personal narrative) are set in Gill Sans.

Texts by other contributors appear in Ehrhardt italic.

Preface

Because I have known Terry Frost for so many years, beginning in 1948, I have taken on the job of writing a personal narrative as a way of stitching this scrapbook of his life and work together. Parts of the story I wasn't there for. I obviously wasn't there when Terry was growing up in Leamington, nor when he was a prisoner of war and began drawing and painting in Stalag 383. I was there in the Cornwall years, 1948 to 1955, and in Yorkshire from 1955 to 1957. I have also been around quite a lot in the later Cornwall years, from 1974 onwards. Fortunately Terry is a wonderful conversationalist and letter-writer, and he has also kept notebooks throughout his life so it has not been hard to use his own words. To give other perspectives, a well-known essay by Adrian Heath, whom Terry first met in the prison camp and who encouraged him to become a painter, has been included. The book also contains essays by David Archer on Terry's prints, by Ronnie Duncan on the Leeds years, and by Linda Saunders on his Lorca project. The aim has been to reflect the richness and diversity of a lifetime of work and, flying in the face of Terry's own trenchant assertion that paintings need no words, to provide some commentary on the art he has produced.

David Lewis

Newlyn

I like the sun, I'm always looking at it. I live where I can see it rise in the mornings and set in the evenings. And I can see the moon out over the water. The moon is another fascinating thing for me. Sometimes I see a black moon – that's marvellous, and a blue moon is wonderful. And it's all there. It's just a matter of letting yourself go and not having any inhibitions or pre-conceived ideas. You've always got to be ready to discover, to find out. There are always possibilities.[1]

Newlyn, where Terry Frost lives on the hilltop overlooking the town, is one of the last remaining fishing ports in Cornwall. It is a matter-of-fact, hard-working place. You won't find many yachts or pleasure boats among the fishing craft moored in ranks four or five deep along its quays.

By contrast with St Ives on the north side of the West Cornwall peninsula, known as Penwith, there isn't much in Newlyn for tourists to do. The biggest shop is the fishermen's cooperative. It offers oilskins, ropes, pulleys, and tall rubber boots. On the corner of the harbour where the main road from Penzance crosses a bridge to enter the town, you will find a couple of pubs, a post office, a fish and chip shop with unpredictable hours, and a little place where you can buy postcards and chocolate bars, and that's about it.

At first it may be a surprise that Terry Frost – whose work may seem to belong more to cities than to landscape – would live in a fishing town virtually as remote from London, New York or Paris as one could get. He has never lived for any length of time in a big city. He first went to St Ives in 1946 and apart from two fairly long periods when he lived in Leeds, from 1954 to 1957, and in Banbury, from 1963 to 1974, his life as an artist has been centred on West Cornwall. From 1974 onwards he has lived in Newlyn.

Over decades of steadily growing recognition he has become one of Britain's most prominent living abstract artists. The forms in his paintings are simple. Although they bear no easy reference to figurative sources, they are rooted in the visible world; his colours are generally bright and exhilarating, and often seem to spark off each other like electric charges. His paintings have little or no pictorial depth. On the contrary, they radiate energy outwards. When you walk into a room where there is a Frost on the wall, even if it's a very small Frost, the chances are that it will be the most dominant object. Its energy will come off that wall at you, exerting itself directly on the space you are in and on your sensibility. The sim-

plicity of the forms, the lack of depth, and the radiance of colour, scale and energy are the principal keys to the meanings of Terry Frost's paintings. There is nothing difficult about his work. The biggest difficulty is getting rid of the inhibitions that may prevent you from opening up to its messages.

His paintings and collages project a freedom and a joy of life, amounting often to sheer exuberance, but then, joy of life and exuberance are the qualities which most characterise the man. There is an openness and a freedom, an energy and a gentleness about him that are contagious. When one is with him the concerns of everyday life fall away like shackles undone. Through painting he has created a language to communicate these qualities. And the courage to project them is increasingly rare in a time when so much art reflects anguish, anxiety and oppression.

For over a century West Cornwall has been a place where artists have come to work. At the turn of the last century they came partly because of the quaintness of its little fishing ports huddled against the rage of the seas – but mostly because the life of the sea, the boats and the fisherfolk around the harbours, provided subjects that were at once humble and heroic. The language of art has changed quite a bit since then and today it is the texture of granite and the wind-scoured rhythms of the land which have attracted artists to Cornwall. Its westerly tip, the Penwith peninsula, has been the workplace of many important figures in British art in the past generation or two.[2] W. Barns-Graham, Sven Berlin, Naum Gabo, Barbara Hepworth, Patrick Heron, Roger Hilton, Peter Lanyon, Bernard Leach, Denis Mitchell, Ben Nicholson, Alfred Wallis, John Wells and Bryan Wynter are some of the names that spring to mind in addition to Terry Frost. When you add the poets W. S. Graham, George Barker, and Robin Skelton, the composer Priaulx Rainier, and the typographer Guido Morris, these decades become remarkable and unprecedented, culminating in the recent opening of the Tate Gallery St Ives.

Critics, who like things to be neat – or, as Ben Nicholson used to say, to 'tack down magic carpets' – have called that time and place in British art the St Ives School. There is no such thing as the St Ives School: it isn't that easy to tack down magic carpets. Other than a geography which has its own powerful characteristics, and the interweaving of lives and friendships extending back over forty years, there is little common ground in the artists' work. Terry Frost, like the others, has gone his own way with unabashed candour and vigour.

The symbolism of Terry Frost living in the furthest house on the edge of Newlyn can hardly escape you. It is also the highest up, where the winds blow free. It gives

The sun rising over the Lizard
photograph by Terry Frost

1. From the Milburn-Foster interview, see page 238

2. See the exhibition catalogue *St Ives 1939–64*
   Tate Gallery, 1985

him the isolation he needs to focus on his work. Yet Penzance station, with its direct line to London, is only a mile or so away.

There is an introverted, secretive quality to Newlyn. It is as though this town, with its granite cottages tightly massed up the steep hillsides above the harbour, wanted the rest of the world to keep away so that it can concentrate on its daily business of battling the ever-changing and often tumultuous sea. When you are down at Newlyn harbour, where the big fish-sorting sheds are, you will find only one narrow lane leading up into the town. Trewarveneth Lane is steep and winding. Cottages, built with hewn granite blocks, line each side. Their firmly shut front doors give nothing away. But every now and then as one climbs one may glimpse, through an iron gate and within a walled enclosure, an intimate garden filled with flowers.

Like the granite of the land itself, the townspeople to this day retain stern attitudes, dominated by Methodist chapels and an abiding sense of rectitude and sin. There is a toughness and a tradition of mutual support lying deep in these Cornish people, doubtless coming from uncounted generations who scratched a living from gale-swept farmlands and battled the surges of the sea in small boats; a hardness tempered by an unswerving warm-heartedness and generosity, once they have accepted you, that have sustained the artists who have come to coexist with them. And so, when you climb Trewarveneth, don't be surprised to find a narrow lane branching off it to the right called Beaux Arts, nor to find along it the old studios where Stanhope Forbes lived and painted a century ago, and where John Wells' and Denis Mitchell's studios are today.

Trewarveneth ends where it meets the road from Penzance that has also climbed sharply uphill from the little bridge at the harbour. Across the road Trewarveneth becomes Tredavoe Lane. As you continue to climb, the houses are newer. Their walls are no longer granite but stucco painted white.

Summer Collage
1976
acrylic and collage on canvas,
85 × 65 in, 216 × 165 cm
(the artist)

The studio

As you turn into Terry Frost's place from Tredavoe Lane the white stucco house is on your right and on your left is the studio, a shed-like building with big windows, which you reach through a wrought-iron gate and along a flagstone path bordered by flowers always in bloom, even in winter. Open the door of the studio and you are immediately assaulted by an anarchy of colour. Colour, for Terry, is everything. Where we see objects in the world around us, he sees colour. Colour determines form, rhythm and space.

The room is more than a studio; it is a laboratory-workshop. Against the far wall are racks of paintings and stretched canvases. In the middle is a huge table – a makeshift affair made up of hardboard panels laid on top of a couple of up-ended trunks and recycled table legs. Every square inch is covered with a profusion of works in progress, paintings and collages in the making, projects for lithography, designs for fabrics or ceramics.

The wall to the right is one huge window. On open shelves, incongruously mounted in front of this window, are bottles of paints, and jars of brushes with the light shining through them, and an untidy row of magazines and books each containing favourite pieces, particularly philosophy and poetry, Karl Popper and Bachelard's *Dream & Reverie*, and Eliot, W. S. Graham, Blake, Lorca. Also on these shelves are colour constructions, some of which rock back and forth when you set them in motion. Below the shelves are drawers full of sketches and past collages, stuffed away as an ideas-bank for future reference. To one side is a cabinet with long drawers filled with completed works on paper, collages, paintings on paper, and prints numbered and signed, each pre-served between layers of tissue. The top of the cabinet does treble duty as a cutting board, a working surface for pastels, and a surface for laying out painted papers to dry.

I know this studio well. Over the years I have spent many wonderful hours there. It is a quirky, happy place. On a recent visit, in the summer of 1993, I found that Terry had been prevented from painting on his usual scale by arthritic trouble in his neck. What a lucky break for the small collages! The studio was full of them. The table was covered with a riot of cut and uncut papers in a variety of sharp colours, black, red, mauve, various greens and yellows, blue; some were smooth and shiny, others matt. Lying on top of them were scissors with curved silver blades for cutting circles and arcs. Several of the papers had brushstrokes through the paint like currents in water, wind-tracks in sand, green sap flowing, sun on the surfaces of lemons.

Here and there were collages already begun. Some were based on drawings in pastels and chalks, marks on paper – black, yellow, blue, grey, red. On top of them, cut out pieces of the coloured papers had already been positioned but not pasted down, set out, so to speak, on trial. Pieces of paper in red, blue and white stripes had been folded into vertical corrugations. (I wondered whether it was a coincidence that the blue Terry was using today was the cerulean of the agapanthus flowering outside the studio door.) On the whitewashed wall opposite the big window were pinned up a dozen or more collages in process, all variants on a single theme. Some were three-dimensional constructions in paper, with coloured planes and in some cases strings. But whether a collage was two-dimensional or three, every colour had its own intensity and texture, sharp as a butcher's knife. I tried to photograph what I saw, including Terry's hands while he drew. Why am I doing this, I asked myself, with black and white film in my camera instead of colour?

In his studio Terry is like his table; he is a battery charged up. A profusion of energetic ideas is ready to take shape: 'The danger is that when you make a mark the wings of imagination could be clipped'. His eagerness for the creative act of working is artesian; 'there are no answers to the possibilities of discovery, otherwise painting would be dead'. If one thing is not working out well he moves without frustration to another, and another, only to come back again to the first. 'Fear is the most terrifying and wonderful thing at the same time. I think that every painting you do, if you are not in total fear at certain stages and you haven't got the courage to take it on, then you just do pretty paintings.'[1]

For years, as far as Terry is concerned, making collages and constructions parallel to painting has always been an art form in its own right. Sometimes collage is incorp-orated in painting. At other times collages are expendable like sketches, working drawings, explorations of colour-form relationships. When Terry pins up a series of them on the whitewashed wall, it's as if a dynamic is set up between them which spins off yet more ideas. Then the time will come when the intensity of exploring particular ideas calls for the larger scale of painting. Although the table occupies so much of the room, there is just enough space to get around it. An area on the tabletop is cleared for the task in hand. Terry sometimes paints canvases in the same way that he makes collages – flat rather than upright, unstretched and merely taped to a board – rotating them as he works, or walking around them. His purpose is to be 'in the best position to make the shape, so that the *paint draws for you*'. When a work seems to be ready, it will be taken into the house to see how it holds up.

Untitled
1988
hand-coloured and collaged etching,
$14 \times 10\frac{1}{2}$ in, 35.6×26.7 cm
(private collection)

1. From interview with Mike von Joel, *Artline*, vol.4 no.8, 1989, pp.16–19

The house

If you want to be formal and enter the house through the front door you will have to go all the way round, squeezing between the breakfast room and a rock garden. Chances are that if it's raining you'll get dripped on as you walk under the eaves. It's much easier to do what everyone else does: go in through the kitchen door, past the washing-machine and the stove, with its kettle for tea always on the boil and with laundry airing overhead.

It is not an accident that almost everyone uses the back door. The Frosts are family people. They have five sons and a daughter, and although all are grown up now (and there are grandchildren) you'd better learn their names – Adrian, Anthony, Matthew, Stephen, Simon, and Kate. Terry and his wife Kathleen are the pivot of a family that has grown up with the uncertainty and often hardship that have been the daily reality of a full-time artist. Indeed one senses that, since their marriage fifty years ago, there has been an unwavering, sustaining confidence in Terry's art on Kath's part.

But if an artist's environment reveals aspects of his inner self, then the inner radiance which one senses – even in the confines of that compact kitchen, with its shelves crammed with ceramics decorated by Terry and its stoneware jars stuffed with red, black and white spoons – has a parallel in the light reflected from the sea on to the pure whiteness of the walls of the house, outside as well as in, bestowing timelessness and peace.

The house is an extension of the studio. Paintings, collages, and constructions are on every wall, not only downstairs, but on the staircases, landings, bedrooms, and even in the bathroom and lavatory. There are a few objects by other artists too, favourite and intimate pieces by close friends, a Robert Adams sculpture, another by Denis Mitchell, drawings by Roger Hilton, Peter Lanyon and Alan Lowndes, two or three paintings by Alfred Wallis. But most of the things are Terry's and some have been in the house for a long, long time. These older things are benchmarks against which new works are sized up.

The dining-room, which used to be a studio and has a huge window taking up most of one wall, has a painting some eight feet by fourteen, so large in fact that it cranks round the corner of two walls. It is made up of a large number of individual canvases, two feet by two feet, and on each of them is painted a spiral, all roughly the same but different in colour, texture and rhythm, some red, some green, some blue, some yellow, so that each has its own vitality, and is interchangeable with any of the others, yet is always part of the whole.

New collages and paintings are brought into the house

Photographs by David Lewis

all the time. Terry will tell you that only when a work insists on taking you by surprise at a moment when your mind is preoccupied by something else, grabbing you, not in the intellect but in the gut, is it likely to be any good. Some of the largest pieces in the house are in the smallest places, such as the dog-leg of the staircase, yet a collage, six inches by two and a half, hung in the living-room is called upon to compete with a bay window overlooking the garden, a sofa, bookcases, armchairs, and the TV, to say nothing of having to hold its own with a dozen other paintings and collages, and to dominate an axis from the hall. One's first impression might be that the extraordinary vitality of these works would be at odds with one another, and with the equilibrium established by the whiteness of the environment. And then one might be puzzled because this isn't the case. This is because, in spite of being so intensely alive, every work, whether it is a painting, a collage or a construction, has an implicit resolution of the parts of which it is made.

The basic forms in Terry's paintings are usually simple: rectangles, circles, semi-circles, spirals, chevrons, quadrants. The colours are sometimes merely white, black and one or more of the primaries, red, yellow or blue. At other times more complex colours are used, pinks, maroons, oranges, greys, browns. Each colour also has its own quality: thinness, thickness, transparency, opacity, smoothness, coarseness. The integration of laces, or other materials such as plastics, adds complexity. But the theory is always the same. Introduce one colour/form on to an anonymous white surface, and it will immediately set up a colour/form/space relationship with that surface, and with the edges of the white. And the white itself will immediately spring to life. Introduce a second colour/form, and more complex colour/form/space/texture dynamics are set up, which begin to proclaim an energy and a discipline. This discipline becomes more intricate, clearer and tighter as more elements come in. A work succeeds only when each element has a dynamic role to play in the energy and holism of the final object. When I am looking at Terry's work I am often put in mind of a remark by Pascale in his *Pensées*: 'Multitude which cannot be reduced to unity is confusion; unity which is not dependent on multitude is tyranny'. But the power of each work only begins in the internal inter-relationships of its colour and forms. In most of Terry's work there is little or no internal illusory or pictorial depth, nor is there a figurative image, at least not one that is immediately recognisable. The vitality therefore radiates outwards. The relationships of scale within each work relate to the actual living space we inhabit as spectators.

Blue Moon and Orange Rhythm
1986 gouache and collage,
30 × 22 in, 76.2 × 55.9 cm
(private collection)

Recollections and movements

Adrian Heath

'The value of a line, of a form consists for us in the value of the life that it holds for us. It holds its beauty only through our own vital feeling, which, in some mysterious manner, we project into it.'
Worringer

The human mind, in order to make its ideas more manageable, is inclined to make basic divisions in its field of study; later, as the focus of attention tightens, further subdivisions will emerge. For example, the Art Historian has drawn a broad division between the Classical and the Romantic not simply to indicate the style of a particular work but to denote some fundamental differences in the technical approach and the philosophical aims of the artist who made it.

In 1908 Wilhelm Worringer published an essay entitled 'Abstraktion und Einfühlung' (which was eventually published in English as 'Abstraction and Empathy'), which proposes another division. Although his text only reached an English public in 1953, his ideas were widely known through his most eloquent followers, T. E. Hulme and Herbert Read. Hulme's book, Speculations, was published after his death in 1929, and it contains a lecture, 'Modern Art and its Philosophy', which was first delivered in 1914. Hulme clearly states: 'There are two kinds of art, geometrical and vital, absolutely distinct in kind from one another. These two arts are not modifications of one and the same art but pursue different aims and are created for the satisfaction of different necessities of the mind.' He goes on to propose that the 'vital' art that had been dominant since the Greeks and throughout the Renaissance to the present was now in decline and that it was to be replaced by a 'geometrical' art closer in spirit to the art of Byzantium and to certain oriental cultures. His hypothesis was based on his admiration for the early work of Epstein and no doubt for some of the Vorticists, and his argument would have been strengthened by the inclusion of such names as Mondrian, Malevich and Kandinsky who formed the first wave of abstract art in 1911. It would be interesting to see, had he lived, how he would have reacted to the artists who formed the second wave of abstraction in the 1930s, led by Nicholson, Moore and Hepworth, in this country.

After the war there was a new generation of artists and students who were anxious to test for themselves the potential of abstract art and to them the writings of Worringer, Hulme and Read, together with the texts of such artists as Kandinsky, Mondrian and Arp, were of vital interest (in 1950 the written word circulated before the artefact).

Although it is easy to be stimulated by these broad generalisations, it becomes confusing if one tries to apply them to individual artists and one wonders if anybody is ever entirely classical or romantic, geometric or vital. However, I held the view in 1947, and I see no reason to change it now, that Frost was largely a Romantic. I based my assessment on my belief that emotion was more important to him than reason and that in his work direct and spontaneous action produced more authentic results than calculation or planning. I also thought that at this early stage of his career a little external discipline, a touch of classical control and reticence would not inhibit the growth of his natural talent. I therefore suggested that he should study at Camberwell. In 1948 the Painting School at Camberwell had been taken over by the founder members of the Euston Road School. William Coldstream was the Head of Painting and he was assisted by Claude Rogers, Victor Pasmore and Lawrence Gowing. The discipline in the life room was based on measurement used as a principle of construction rather than as a correction to a faulty eye. One could spot the work of the serious student (and Frost enjoyed the company of many serious students between 1947 and 1950) by the way a crop of marks would initially appear, like a rash, on the canvas.[1] These marks were reference points on the model that would correlate with other points of reference in the background and it was some time before the artist could risk stating a contour line. For the success of the operation it was essential that the model should hold the pose unflinchingly from session to session and that the student should mark the position of his own easel and footmarks on the floor before starting to measure with stick and plumb-line. It was thought that this system might promote a search for truth along objective lines and that it would discourage the vulgar virtuosity that comes from a mastery of traditional conventions, as well as those brash simplifications that laid claim to expressionism. It was a training founded on direct observation but it did nothing to foster the claims of imagination. Frost attained considerable competence but it could not be said that he relished this approach to art. When he worked at home on both his nude studies and his portraits they reverted to an expressive particularity of form.

But there were many other sources of study in London that were quite unconnected with the life class at Camberwell. The national galleries and museums offered him the chance of seeing works that had only been known to him in reproduction and the private galleries of Bond Street and Cork Street were places where he could encounter works by the key names of this century. We both noticed that Cubist painters, like Juan Gris and Jacques Villon, measured the proportions of the canvas rather than their particular view

1. See page 40

of the model. It was a practice that threw another light on our understanding of the works on proportion that we had been reading by Jay Hambridge and Matila Ghyka. It also deflected Frost's attention away from things perceived and concentrated it on the forms constructed, and the relationships established between these impersonal areas.

In 1949, while still a student, he painted his first abstract: a picture called 'Madrigal'.[2] I can remember seeing two versions of it in his flat at Battersea; both were composed of squares and rectangles, some of them tilted through 45° but the impact was far from being geometrical and cool. The use of the diagonal, the dark colours and the emotive handling of the paint, created a mood and a sense of space that could only be described as poetic. To my surprise he said that he had been inspired by a poem by W. H. Auden, 'O lurcher-loving collier black as night'.

The next few years was a period of self-discovery. When he left Camberwell in 1950 he returned to St Ives and took one of the Porthmeor studios adjacent to Ben Nicholson. With a wife and child to support it was always a struggle to make the best use of it. The artistic climate of St Ives was still dominated by Ben Nicholson and Barbara Hepworth, the only names of national importance still working in West Penwith. Adrian Stokes and Gabo had left in 1946 for London and New York respectively. By 1950 both Ben and Barbara had relaxed the austerity and the purity of their ideas of the 1930s and the pursuit of the 'Absolute' as defined by Gabo in CIRCLE:

'The shapes we are creating are not abstract, they are absolute. They are released from any already existent thing in nature and their content lies in themselves.'

After the war neither Nicholson nor Hepworth held these views, in fact they saw no difference between abstraction and figuration. Nicholson would combine a still life group (some of them from a much earlier period) with a view through the window, while Hepworth would attend operations at the London Clinic with sketch book at the ready. Ben also made sketching expeditions around the coast. At the same time they could each return to their studio to make totally abstract paintings, reliefs or sculpture. Lanyon, on the other hand, when he was demobbed from the RAF and returned to his house in St Ives, renounced abstract art and described himself as a landscape painter in the tradition of Constable, rather in the same way that William Scott was frequently described as a descendant of Chardin.

Frost not only knew Nicholson well, but he also worked for Hepworth as a carver, and when teaching at Corsham he worked with Peter Lanyon, Bryan Wynter, William Scott, Bill Brooker and Kenneth Armitage. Corsham thus presented yet another mix of creative talent but definitely of a Romantic order. Scott and Armitage both worked with metaphor and analogy in a way that allowed the most

mundane objects to merge and to create an image of quite disturbing implications: magic was Scott's word for it. During the terms at Corsham Frost would commute from London so that he was able to keep up his friendship with Pasmore, Hill, the Martins and myself. In the terms of Hulme it was definitely the 'geometrical' part of the week. I shall quote a few sentences from Kenneth Martin, taken from Broadsheet No. 1, 1951. It starts by making the same point as Gabo that abstract art should not be confused with 'abstraction from nature': 'Just as an idea can be given a form so can a form be given a meaning. By taking the severest form and developing it according to strict rule, the painter can fill it with significance within the limitations imposed. Such limitations of form have been constantly used in poetry and music.' This is a very different view of art from the one prevailing in St Ives or at Corsham at this time. Martin talks of the painter, but in a very few years both he and his wife Mary, Pasmore and Hill had given up the use of paint on a flat surface in favour of reliefs in new materials or in metal for mobile sculptures.

How did Frost react to this variety of stimuli coming from diverse directions? It is true that he made a few constructions, one of which survives from as early as 1952, but it is a playful object, fabricated from wood and cord and it is closer in spirit to Miró than to the precise aims of the constructionists. Frost was unmoved by 'new materials' and continued to use oil paint. Even with his early pictures there is always a tendency to distract the attention away from the surface, either back to the artist and his emotive handling of paint or outwards into a world of recalled sensation. Even the single geometric shapes that he used as structural elements in the early 1950s seem dissatisfied with their role, especially the circles which always seem anxious to play the part of a moon or a sun. However, these interpretations are never forced upon the spectator but they must be read as indications of his desire to relate his art to the world that he knows and enjoys. If we look at the titles he gave his pictures at this time, it is another clue to this intentions: 'Green and White Movement', 1951;[3] 'Movement, black and white', 1951; 'Blue Movement', 1953; the colours are simply descriptive but the insistence on the word 'movement' is ambiguous. E. J. Power in The Moving Format had considered area displacement as a method of composition, with special reference to Juan Gris, but if we read the artist's own words we see that the movement does not solely relate to the forms on the canvas but to the form of things seen and remembered:

'I had spent a number of evenings looking out over the harbour at St Ives in Cornwall. Although I had been observing a multiplicity of movement during those evenings, they all evoked a common emotion or mood – a state of delight in front of nature . . . The subject-matter is in fact the sensa-

Paddington Station
1948
painting, oil on board,
$7\frac{3}{4} \times 11\frac{1}{4}$ in, 19.7 × 28.6 cm
(Belgrave Gallery)

study, pencil and ink,
$11\frac{1}{4} \times 14\frac{1}{2}$ in, 28.5 × 36.8 cm
(the artist)

2. See page 46

3. See page 51

Construction
1951–52
painted board, card and twine,
$9\frac{3}{4} \times 18\frac{3}{4} \times \frac{3}{4}$ in, $25 \times 47.5 \times 2$ cm deep
(whereabouts unknown)

*tion evoked by the movements and the colour in the harbour.
What I have painted is an arrangement of form and colour
which evokes for me a similar feeling.'[4]*

He then goes on to describe the actual evolution of the picture from an initial linear drawing, to a small monochrome painting, a series of lino-cuts, and a smaller version on a canvas of similar proportions. When looking at the final work one might not guess the classical stages of its development.

Movement is also the subject of an earlier work, 'Walk along the Quay',[5] which was painted in 1950. In this case the situation has become even more complex as the artist has added his own movement to the equation, not on a single ocasion but on many, for the walk was in fact a daily stroll. It became an exercise of Bergsonian complexity with memory fuelling the imagination and only formal structures remaining to censor the unpaintable, as there was no specific mood in the artist's psyche to demand expression or the light and weather of a special day to unify the whole. Possibly the most specific demands were made by his choice of a long, narrow canvas to symbolise the strict limitations of his daily walk. In the painting the weather is set fair, and the mood is optimistic. A central panel in the upper half of the picture is a gradation of blue tones, cut into by an area of white. The relationship between these tones in their context acts as a quotation from a summer seascape. The near vertical lines that enclose this area are ropes, the rigging of the moored boats, while the canvas which gives rhythm and movement to the picture at a formal level also evokes by its shape memories of hulls and rudders. The composition as a whole shares some of the qualities of Nicholson; the sparse strength but not the suave elegance.

In 1954 Frost was awarded the Gregory Fellowship in Painting at Leeds University, so he moved to the North taking his family with him. The Fellowship was for two years and it included a house and studio so that for the first time he enjoyed a respite from financial worries. He made new friends and enjoyed the Yorkshire landscape, especially the Dales under winter snow. He seldom recorded his impressions with drawings made on the spot, but in words: letters to friends, but more frequently with the spoken word, in anecdotes to amuse friends or in stories to instruct or stimulate students. The narrative has always been a method of keeping the past alive in his mind. 'Winter 1956', was started off by an afternoon tobogganing with friends. Movement again, but of a more violent nature; action rather than contemplation. A line is a point in movement; Frost enjoyed 'living' his lines that afternoon. There is another story of an afternoon walk in the snow with Herbert Read, when suddenly Frost turned and looking up saw 'the white sun spinning on top of a copse . . . A naples yellow blinding circle spinning on top of black verticals'. Unlike most of his stories this incident concerns a moment of truth, in which the image

Walking Along the Quay (Blue Movement)
1952
oil on canvas,
$13\frac{3}{4} \times 13\frac{3}{4}$ in, 35.5 × 35.5 cm
(Lancaster University)

▷ *Winter, 1956, Yorkshire*
1956
oil on board,
$97\frac{1}{8} \times 49\frac{1}{8}$ in, 246.7 × 125 cm
(Tate Gallery, London)

4. See page 60 for the context of this quotation, from Lawrence Alloway's *Nine Abstract Artists*

5. See page 47

6. See page 67

*is presented to him ready made. 'Red, Black and White',
1956 was the first painting to stem from that experience.*[6]

*How can one assess Frost's response to nature or the con-
tribution that it made to his art? Nature certainly did not
serve as 'motif' in the Cézanne sense, a selected section of
landscape that would yield the basis of a composition, neither
did it fire his curiosity as in the case of Ruskin, who peered,
recorded, deduced and finally explained. Frost himself
simply accepts the outside world as a source of 'kicks'. He
could never predict his own reactions or arrange for their
recurrence: either it happened or it did not. But the moment
of awareness when it occurred provided a stimulus that was
essential to his work.*

*His reaction to art and his debt to other painters is equally
difficult to determine as there are no obvious links of a technical or stylistic nature to suggest a name. Without doubt other
artists have played an important part in his development but
their influence has worked at the profound level of thought,
and an attitude towards life, rather than through their
technical procedures or painterly mannerisms. Pasmore,
Nicholson and Lanyon were artists who were important to
him at the beginning of his career, while a little later it was
the personality of Roger Hilton that he found both provoca-
tive and stimulating. In 1957 they paid a visit to Paris
together. For Hilton, who had studied before the war at the
Académie Ranson, it was a return to familiar haunts but to
Frost it was all new and exciting. The Musée d'Art Moderne
gave him an introduction to the twentieth century that was
different from that offered by the Tate. He was able to see
their considerable collection of Robert and Sonia Delaunay,
and the 'Plans Verticaux' of Kupka more than lived up to
the impression it had made on him in reproduction. The
brightly coloured compositions of Herbin have remained in
his memory together with some works by the young Tapiès
representing 'art informel' at the other end of the aesthetic
spectrum. He was struck by the whole gallery scene in Paris
at this time, and their dedication to selling their artists'
work. He was equally impressed after a visit to the studio
of Soulages with the artist's ability to produce the goods in
quantity and on time. He was impressed but felt uneasy at
the same time.*

*In 1956 Frost had a further opportunity to widen his
horizons when the 'American Exhibition' came to the Tate.
Until this period Paris had always been the Mecca for the
English avant garde, but suddenly the attention and the
interest of young artists was focused on New York. The
myth generated by Pollock, Rothko, de Kooning, had
already been promoted in England through magazines but
only a very small number of English painters had seen their
work. The Tate show divided the British art world: there
were those who blindly accepted it and there were others who
jealously denied its qualities. Popular subjects for discussion*

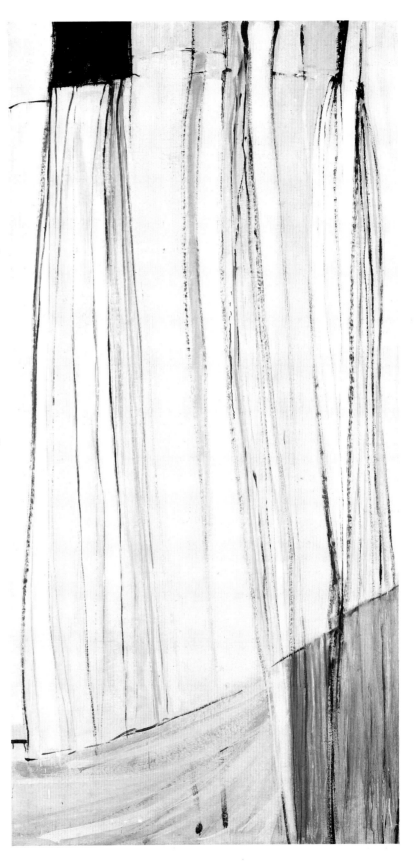

were those concerning size, skill, and finish.

At this stage of his career it is not surprising perhaps that Frost's favoured artists were Motherwell and Tomlin, two American painters who were among the most fully steeped in a European tradition and yet whose roots in American soil were deeper than most. In 1960 Frost was able to test the climate of New York at first hand. Bertha Schaeffer gave him his first one-man show which he attended, staying for three weeks. He met de Kooning and visited the studios of Barnett Newman and Motherwell; the critic Greenberg introduced him to Kenneth Noland and Olitski who were painters from the younger generation that he was promoting. It was the spirit of optimistic confidence and the practice of hard work that he found encouraging. After this visit Frost could no longer be considered a provincial artist; he was aware of a situation prevailing beyond these shores; not by reading but by direct contact and experience.

It is difficult to speak with authority about the development of an artist's work over a period of thirty-five years entirely from memory; one needs the presence of the pictures hung in chronological order to confirm one's understanding of the progression. Fortunately the Arts Council Retrospective of his work is only nine years ago [1976] and it can act as a useful guide. By the standards of the twentieth century it is a very consistent body of works: for example, since leaving art school in 1950, he has always worked as an abstract painter. Unlike those well known Americans, de Kooning, Guston and Diebenkorn, who alternated between the figurative and the non-objective means of expression, Frost remained constant to abstraction and, as I have tried to make clear, he has done this with his eyes open to the world about him; he has not adopted an idealist attitude to pure form or resorted to a mathematical or a systemic approach to the creative act. 'Nihil est in intellectu quod non fuerit prius in sensu' (there is nothing in the mind that was not first in the senses) is not a quotation that he frequently uses but I am certain that it would have his backing. However, having appreciated the world with all his senses he has never felt inclined to reproduce his perceptions directly but he has always preferred the alternative task of inventing symbols to do justice to the experience. Even during the early years in St Ives we see him groping towards that end. Shapes were first drawn on the canvas – form preceded colour – to be changed inevitably in the process of working, but the movement we have referred to was initially conceived in linear terms. The actual painting of the work was simple and direct; completely lacking in those laboured refinements of some of Nicholson's admirers who would scrape and pumice a panel till it evoked a moorland space or the texture of weathered rock before a line was drawn.

When he was in Leeds his painting became increasingly direct, and painting and drawing merged into a single process

Arrowed Figure
1959
oil on canvas,
72 × 96 in, 183 × 243.8 cm
(the artist)

to produce results that were always forceful but at times looked harsh and crude to eyes trained on French art and still unfamiliar with American painting. Frost was always suspicious of the charms of 'la belle peinture', especially when translated into abstract modes of expression where it smacked of 'haute cuisine', where it produced not images but logos by which its maker could be instantly recognised. It is one of the penalties of commercial success that a dealer frowns on any deviation from a selling line. Frost has always worked on a theme till his interest in it wanes and then he moves on; he has resisted the temptation to repeat, polish and refine on a particular series. One may regret that he did not stay longer with some of his discoveries of the early 1960s: 'Gwennor', 1960, and 'Black Arrow', 1960, are among the best works of the period. They are the outcome of direct spontaneous painting where a sudden flurry of excitement can weld together some sweeping brushstrokes to produce that contradiction in terms, a 'non-objective' image that can haunt our memory and create its own significance in our minds.

The 1960s was a moment when I thought the work of Frost might take on the representational connotations that seemed to hover close to the surface of his paintings. He would have been following the example of de Staël whose abstract became figurative as early as 1952, and preceding

by a few years a similar change in the work of Roger Hilton.
It would have been a move that would have been consistent
with the romantic side of his nature. Frost, in fact, reacted
rather differently and began to think of the canvas as an
object once again. He writes of 'Laced Grace' (oil, canvas
collage, cord on canvas) and other related pictures in the following terms: 'I did a whole series of laced paintings, in gouache, on canvas and in lithograph. I think I was trying to
tighten the form. I remember thinking I would like to use
a spanner.

'I had the two semi-circles or half semi-circles collaged on
and they always made a tension between each other, so much
so that I decided to tighten them up. I laced them up and
pulled them tight so they could not escape this tension. Like
sails pulling against the wind and my grandmother's stays.'

These few sentences afford us considerable insight into his
approach to art. For example, the stress he lays on the condition of tautness. If he says (which he frequently does) that
a painting is as 'tight as a drum', he is bestowing high praise
for he considers the tensions between the forms are stretched
to their utmost: 'tight-laced' is an expression signifying
rigorous self-control, which is an artistic virtue in classical
terms, and which is here symbolised by the actual object
through which the tightness is achieved: the lace.

The next change of direction showed itself in his attitude
towards colour. During the late 1950s and the 1960s his use
of it was emotive, the colours he used were those that one
can perceive in landscape, evocative of space, light and air,
and they would surround and suffuse a linear structure in
much the same way that light can transform the structure
of a familiar landscape, or a colour wash can change a
drawing. At some moment in the 1970s there was a change.
Pictures such as 'Orange Moonship 74', 'Tall Collage 73–
74', and 'July Jungle 72–74', are works in which colour has
been used as a basic structural element. Simplified forms
have been cut out from strong primaries and used directly
as collage: colour is no longer an element to reveal, conceal
or disguise structure, it becomes the structure. It is difficult
to pinpoint the cause of this quite significant development.
It may have been a bonus from his own teaching methods
coupled with a reassessment of the work of some of his
favourite artists of an earlier generation; the names of
Matisse, Delaunay and Léger spring to mind.

Frost's work has always been notable for what can best
be described as a 'strong gestalt' – a powerful configuration
of form. 'Summer Collage 76',[7] fundamentally a combination of squares and circles set against a strong yellow ground,
must serve as an example of what I mean by a work carrying
visual impact. It is contemporaneous with works of a very
different order: 'Through Blues 69', 'Through Blacks 75',
and 'Through Yellows 75'. Are these the result of some personal research into the affective role of colour or are they

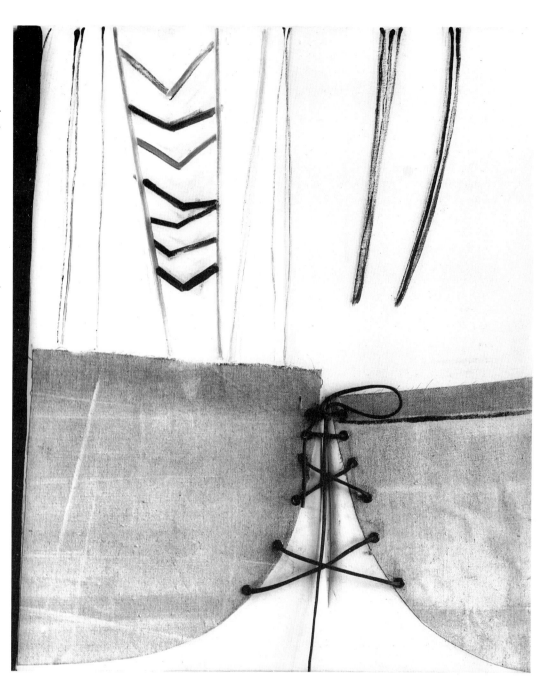

Laced Grace
1962
oil and collage on canvas,
24 × 20 in, 61 × 50.8 cm
(Belgrave Gallery)

7. See page 11

a belated acknowledgement of a link between music and abstract art? In 1977 Frost wrote down a note after listening to some music on the wireless: 'How can I do something as good as that with colours? It ought to be the same as writing music, putting my shapes and colour together.' I have called these paintings work of a different order because they have moved, to use a phrase of Mondrian's, from the world of 'particular form' into the world of 'determined relationships'. They are moving into the aesthetic of the 'all-over' painting. The scale of the mark has not been reduced as drastically as it was reduced by Pollock or Tobey (where the surface reads as animated texture) but the units have been reduced in size and increased in number so that they lose individual significance and only work in unison like notes of colour. Pictures of this nature invariably lose their impact as memorable form but they invite careful inspection and lengthy perusal. For the spectator their enjoyment becomes a time experience as it is with music. It seems that the element of movement that plays such an important part in Frost's appreciation of life has now reappeared as a structural ingredient in his art.

Through Yellows
1975
oil and collage on canvas,
78 × 102 in, 198 × 259 cm
(the artist)
For other 'Through' paintings, see pages 189–191

This essay was written for the exhibition catalogue
Terry Frost: Painting in the 1980s, Reading University
1986

Precedents

There are, of course, well-established precedents in the broad stream of the Modern Movement for organising the colour/space energy of a work of art to expand outwards into the actual space we live in, rather than focus inwards on the internal (fictional) space of the work itself. Their origin lies in the early Cubism of Picasso and Braque, 1906–12; the traditional interior space of painting was flattened so that forms were not only built up to appear in relief, but also offered multiple viewpoints at the same time. In the later Cubist period, 1912–16, Picasso made a series of painted reliefs from assorted materials, wood, metal, and wire, which thrust the Cubist idea outward in three dimensions.

In Mondrian's paintings there is no internal space. In order to emphasise the expansive power of his work outwards, he mounted his canvases in 'reverse section' frames so that the picture-plane stood away from the plane of the wall. The organisation of Constructivist sculptures by Antoine Pevsner and Naum Gabo was similarly based on a conscious effort to radiate rhythms into the space of our living environments. Their sculptures coincided with new discoveries in physics, such as Einstein's theory of relativity, which placed our planet and the reach of the human mind into ever-expanding geometries of space. Curvilinear rhythms, constructed in modern man-made materials, metals, glass and plastics, are a visual language expressive of our oneness with a universe in perpetual movement and change and yet in perpetual balance, an ever-shifting metamorphosis which is perpetually recreating stasis.

Like Cubism these were watershed events. They marked a clear alternative to illusionistic perspective art. Both Mondrian and the Constructivists sought to acknowledge a heightened sense of order – termed by Mondrian 'dynamic equilibrium' – and to relate that order directly to architectural space.

These events, most of which were taking place in Paris, affected British art almost as soon as they occurred. Wyndham Lewis's Vorticism at the start of World War I was a development of Cubism which included time and motion. Ben Nicholson began a series of post-Cubist paintings in the early 1930s. By the mid 1930s he was doing hard-edge geometric paintings and white reliefs. In 1937 he, Naum Gabo and J. L. (later Sir Leslie) Martin edited and published *CIRCLE*, subtitled 'an international survey of constructive art'.[1] It was the first book to bring between single covers the notion that occupying and ordering space is the factor unifying modern painting, sculpture, and architecture.

Interrupted by World War II, the debate resumed in the early 1950s over whether architecture, painting and sculpture should merge. It was occasioned in part by the writings of the American Charles Biederman, and in part by the evolution of Victor Pasmore and other British artists from painting into constructed reliefs and free-standing or suspended constructions. But Frost was too much of a painter to be drawn deeply into the debate. He stood on the sidelines while many of his friends, Pasmore, Anthony Hill, Kenneth Martin, John Ernest and others in London, and Constant, Stephen Gilbert and Nicolas Schoffer in Paris, explored how artists and architects could be integrated into teams. But he was nevertheless deeply affected by it. These were more than fellow artists, they included his mentor Adrian Heath and they were his friends; the arguments swirled all around him, in the studios, in the galleries, in the pubs. He and Roger Hilton exchanged letters about it and about the basic issues of abstraction. Hilton was so torn that he briefly considered relinquishing art altogether. It was reassuring to him that Frost, whom he admired, refused to give up being a painter. The common challenge tightened the bond of friendship between them. Although Frost has made painted constructions and three-dimensional painted collages as part of his output throughout his mature years, he would not give up the one thing which for him lies at the core of his art, namely *the physical act of painting*, of using hand and brush and the tactile quality of pigment to communicate thought. He did not make constructions because he was moving towards architecture; he made them because they rely primarily on structure, whereas in painting

'. . . it is the layering of paint within a structure which comes after years of practice that is important to me – so that structure and spontaneity are simultaneously contained within a brushstroke carrying a particular colour, which in turn is in a structured relation to all the other parts of the painting.'[2]

He could never give up the *action itself* of making a work of art, of letting the paint and the brush transmit with naked immediacy the emotional and spiritual excitement of working on a flat surface, and of making every element – colour, line, texture – sing emotionally and spatially.

Although Frost's work is very different from Pasmore's constructions of the mid 1950s, to say nothing of being different from Mondrian's, his paintings and constructions are rooted in basically similar principles. They are physical objects. They are made up of clearly stated parts. Each of these parts has its own character and vitality.

Yorkshire Landscape Study
c.1954
pencil, 9 × 8 in, 22.8 × 20.3 cm
(the artist)

1. *CIRCLE*, ed. Naum Gabo, Ben Nicholson and J. L. Martin, Faber and Faber, London 1937

2. From interview with David Lewis, October 1993, see page 238

. . . the brushstroke makes the best line in the world
. . . When it is right, there it is, in a single sweep or
stroke, definite, sharp, and absolutely right.[3]

The work arrives at 'completion' when all the parts inter-
relate in such a way that the vitality of each part is
brought out and is actually increased. Because his paintings have little or no depth, it is the scale relationship
which each work establishes with everything around it –
and especially us, the spectators – that enables us to
experience its holism in an absolutely direct way. The
seeds of this approach can be found in his very early
work, even when he was a student, although at the time
he was only dimly aware of his direction. As he matured,
he became more and more confident and daring.

Quadrant Study
c.1966
charcoal,
$8\frac{1}{4} \times 9\frac{1}{4}$ in, 21 × 20.5 cm
(the artist)

Leeds Landscape
c.1956
pencil,
$22\frac{1}{8} \times 5\frac{5}{8}$ in, 56.2 × 14.3 cm
(the artist)

Suspended Forms
c.1959
ink and watercolour,
10 × 8 in, 25.4 × 20.3 cm
(the artist)

3. From interview with David Lewis, October 1993,
see page 238

Landscape and tradition

In Terry Frost's house, the living-room window frames a view of Mount's Bay. Far below, beyond the pitched roofs of houses terraced up the steep hill, lies Newlyn harbour. From this height the fishing boats moored along the quays look like toys. The wind-ruffled sea has the appearance of glistening slate as it slides to the far horizon where it merges with the sky. To the east, beyond the granite tower of Penzance church two miles away, is St Michael's Mount, glimpsed below the bough of an ancient pine at the foot of the Frosts' garden. Overhead, grey clouds are driven by west wind gusts which swirl them and then, as though on a whim, shred them like rags.

There are some regular events in my life which are predictable and I don't have to search for them. The sun comes up over the Lizard in the morning. St Michael's Mount starts off like a Japanese woodcut, a triangle of island and castle nudging through a shroud of mist, and then to the right is a red glow, and if you wait and watch as the sun comes up, first as a semi-circle and then a circle behind the Mount, there is a red reflection shimmering in the water, and that's my morning treat. I've photographed it a hundred times.

And then at the end of the day as I go back to my studio, there it is again! This time there are the two granite pillars, one on each side of the lane, and the yellow sun moves to orange and then to red, and when it is red it is bang in the middle between the pillars. And below the pillars are three parallel strips of granite, eight feet long and set in the ground as cow-stoppers; and you have the broccoli smell and deep green on your right and the gold of the corn on your left, and then the fields open up and out to the moors.[1]

Stabs of colour punctuate the green foliage of the garden, hydrangeas blue and purple, white shasta daisies, orange montbretia, African daisies yellow and mauve, verbena and deep red bougainvillaea, without doubt an exotic inventory of flowers to flourish in the open air of an English garden, thanks to the micro-climate of this peninsula which juts into the warming currents of the Gulf Stream. From a silver slit in the clouds the sun glances into the garden for a wink and the white stucco of the house awakens into textured life.

The garden is protected by a high stone wall and the shoulder of the hill. Upland, behind Terry's house to the north, the moors begin. Open to winter gales raging from the Atlantic, the moors are treeless, scoured. Granite boulders jut from the wind-moulded contours as though the bones of the planet are breaking through the earth's skin. The palette is sable, rust brown, sage and ivy green, and greys, with stabs of gorse yellow, mustard yellow, foxglove pink and lichen orange.

In spite of his being a non-figurative artist, Terry's paintings have always been affected by the environments he has lived in. Aspects of landscape have provided moments of clarity, of vision, for much of his work. To the uninitiated this may seem baffling. It is not a question of representation, but of vocabulary. Wherever he has lived, in the Midlands, in Yorkshire, and in Cornwall, he has found landscape vocabularies which he has then transformed into non-figurative paintings. When he lived in Leeds in 1954–56, for example, the stone walls running up the steep contours of the Dales, separating fields, became the theme of a succession of non-figurative paintings. Similarly, sojourns in Cyprus have produced a series of paintings and collages in which the sun, the moon and the Mediterranean have produced a vocabulary of circles and crescents with a sharper palette of blacks, orange, blues and lemon yellow.

Traditionally, English art has been an art of landscape. Constable and Turner, contemporaries almost a century and a half ago, showed two contrasting sides of the English temperament towards landscape. Constable's paintings of Suffolk – of ploughed fields, summer elms, wind-rippled streams, and cloud formations overhead with their moods ever-changing from the drifts of soft cumulus to the dark portents of thunder – were direct, immediate and physical. His method of painting was similarly physical and direct. Even if his larger paintings were not painted out of doors he wanted to create the impression that they were. His masses were firm and unequivocal; wet surfaces shimmered; shadows were dark; his brushstrokes were muscular and strong. As a spectator you are drawn physically into his landscapes with all your senses going full blast. In the words of E. V. Lucas, 'he brought English people face to face with England; the delicious, fresh, rainy, blowy England that they could identify.'[2]

Turner's paintings on the other hand were ethereal, floating, translucent. Unlike Constable, he did not want to project us into the landscape, but rather to detach us from reality and project us into the poetic realms of the subjective. He made thousands of sketches in his lifetime; and he used them to condition and develop vocabulary. He understood that memory is highly selective and creative, and that forgetting and recreating are two sides of memory.

In Turner's paintings nothing is firmly anchored. Recognisable objects, such as a ship, a cathedral, a mountain, a swirling sea storm or drifting veils of mist across

1. From interview with David Lewis, October 1993, see page 238

2. E. V. Lucas, *John Constable the painter*, quoted by Cyril G. E. Bunt in *John Constable, the Father of Modern Landscape*, F. Lewis Ltd, London 1948, p. 7

the reaches of the river Thames, are made airborne by waves of translucent colour filled with pale light. They are there to be points of origin from which we are transported by the rhythms of the painting and on wings of light into poetic realms within our subjective selves, our emotions, and our dreams.

Constable and Turner were revolutionaries in their time. They taught us to look at art in new ways. Turner brings us to the threshold of the non-figurative; his world is subjective, poetic, associational. It does not stretch our credulity too far to see in him a forerunner of some of the modern colour-field painters, such as the Americans Sam Francis and Helen Frankenthaler. Constable, on the other hand, had a genius for direct expression, down to earth, uncluttered by convention. It is small wonder that he made a powerful impact on his French contemporaries, Delacroix and Géricault, and through them became a forerunner of Impressionism and van Gogh. Both of these aspects of English landscape are strongly present in Terry Frost's art.

But Constable and Turner present only two aspects of the English attitude to landscape. Henry Moore's sculpture reflects another aspect, our oneness with the land. Human imagery merges with images of hills, bones, and rocks, scoured by countless seasons of wind and storm, like the uplands of his native Yorkshire. And Ben Nicholson's post-Cubist paintings are landscape of a different sort. Here the eroded landscape – in this case Cornwall – is the basis on which a construction of coloured planes is built up, as though setting our modern technological world within the timeless rhythms of nature. In spite of Terry Frost's relation to each of these four aspects of British landscape, he presents a new and different attitude and message. He creates wholly new images. Like Constable and Turner in the nineteenth century, and Moore and Nicholson in the twentieth, he teaches us to look at art in new ways.

Yorkshire Black and White
1955
oil on board,
23 × 60 in, 58.4 × 152.5 cm
(private collection)

Force 8
1960
oil on canvas,
$87 \times 68\frac{1}{4}$ in, 221×173.4 cm
(Ferens Art Gallery, Kingston upon Hull)

Early life

Terry Frost was born in Leamington Spa in 1915. He lived with his grandmother. He was clearly a happy boy.

I had an Uncle Fred, an Uncle Tom, and an Uncle Don. My Uncle Fred and my Uncle Don were into sports, so I was taken to all sorts of matches, soccer and cricket. I saw Dixie Dean, Don Bradman, Wally Hammond and Joe Grimmet. My Uncle Fred did a lot of drawings from magazines and photographs, so I did drawings from *Boys' Own Magazine* and I could do better than Uncle Fred. Of course we never talked about art because nobody knew anything about that. The only picture we had was a reproduction called *Leading the Horses to Water*.[1]

At school he loved particularly to draw and to write. He would get completely engrossed in what he was doing. In his notebook he recalled:

One of the reasons I gave up writing was because I was given bottom marks for my composition on making a Christmas pudding, or cake, I can't quite remember which. We had about two hours to do the exam composition and I was nearly always in the top half-dozen for composition at the age of eleven. I really thought I knew all about Christmas puddings and cakes, for every Christmas I would help my Gran. I loved it. Wash the currants, chop up the candied peel, grate the nutmeg etc. etc. I really knew what went on. And at the end of the period of time allotted I had only just got all the ingredients together on the table with the description of the bowls and trays. I'm sure it was a Proustian description — but it failed because I never actually got as far as making the pudding, or cake. And so I was bottom of the class. That was a shattering blow because I loved what I was writing about. I had been completely absorbed and had not stopped writing for a second. Looking back after sixty years I still feel the hurt and the injustice of that marking. No recognition at all for the descriptive work I had done. Captain Billingham, that was. I shouldn't think he could have read much himself.[2]

I was art editor of the school magazine at the age of eleven. Titch Eveleigh was our art master. He was very good at lettering. I always came second in art because I couldn't letter. I could never get my letters to look proper. Frank Unitt, the boy who always came first because he could letter better than me, became after the war the best women's hairdresser in town.[3]

Like most of the boys at his school he was expected to grow up to work in one of the Midlands industries, most likely a car factory in Coventry. By fourteen he was already earning his living, first in a cycle shop, then a bakery, and then an aircraft factory. Just before World War II broke out he was a salesman for an electrical and radio components wholesaler in Birmingham.

I left school at fourteen and went to work, which is a natural thing to do in the Midlands, a working-class family, you go to work, everybody goes to work. That's what it's all about.

I worked at Curry's the cycle shop first of all and I had a terrible job. You know in the old days Curry's used to have glass shelves in the windows, beautiful curved glass shelves, on which they'd put brake blocks, radio and lamp batteries, bulbs, every little thing, and I used to be in the window doing all those shelves. Didn't know I was going to do any art of course, but when I look back I realise I was, because I used to use tubes of crepe paper and I learned to make all kinds of shapes, crinkle them up, and do it in green and yellow for Easter and all that kind of lark. I cleaned the windows as well as polishing the floor and delivering bikes out in the country — you know, ride one and push one — because they were only £2 19s 6d in those days. I also killed rats in the cellar, charged the batteries and all the rest of it. That was my first job.

I had about seven jobs; I never got the sack in those days which is rather amazing. I switched jobs and I can't remember the order of things but I know I worked in a bakehouse for a time. That was a bit arty because I used to put the jam and cream in the doughnuts.

I had three uncles. One of them aspired to be a linesman in a first division match once, so he got on very well. He took me to football and cricket matches. Aston Villa was my team. Another was a toolmaker. He actually did a lot of drawing but I never took any notice at the time because I was more interested in cricket or football. They all played. Well, he copied from photographs so I tried copying from his copies. I copied Billy Bunter and things like that from magazines. At school when I was eleven I wasn't thinking about art. I mean the only posters we had were Terence Cuneo's trains and the great thing I remember about art was I spilt some water on the paper when I was doing a rose and got a cuff across the ear. I resented that very much and I still resent it from that day to this. We never got very much encouragement at school. I mean art was always treated as a minor subject and still is in most schools which is a tragedy. If we had more art we might get less bloody murder. But it don't make a profit so much as other things.

Anyway I became unemployed for a short time. It

1. From interview with David Lewis, October 1993, see page 238

2. From a notebook, late 1960s

3. From interview with David Lewis, October 1993, see page 238

was in the 1930s, the depression. I had to go to evening
classes, it was one of the conditions otherwise you
didn't get your dole, and I took drawing, the art class.
But it was only for about three weeks because then I
got a job making cakes and I got quite decorative putting the crosses on hot-cross buns. Two thousand
bloody crosses is a lot to do at about four o'clock in the
morning, and then paint them with a bit of glaze. So I
had plenty of practice. Then I joined the Territorials
when I was seventeen and one of the other members,
Roger Hadland, got me a job at Coventry, at
Armstrong Whitworth where they made the fighter
planes and bombers. I was in the part where they put
the red, white and blue targets on the wings – now isn't
that interesting? It was a little bit before the Americans
were doing them. Kenneth Nolan – that's the first
thing Clement Greenberg ever showed me, he un-
rolled it and showed me, and nobody had ever heard
of him then. It was four foot square or a bit less and
I thought, Wow.

My job was not to do the targets but to make the tea
and prepare the paints for the painters, who were
wonderfully skilled at doing those targets by hand.
Then I had to clean up afterwards. I was put into a
secret hangar where the Wellington bombers were
built and I had to paint the electric wires in the planes
different colours, red here, blue there. This gave me
the privilege of joining the other workers in the hangar
to watch and cheer the test pilot as he took our bom-
ber up on its first flight. Meanwhile the newspapers
announced that there'd be no war, not this year, not
next year, nor ever.

After that I got a job in a radio firm, making simple
repairs and driving a van. Then I was called up straight
away in 1939 because I was in the Territorials, you see.[4]

4. From interview with Dave Lee, 1993, see page 238

Terry Frost with his Gran and a neighbour

Terry Frost the soldier in Cairo

The war years

After service in France, Palestine and the Lebanon, Terry Frost transferred to the Commandos and served in the Sudan on the Abyssinian border. He was captured in Crete in June 1941. He was imprisoned first in Salonika, then in Poland, and finally he was moved to Stalag 383 in Hohenfals, Bavaria, where he spent most of his four years as a prisoner-of-war.

Stalag 383 was a huge camp. It held hundreds of prisoners. To fight the boredom the prisoners organised a variety of activities. There were fourteen men in Terry's hut.

'Hobo' Challis, a professional tramp but a very intellectual man. He used to read aloud to us whenever we got a book through the Red Cross, and he did caricatures. I thought 'I can do that'. But I couldn't. I could do a likeness – but I couldn't do the exaggerations like Hobo could. As soon as I got a likeness all the lads wanted one. I used old pieces of cardboard, or bits of paper left over by the Germans when they blacked out our windows . . .

One day I was busy drawing the back of a sitting figure on a piece of the black-out paper and I was being very hesitant, tentative when I heard a voice behind me saying 'why don't you *put it on?*' and that was the first time I met Adrian Heath. He invited me to his hut where he was doing figure studies, and he was the first person to talk to me seriously about art. He introduced me to about six other blokes who had made a sort of art school, and to Basil Marin who had been at Madrid University and had a book on Velasquez. Marin was more of an art historian than a painter, but he was very keen on poetry and I supplied him with lines from Keats and Shelley to write to his pen friend in England: 'Bright star as steadfast as you are . . .'. He told us all about the use of angles and geometry in Velasquez, which was a revelation to me. Then I got hold of Irving Stone's book on Van Gogh, *Lust for Life*, from Challis via the Red Cross and that was the first art book I'd ever read . . .

One of the German guards had been in an art school before the war. He used to have to put handcuffs on us if one of the SS officers came to inspect because we were ex-Commandos and some German prisoners who had been captured by the British had been found with their hands tied, but Smudger Smith, who had worked in dentistry, picked the locks in a moment, and it became something of a joke because after that when the SS officers were seen the bugler played the double and we'd put the handcuffs on ourselves without locking them and walk around looking abject, and then take them off as soon as the officers' backs were turned. Anyway the German guard was a nice chap and he gave me some ochre and other oil colours . . .

When we got a parcel from the Red Cross I would collect the oil from the sardine tins to mix with my paints, and I found that the barley which the Germans made our soup with made really good size. We had hessian pillows in our beds, so I would swap a portrait for a pillow, and I would cut it up. One side I'd use for the chap's portrait, and the other side would be for me. Then there was a Scottish lad who made brushes for me in exchange for a portrait; he'd snip the hairs from the horses' fetlocks when they were brought in to clear the sewage and whatnot, and he'd secure the hairs to a piece of wood with tin from the sardine cans. I got other oil paints from Red Cross parcels and through a central exchange that Mick Moore had set up among the prisoners. He ran a kind of stock exchange based on barter. If you wanted a map of the German defences, an elephant or a pair of knitting needles he'd get it for you in exchange for something you had. He had the values of things written on a blackboard, for example one pair of socks = one tin of bacon. Mick Moore was also in charge of the theatre group's costume shop where they had a sewing machine and a tailor's shop that could make costumes out of anything. When I did Mick Moore's portrait in his hut I didn't know that we were sitting on the floorboards over the underground room the lads had dug to plan and train for the escapes . . .

I did in the end about two hundred portraits. It was a very good training. Fred Mulley[1] was our art critic. Of course, everyone else was an art critic too: 'What the hell's he got blue hair for?' I did a portrait of WO Wright, but I didn't know at the time that he was in charge of the escapes (about a month ago his widow sent me a letter with a photo of the portrait which her daughter had found when she was clearing up).

I was in the last row of huts nearest to the wire while the lads were down there digging a tunnel. I would lie in the sun in the grass under the sentry box pretending to be sunbathing and reading but my job was to watch the guard. The corporal in charge was a tough disciplinarian. I was watching him at the changing of the guard and I saw him hesitate just for a second, and I knew he had heard something from under the ground, the slightest sound of a pick on a rock, something like that. So I dropped my handkerchief, which was the pre-arranged signal to one of the boys in the hut so that he could stamp on the floorboards and alert the lads in the

Interior, Hut 295
1943
watercolour,
$8\frac{1}{2} \times 12$ in, 21.6 × 30.5 cm
(the artist)

Guard Tower and Fences
1943
watercolour,
$9\frac{1}{2} \times 12$ in, 25.2 × 30.5 cm
(the artist)

1. Now Lord Mulley

tunnel. But they never got the message. A couple of minutes later the guards were all over us in the hut . . .[2]

So the British lads made disturbances in all directions, yelling and waving their arms and running hither and thither, distracting the guards so the tunnelling tools could be passed out and hidden away for the next effort. And the person doing the passing was Adrian Heath. Adrian was the bravest man I have ever known. Well, before Adrian could get out, the guards were into the tunnel with flashlights. But the tunnel turned a slight corner and Adrian hid there for a moment, hanging on to the floorboards which the lads had used to shore up the tunnel. And when the Germans crept forward to the bend Adrian leapt out at them barking like a mad dog. Scared the living daylights out of them! Twenty-one days bread and water he got for that. Nothing new to Adrian: he got bread and water regularly. The sad thing was there was only a yard or two to go before the tunnel would have broken earth beyond the barbed wire . . .

But there were escapes. One night I was in the wash room right opposite when one of our lads, a Spanish Freedom Fighter named Barosso, tied a brick to a rope and tossed it over the electric wires above the barbed wire enclosure and gave a sharp pull, dragging the wires together and fusing the entire camp. A previously picked number of fellows rushed forward with a ladder and back packs and attempted to get over the top, only to be caught in the emergency floodlights which we hadn't known existed. Three of the lads got away as far as Graz. One was dressed as a woman, lovely curly blonde wig he had. Another was dressed as a Bavarian. But they were caught because their contact had been caught the day before, and they were brought back. Mick Moore had the sewing-machine and had made their disguises, pretending he was making costumes for the camp theatre . . .[3]

As the Allied forces moved swiftly forward in the final days of the war the prisoners from Stalag 383 were marched towards Berchtesgaden to be used as hostages, but the swiftness of the Allied invasion foiled this attempt and the prisoners were freed to come home.

Talking to students at King's College, Newcastle, in 1954, Terry summed up his wartime experiences:

First of all I was self-taught, and worked painting POW friends' portraits, still life, landscape, etc. A very exacting task; if the portrait wasn't liked, then you heard about it in much stronger terms of abuse than the critics dare to use now. Good training that was. The sunsets, pine trees, frost, every blade of grass, I looked

2. From interview with David Lewis, October 1993, see page 238

3. From interview with David Lewis, July 1993, see page 238

at intensely. Certainly I learned how to see things around me for the first time . . . I am sure that was the best education I could have had before becoming a professional painter.

When Terry Frost returned home from Stalag 383 he wanted only to become an artist. His family could not understand it. The war had shattered Britain. Its industrial cities had been bombed. Coventry lay in ruins. Food and clothing were in short supply and were rigidly rationed. Tens of thousands of soldiers, sailors and airmen were returning to an economy in the turmoil of shifting from armaments and war to reconstruction. Terry's family simply could not grasp why in such circumstances he would want to be an artist. It seemed to them to be frivolous and irrelevant. His male relatives, all of whom had worked in industry before and during the war, and had endured hardship and terror, were not bashful in telling him that drawing and painting were 'sissy'.

Uncle Fred, who was a really good friend, was in Coventry all through World War II and he'd been absolutely bombed to pieces. When I said after the war that I wanted to be an artist he said, 'We all thought you'd gone nuts because all you wrote about in your letters were the colours of the blue jays and the green of the trees'. But you've got to understand that when you're on patrol or lying alone in a forward position, or when you're a prisoner surrounded by wires, and there are the birds so free and the trees and the clouds, it puts everything in perspective . . .[4]

DL: In 1945 you were demobbed?

I went back to work for a bit. They had to keep my old job open for me. I lived in Leamington but worked in Birmingham. I was employed in an electrical components wholesalers. I'd moved up the ladder a bit from my little job in Coventry. Fluorescent lights had just come out and I was standing waiting for them to come off the line and flogging them fast. Then I went to Birmingham art school at night. It made me quite tired.

DL: So by this time you were hooked?

Oh yes, I was hooked. I went into hospital and I knew the reason I was ill was that I wasn't doing what I'd promised myself – as simple as that. I'd been through so much. I only remember the good things. I could tell you a lot of bad things but I don't want to. I'd promised myself that I'd paint, because that's what I wanted to do and I didn't have to do anything else. After all, I'd seen a lot of my mates killed. I'd seen all kinds of things. At first, I didn't have the guts to do it because you come back to a conventional family life and it's very difficult.[5]

To Terry Frost painting and drawing were far from irrelevant. He wanted to express a new-found freedom. He wanted to learn how to be an artist and to be in an environment where artists were not despised. In 1945, when he had returned to work in Birmingham, he met and married Kathleen Clarke, and took art classes in the evening. He was interviewed, by an Army major for an ex-serviceman's grant to go to art school as a full-time student, but was told that as he hadn't got School Certificate he hadn't a chance. His frustrations mounted.

Terry and Kathleen at the time of their marriage in 1945

Flowers in a Vase
c.1945–46
watercolour,
$11\frac{1}{4} \times 7\frac{1}{2}$ in, 28.5 × 19 cm
(the artist)
A still life in his Grandmother's house

4. From interview with David Lewis, October 1993, see page 238

5. From interview with Dave Lee, 1993, see page 238

Marrows
1943
oil on paper,
9 × 13 in, 22.9 × 33 cm.
(the artist)

St Ives 1946–49

Frost hitch-hiked to London (it took two days) and visited the National Gallery, intending in the afternoon to go and see Adrian Heath. Walking up Duncannon Street he popped into a pub, where he was astonished to see Fred Mulley and some of the lads from Stalag 383. One of them who was still a Regular and in the Education Corps told Terry to keep trying to get a grant to study art, as there was a clause in the guidelines allowing for special exceptions. That afternoon, Heath also encouraged him to persevere. Eight months later Terry got his grant and with Heath's help got a place at the Camberwell School of Art in London.

Meanwhile, Heath also advised him to get as far away from his family as he could, and suggested St Ives. He himself had studied briefly in Newlyn before the war with the then aged Stanhope Forbes at his studio on Beaux Arts Lane: indeed, Heath was probably the last of a long line of Forbes students.

Adrian Heath, being my friend in the prison camp, said the best place for me was St Ives or Newlyn because there were a lot of studios and painters there. I'd never heard of the place. So I whipped Kath off quickly and we took the train to St Ives. Our trunk got lost at Bristol on the way down and we arrived without anything except what we stood up in. All our possessions were in that trunk, which my grandmother had stored her onions in for years, so when we did get it our blankets were absolutely reeking of onions.[1]

We went to the local reference library and looked up places that were available. We went to one or two bed-and-breakfast places but we didn't have enough money really. Eventually we saw in the local paper in the library a caravan to let in Headland Road in Carbis Bay, for 30 shillings a week, which we took. It was only a little caravan on a bit of spare ground up there, in an empty field opposite a large house occupied by Miss E. M. Hodgkins, known to everyone as 'Hodgy'. This was before she (who was well off and already in her sixties) began putting together the collection of modern paintings and sculpture which she ultimately bequeathed to the Tate. Her house was a few doors from Chy-an-Kerris, the house occupied by Ben Nicholson and Barbara Hepworth and not far away was the bungalow where Naum and Miriam Gabo had lived. Once when the chickens were eating my sausage out of the frying-pan and I shooed them off, Hodgy said 'what are you doing feeding my chickens?' I said 'that's my breakfast they've just eaten'. She saw my paintings and

remarked, 'Oh, if you're a painter, do you know that Ben Nicholson and Barbara Hepworth live along this road?' 'No, I didn't,' I said, because I'd never bloody heard of them. Hodgy was interested in painting and she found us digs in another house in Carbis Bay. It was very difficult to paint there though so I went to Leonard Fuller's school – he said I could come at half price and I went in the mornings. Then we got a job in domestic service. I was the butler and Kath was the maid. We used to have to wait on the paying guests, who happened to be young Commando officers. I got into trouble with the washing up because it was all posh silver, which I'd never handled before and I rattled it together in the water. I painted a bit in my bedroom there.

I used to work early in the morning and then go down to Leonard Fuller's at ten o'clock. Well, of course, I met people like Sven Berlin, and John Park. Sven was particularly good for me because he was my first modern artist. He was using bits of glass in those days and doing wonderful drawings of lobsters and things like that. He was a very good draughtsman and he was modern for me. Then there was Leonard Richmond, who told me to paint a polished table, a bowl of fruit, running water and bridges: 'that's what people want', he said.

I painted portraits – I'd do a portrait for thirty bob to survive – or boats in the harbour. I shared a studio with Wing-Commander Bunny Stone, who had a bit of money. We managed to find a studio for seven shillings and sixpence a week each and I painted with him. We got on very well together. Then through Sven I met Sydney Graham the poet and Norman Levine, the Canadian writer. They were all optimistic in those days just after the War. Everybody was equal. It was a totally different scene to what it is now. I met the people who had a show in the Crypt, Peter Lanyon, Sven, Adrian Ryan, Johnny Wells, Willie Barns-Graham. Lanyon was very good. He used to take me out into the landscape; we used to go drawing together. He and Sven were great supporters. They encouraged me. But you must remember these were the young ones then, they were nothing.[2]

Kath got a job in the post office delivering telegrams on her bike. It didn't have any brakes and you know what those hills were like – it's a wonder she's still alive. Add to that she didn't understand what people were saying a lot of times, you see the Cornish accent is quite a beautiful sound but difficult to understand at first, but she got tips, threepence here and sixpence there. Then, the people who owned the caravan wanted it back for the holiday letting season and they

Terry and Kath, Adrian and Anthony on a day out at Port Navas

1. From interview with Sarah Fox-Pitt and David Lewis, April 1981, see page 238

2. From interview with Dave Lee, 1993, see page 238

Photograph by Roger Mayne,
boys in the harbour at St Ives

Street in St Ives
1947
oil on canvas,
18 × 14 in, 45.7 × 30.5 cm
(the artist)

found us another place in Carbis Bay. Later Kath and I worked as housekeepers for Mrs Finlay until Jim Holman and Linden Travers took over the house.[3] Then Kath got pregnant: it was get up, get the Aga going, clean up, feed the dogs . . . then I'd go to Fuller's.[4]

Leonard Fuller was an academic painter who ran the St Ives School of Painting in a converted sail loft on Back Road West. Peter Lanyon and Sven Berlin occasionally used the school for some life drawing.

At Fuller's I met Pippa Renwick. She owned 12 Quay Street. She had Tatts Fielding as a tenant. Tatts' son Paul was a model at Fuller's. Pippa let us have her top room. Tatts was a glamorous and educated lady; every month she received a small pension of some sort, but of course she never paid her rent. She had all her bills and court orders pinned up like decorations around the fireplace. It was rather embarrassing to be caught in the middle between Tatts and Pippa. When Tatts' pension came in Pippa would say, 'Tatts, I want the rent. You owe me £25.' Tatts would have it all written down in a little book; and she would say, 'and I've added on the interest!' – as though to give Pippa the impression how honest and generous she was. Then she would find a way to put off paying once again, and end up never paying at all. Finally Tatts got ill and was admitted to St Mary's Hospital in London. Pippa took the opportunity to write and tell her not to come back, but I don't think Tatts wanted to come back. And that's how Kath and I got the house.

Leonard's was really my studio. But I used to paint in my bedroom also. That was where later on I did the *Walk Along the Quay* painting, the big one that Adrian Heath had. I found myself working next door to Harry Rowntree in 1947, when I shared a studio with Bunny Stone. There was Bunny (who was very posh) with his overcoat and his cap on, painting fighters and bombers which he copied from magazines, and there was I painting chipped teapots and Vim tins. Then there was Sven Berlin. Sven was a brilliant draughtsman and he was very kind. He lived down by Porthgwidden Beach where the kipper lofts were. He told me about Gabo, and what Gabo had said to him about how, when you throw a cow-pat against a whitewashed wall, that's art! John Park and Sven would buy me half a pint of beer in the Sloop and when I left I'd find half a crown and a packet of Woodbines in my pocket.[5]

A good spirit prevailed among all the people in the art community at that time. Without doubt the mood was related to the aftermath of war. Britain was faced, not only with the vast task of rebuilding its shattered cities

and industries, but with economic and social reconstruction. The ills of the 1930s were as fresh in people's minds as the destruction of war. Artists seemed to be a mutual support group and they respected each other in spite of deep differences in their approaches to art, most notably between the traditionalists and the moderns. These were generous times. Unfortunately, although we did not know it then, the generous times were not to last.

The evil of war brought out the goodness in individuals. Class distinctions were undermined; everybody tended to try and help one another. People were trying to get through. The worlds of drama, writing and painting, which before the war were very much a closed shop, were opened up to people who never thought they could be part of them – people who wanted to do things for real reasons.[6]

The importance of St Ives as a centre was not only because a large number of artists lived there or thereabouts but it had a tradition and it had the necessary elements that help. Studios were in former fishermen's lofts, rents were cheap, money was in short supply. The odd working hours of the fishing men allowed for the meeting of artist and fisherman. Perhaps the self-employed part or the independence part made for toleration and often genuine friendship. I think this independence of locals and artists played a part in creating the right atmosphere for work. The 'season' had not become so hectic and was looked forward to as a bit of a break. Most people got jobs and most houses did B and B. Most visitors looked for art and fishing boats, plus the exhilarating discovery of the West Penwith dramatic seas, landscapes, winds etc. So there was a fierce encounter with visitors, art and fish and environment. This fierceness was a welcome, or I would say, beneficial necessity – perhaps it acted as a catalyst to more endeavour on the part of the artists, fishermen, B and B workers. The place hummed with a certain stirring happiness – good for work.

Visitors came from all over the world. Critics, artists, poets etc, visited Cornwall, also most London and North Country artists came down for spells. Usually to be scathingly critical of all the artists down there (but always they came back for more). This continual influx of people connected to the arts was most important. It got the artists known. It provided stimulating discussion. It meant that the studios were visited and a genuine interest was shown in what was going on. This I believe, this genuine interest, is what is most valuable to young unknown artists who are trying to do all that they can within their abilities. This

Still Life with Vim Tin
c.1946–47
oil on canvas,
$15\frac{1}{2} \times 10$ in, 39.3 × 25.4 cm
(Belgrave Gallery)
Leonard Richmond, who had exhorted Terry Frost to paint attractive subjects like fruit and bridges, told him he'd never get anywhere with a cracked teapot and Vim.

3. Linden Travers was an actress well known for the title role in the film 'No Orchids for Miss Blandish'.

4. From interview with David Lewis, December 1991, see page 238

5. From interview with David Lewis, December 1991, as above

6. From interview with Sarah Fox-Pitt and David Lewis, 1981, as above

was a step above London. I think London could be very lonely and the effort to get anyone to see you was heartbreaking. Either you were in with a small clique or you were right out. At least in West Penwith nobody could really hide anyone from anybody. And the regular exhibitions in bookshops, hotels, pubs, the Crypt, shop windows, meant continual exposure of everybody's work. Everybody's work because obviously one shop, such as Robin Nance's, would have a Lanyon in the window but the next would hate that modern stuff and so you had your traditional flowers or the harbour. A great place for art to flourish; it was optimistic.

Winter gave the test of intention. It sometimes caused serious distress through lack of money. But let me say the St Ives people did have a way of pulling together in spite of strong antagonism on lots of points between locals and artists and abstract and non-abstract artists. Don't mistake what I'm saying for sentimentality, for I know from experience the great help that people gave to each other during hard out-of-season winters. This in itself is again one of the reasons why so many young artists have been able to live and work down there for long periods of their formative years. And this does not apply only to painters, for many young craftsmen have found encouragement in the area – for metalwork, pottery, jewellery, weaving and so on. That's a bit of an idea of the help the place has to offer, not through its landscape or light, but through its people, its intimacy.

Of course, you can't separate people from their environment like that for it is the limitations forced on one by the landscape that make people come more together, or if not more together, at least more aware of one another, for better or worse. It's almost impossible not to know what is going on with everyone. The sea contains such a narrow strip of land, it dominates by gale and wind, by pressure on the sand and rocks, and it lulls by blue and calm and sun and colour. Extremes: breaking points and warm cuddles of encouragement.[7]

Self Portrait
c.1946
oil on canvas,
18 × 14 in, 45.7 × 30.5 cm
(the artist)
The figure on the right is Bunny Stone

7. From Terry Frost's notes on St Ives

David Lewis in Cornwall, Peter Lanyon and landscape

I came to Cornwall in the autumn of 1947. I knew no one. I lived that winter in a primitive granite cottage at Bosporthennis, near Gurnard's Head, and did piece-work cropping potatoes on a farm belonging to Mr Carne. It was back-breaking work in heavy mud and driving rain. Everything was rationed, food was short and I had little money. Mr Carne lent me a gun to shoot rabbits so I could get something extra to eat, but the gun was rusty and I was a lousy shot, so I had potatoes instead.

The Atlantic gales were dramatic and beautiful. I loved the brown bracken of winter and the driving mists. · Whenever I could I would walk to the hilltop above the farm and nestle into a pocket of soft grass behind huge granite rocks to read a book away from the wind. It was up there that I read James Joyce's *Ulysses* and the poetry of Pound and Eliot.

I got a job with the Workers Education Association (WEA), teaching modern literature at Hayle one evening a week. I was paid seven and sixpence but was responsible for my own bus fare. The nights were cold and blustery waiting at those bus stops. One Friday evening I walked down to the Gurnard's Head pub for half a pint. At the bar two men were talking about painting. One of them kept looking at me as though I was strange. He leaned over and asked me who I was and what I was doing. His name was Peter Lanyon, a young painter, and his companion was John Wells. Johnnie had been a doctor on the Scilly Isles, but had given it up to become a full-time artist. Perhaps it was my general appearance or maybe he and Johnnie were down wind from me, but Peter suddenly asked me: 'Would you like a bath?' A bath! I could hardly imagine anything more luxurious! 'Come over next Friday', he said, 'and I'll ask Sheila to cook supper for us.'

This was the first of several visits to Peter's Attic Studio in St Ives. I hadn't enough money for bus fares so I would walk the five miles each way on a public footpath along the cliffs, across stiles and rain-saturated fields edged with granite hedges. More than once Peter and Sheila invited me to sleep overnight in the studio. They were unforgettable evenings, discussing art and looking at Peter's paintings and drawings. With him I met Ben Nicholson, Barbara Hepworth, Bernard Leach, Bryan Wynter, and Terry Frost, and heard about Naum Gabo who had left for America only a few months before.

The following spring I moved from Bosporthennis to Higher Tregerthen. This was a group of cottages below

Eagle's Nest, where the painter Patrick Heron now lives, and near the village of Zennor. The cottage I rented had been occupied during World War I by Katherine Mansfield and Middleton Murry, and the next door cottage had been where D. H. Lawrence and Frieda had lived at the same time. During the time I lived there, the poet George Barker was living in Zennor and Bryan Wynter lived high above in a hilltop cottage.

I got occasional summer piece-work in the broccoli fields but in the winter my only income was from my WEA class. I became very ill from malnutrition, and urged on by Peter Lanyon, a young local doctor, Roger Slack, brought his car down the almost impassable lane, carried me out of the house, laid me on the back seat, and carted me off to the Edward Hain Hospital and recovery. Meanwhile my contacts with the younger artists broadened and I spent increasing amounts of time in St Ives. In the summer of 1949 I married the painter Wilhelmina (Willie) Barns-Graham and moved from Higher Tregerthen to St Ives; Peter Lanyon was our best man. Willie and Peter were both members of a small group of younger artists who recognised themselves as the next generation beyond Nicholson, Hepworth and Gabo. Their meetings were held in Willie's studio. At the time the only large gallery in St Ives was a converted church, once the old Mariners' Chapel. It was operated by the St Ives Society of Artists and dominated by old guard academics. The 'moderns', as Nicholson, Hepworth, Lanyon and others were referred to, were relegated to a small area behind the main door. Restive at being treated in this way and spearheaded by Lanyon, the younger artists pressed for and obtained exhibition space in the crypt below the church. The Crypt Group, as it came to be called, included Lanyon, Wells, Wynter, Berlin, Barns-Graham and the printer Guido Morris. Several paintings now in the Tate and other public collections were first shown in the Crypt exhibitions.

Willie and I lived first on Bethesda Hill, close to St Ives harbour, and then at 4 Teetotal Street, a few doors away from 12 Quay Street where Kath and Terry Frost lived, and who by that time were renting the whole of that small house. We were all quite poor; it was hard to get work, except in the summer season. Terry and I were lucky. I worked the breakfast stint as a waiter and short-order cook in Rose's Café on the harbour front and in the summer season Terry worked as a waiter at the Sunset Bar and at St Christopher's guest house – thus we were neighbours and had things in common. When I first knew Terry Frost he was in transition between being a figurative painter and moving into abstraction. While Kath continued to live at 12 Quay Street, Terry was commuting back and forth to the Camberwell School of Arts.

In the summer of 1947 Peter Lanyon had introduced Terry to Ben Nicholson, with whom Terry maintained a correspondence while he was away. At that time Peter Lanyon liked being the link between us all. He was absolutely passionate about Cornwall. He had an independent income which allowed him to devote himself entirely to painting. He loved exploring the landscape.

Peter would drive me all over the place, along the coast and up on the moors, talking all the time. He was so proud of the Cornish landscape. Then we'd sit down and draw together . . .

The most important thing about Peter was that he taught me to *experience* landscape. Perhaps he wasn't really telling me what I should do so much as telling himself what to do and reassuring himself that this is what he needed to do. So you lay down in the landscape, you looked up into a tree to see whether it was an umbrella shape inside or a blown-out inside-out umbrella, you walked over the landscape so that you understood its shape, you looked behind rocks so that you knew what their shape was all the way round and what lay beyond them, you walked over the hills and the high ground so that you knew what was above and below you, and what was above and below the forms you were going to draw, and all the while you're feeling those forms all through, you're travelling through the landscape.

I found it very interesting to see Peter draw because he was so expressionist while I was very tight-arsed, because of Camberwell. He just roared into his drawing, and rushed the waves over, and everything was leaning, and the rocks went in black, just like that. I was in awe of him and much quieter. I walked round and round, trying to draw the experience of the landscape in a single moving line, totally different from Peter. And I would be thinking about what sort of canvas I would use to paint this experience later on: if it was a 36 × 12 inch upright, I had to read it that way, flat to begin with, and then I had to have the nerve to start with my thought after studying all my drawings.

We went to Mullion, and there were black rocks and blue sea, and a little quay jutting into the sea, and a slanting lamp-post to the side, and sea water smashing over the rocks. So when I did my blue and black painting I was walking along that quay to look at the rocks. Peter went back to his studio and did drawing after drawing from the drawing he made at Mullion that day. And that's when he incorporated boot-black into the drawing (I have it in my studio to this day), to make the *blackness* of the rocks.

Gunwalloe was the church out there in the sand. There was a post with a black semicircle and a white semicircle. I did a drawing inside the church looking out. Recently I found that drawing again and I went back to Gunwalloe and there the church was, and the post, exactly as they were forty-five years ago. In the drawing I've got Grace Hendy Lugg on a tombstone. But I couldn't have seen Grace Hendy Lugg from that window. The tombstone was below it on the outside. So I would have had to find that grave on the outside and draw it, and then bring my drawing in and incorporate it into the drawing I was doing inside the church, a sort of time/motion study I suppose.

I would set out my geometrical divisions and then find a way to express something like Mullion Cove by putting colour references to what I'd seen and what had moved me, blue black where the rocks are wet, and the little bay at the bottom, and so I would build up and build up until I had rediscovered my experience, and that's what I did then. And I found out that in a way one loses one's innocence after each discovery. You can never repeat it. It's not the same.[1]

Gunwalloe
1954
pencil,
18 × 21 in, 45.6 × 53.3 cm
(the artist)
The church in the sand dunes is at Church Cove, just south of Gunwalloe fishing cove, on the Lizard peninsula. The black and white sign was set on the 'blue and green undulating space' of the nearby golf course.

1. This text is taken from three interviews with David Lewis, December 1991, July and October 1993, see page 238

39

Camberwell

I went to Camberwell in 1947 after two years in St Ives, when I'd met Lanyon and Nicholson. Adrian Heath knew what was going on there, and I used to go and see Pasmore on a Saturday morning because he was always there then. He was my god because Adrian had introduced me to his work. I'd been in the class, doing what was expected, for about an hour and Pasmore said 'I see you've finished'. I said 'this is what I really do' and I turned the board over to show him my own work. He told me not to come in any more – 'go round the National Gallery, go round the modern galleries'. I said, 'it's taken me two years to get a bloody grant, and anyway I have to sign in in the book'. 'Get someone else to sign you in' he said – and that was the great man, that was my advice from Victor Pasmore. He liked what I was doing and he didn't really want to see me in an art school.

Although I was still doing quite straightforward stuff myself, I was very interested in what the boys were trying to do. Lanyon for instance was into the landscape in a different way. He said you had to get intimate with it. It was really a different way of putting yourself down and looking: a much wider vision of things. And I think that has lasted me all my life.

By 1949 I was doing my first abstracts, very quietly because I still had to do my exam piece. I went into the lithography department and did an abstract theme and when the tutor saw it he said 'that's all bullshit', which of course put me off a bit. But I got another twelve months doing what I wanted, which was fantastic. We were a red-hot lot at Camberwell, and a crowd who knew a lot about art history. We'd all been analysing, because we were very tight on structure, Piero della Francesca. I'd copy Rubens, 'The Three Graces', so we were right on the ball about structure. It was natural that I should continue to do that and see the possibilities in spite of what was going on round me.

I was aware of Picasso and Matisse, though of course they were all into dot-and-carry-one drawing at Camberwell, and that was very dangerous. You must remember the Slade hadn't got past Cubism in those days. It was a pretty tricky time, you know.[1]

At Camberwell, Pasmore told Terry Frost to cut the figure-drawing class and spend time in the National Gallery looking at the old masters, seeing them freshly, without inhibition. This became an important experience for him. It laid the foundation for a personal and non-academic understanding of how the Old Masters worked

that was never to leave him, an understanding based on direct experience of the paintings themselves with a minimum of intellectual conditioning.

I learned every room in the National Gallery, one room at a time. There were particular pictures, one or two in every room. 'St Jerome in his study' was an important painting for me, a little house, which has St Jerome's study, inside a bigger house with a window on each side leading the eye out into the landscape, and I am inside and outside at the same time. Then there was the Rubens room, with 'The Three Graces'. They are the same girl, front view, back, and side. And if you draw the direction of the glances, the glance of the girl in three positions, and the glance of Paris over on one side, you have a wonderful series of geometrical forms informing the structure of the painting. You have the figures doing a semicircle, lights and darks and three flashes of reds, giving a series of time-space-colour movements forming a structural continuity. The geometry is the discipline which gives you the assurance, the confidence, to take risks and make the moves. The Rubens teaches you that.[2]

In spite of following up on Pasmore's suggestion, Frost assiduously attended figure-drawing classes too. We have to remember that although he had got to know Nicholson, Lanyon and others in St Ives, he was still doing orthodox landscapes and portraits. He had come to Camberwell to learn. Like most of the students at Camberwell in 1947, Terry was on an ex-serviceman's grant. The training was rigorous.

We did the Intermediate with a teacher named Walway who was brilliant architecturally at the geometries of perspective. He was in love with the Golden Section and the Greeks and put us through it pretty toughly . . . We started with pure divisions of the rectangle, and we did analyses of the Old Masters from Piero and Carpaccio to Seurat. I also went to Kenneth Clark's lectures . . .

I was with a crowd of what I called the 'Coldstream Guards'. They hadn't got past Cézanne and they weren't going to. They were plumb-line happy, and you have to have everything on the Golden Section, and you have your chin in a chinstrap and everything has to be accurate. You couldn't talk about Cubism or anything like that. You mark where you're standing and where your feet are and where your easel is, and you can't make a mark on an ear without relating it across to the nose and so on and so on . . .[3]

While he was at Camberwell Terry lodged in a house in Albert Bridge Road and would go over to Adrian Heath's

Self-Portrait
1948
oil on board,
(Belgrave Gallery)
Painted in the flat at 57 Albert Bridge Road

1. From interview with Dave Lee, 1993, see page 238

2. From interview with David Lewis, October 1993, see page 238

3. From interview with David Lewis, July 1993, see page 238

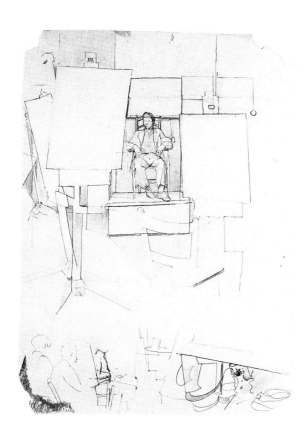

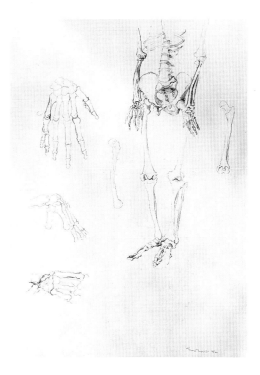

Camberwell Life Drawing
c.1947–48
pencil,
15 × 11 in, 38 × 28 cm
(the artist)
The figure second from the bottom left-hand corner
is Howard Hodgkin, also a student at that time.

Life Study
c.1950
pencil,
$13\frac{1}{8} \times 8\frac{1}{8}$ in, 33.3 × 20.5 cm
(the artist)
Drawn in a life class in the Penwith Gallery, then
in Fore Street, St Ives.

Camberwell Anatomy Study
c.1947–48
pencil,
$15\frac{1}{8} \times 11$ in, 38.3 × 28 cm
(the artist)

from time to time. When Heath bought a house in Fitzroy Street he let Terry have a studio in it, which had previously been occupied by Bryan Wynter before he went to Cornwall. There Terry met Colquhoun, McBryde, Prunella Clough and other friends of Wynter's and Adrian Heath's. Two paintings he made in the 1948–49 period were key transitional works, one a nude and the other an abstract composition 'Madrigal'.[4] The nude was based on the Camberwell model Miss Humphries, or Humph, as she was known.

I didn't want to rebel against what I'd been doing [in the figure-drawing classes] but somehow it didn't seem quite right. So I got back into my studio at Adrian's house and I got all the drawings that I'd done of Humph – I'd been drawing her for a couple of terms – and I decided to paint her, not from life but from my drawings. That became one of the most important paintings of my life. I had to stop being descriptive and start being pictorial. I had the drawings but I had to *make* the painting. And that's when you realise that you have to go back and make more drawings. It's the same line – but you have to go back for more information, more form, more reality. And I did the whole thing, not in front of the figure, but built up from drawings. Anyway it was a good break for me from the continual grind in front of the model. I don't think I showed the painting to anyone at the time as it was so out of line with the Euston Road. I know I was fond of terre verte and naples yellow for the figure in those days.[5]

'Madrigal', painted over a year later, was a composition assignment set by Claude Rogers for the students to do over the summer. There were two subjects they could choose from, 'Joseph's Coat of Many Colours' or 'A Madrigal'. At Leamington Spa, where he and Kath were visiting their families, Terry went to the Reference Library to look up 'coat of many colours', and found to his amazement that the scholars disagreed. A prevailing interpretation was that it referred, not to a coat at all, but to a person's character – the colours of a many-faceted mind. Not knowing what to make of that, he turned to 'madrigal', and discovered W. H. Auden's poem:

O lurcher-loving collier, black as night,
Follow your love across the smokeless hill;
Your lamp is out and all the cages still;
Course for her heart and do not miss,
For Sunday soon is past and, Kate, fly not so fast,
For Monday comes when none may kiss:
Be marble to his soot, and to his black be white.[6]

Terry was immediately drawn to this poem, not only because of the beauty of its rhythm and the colours it

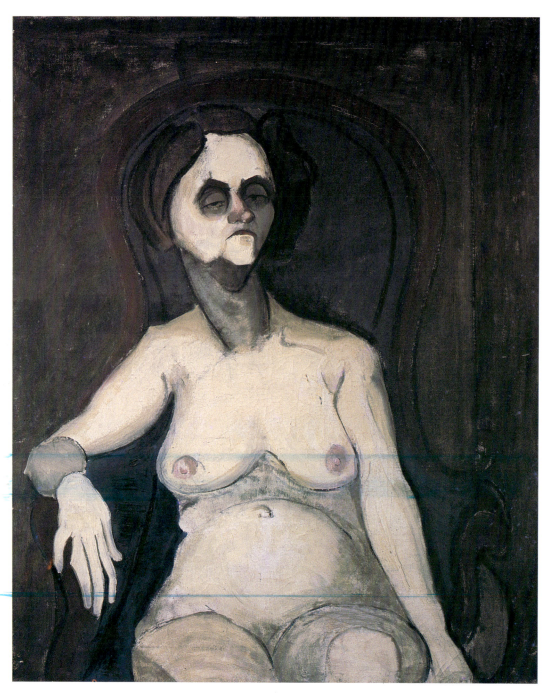

4. See page 46

5. From interview with David Lewis, July 1993, see page 238, and from Terry Frost's notes on the painting

6. From 'Madrigal' by W. H. Auden, courtesy of Faber & Faber

Miss Humphries
1948
drawing, pencil,
$7 \times 4\frac{1}{2}$ in, 17.8×11.5 cm
(the artist)

◁ painting, oil on canvas,
30×25 in, 76.2×63.5 cm
(the artist)

The Chair
1947
oil on canvas,
24×20 in, 61×50.8 cm
(the artist)

evoked, but because of the coincidences of the collier coming back to his Kate.

I subdivided the flat surface with the Golden Section and the square so that every geometrical shape was related to every other shape, and then I used colours emotionally. Apart from the poem, they were very much the Camberwell colours of the time, bottle green, maroon, deep brown, and very much like the dullness of the life room . . .

I pushed in the warmth when he came up from the mine to meet Kate. It was pretty obvious he wasn't coming out of the bloody mine to have a cup of tea.

It was the only abstract on the wall when Daniels, the Principal, came in to give his talk on our work. But having spoken about all the others he found he finally had to say something about this one, and he said: 'This kind of thing is alright, as long as it's not an end in itself.' And that was the only comment I got . . .[7]

Perhaps the most significant aspect of both these paintings is their exploration of the impact of colour and paint quality on geometrical subdivisions of the flat surface. In the painting of Humph, drawing and descriptive painting are not enough. It is colour, and the *shape* of colour, which spell out lightness or weight and spatial depth or advance. Appealing to William Coldstream for help in a drawing class, Terry had said, 'I don't know how to get the head back,' and Coldstream replied, 'think it back'. For Terry this was an unforgettable piece of advice. In 'Madrigal', following Auden's injunction '. . . and to his black be white', the white assumes a power and a textural plasticity which have to be held by the colour-density of each of the other elements of the composition.

The shapes in my first abstract paintings were accurate in relation to other shapes, but I found that if you turned an angle or an axis slightly off the vertical it immediately set up a tension and a rhythm with the other shapes, and brought the whites into play as positives. And then you might pick up a bit of orange paper off a tea packet, or something like that lying around in the studio, and a bit of blue, which you'd cut into a shape, a triangle or a semicircle, and you'd lay that in; and you realise that you've set up a new series of tensions and possibilities, and so the composition would begin to grow . . .[8]

. . . as far as work goes I am perhaps as confused as ever but I have made some advancement. Getting more strength and architectural construction into the pictures . . .[9]

I am now mixing – or should I say, am able to work on, representation and abstract art. This I feel is much better for me, for as you well know I was always moved by things around me, though of course the abstract and subjective work that I have spent so long on has been very valuable to me. For one thing, I did not know that I had any real imagination or deep subjective feelings and I have been able to develop those senses enormously. Now I have to battle on and find the method in which I can express all these emotions best. Whether it be by abstraction or representation remains to be seen.[10]

. . . It looks very much as if the end of the grant will be the end of my full-time painting. At the same time it will probably cause me to fight to live once more and then perhaps I'll paint with something to say again. . . . We shan't know until the end of this month whether I've passed my painting exam or not. It will be touch and go, I know that. If I pass then I suppose I slog on for another 12 months on architecture, anatomy etc for another exam. If I fail then I shall have to take the painting again next year but I wouldn't mind that as I should spend the next 12 months just painting for my own sake and do my swotting in the evenings. You make me laugh when you say you looked in the papers to see if I was mentioned. I don't show anywhere now. The St Ives Society has split up . . . the Crypt boys opening a new gallery next to the Castle Inn. It's called the Penwith Society and I've been invited to exhibit but so far have declined because I don't think they would accept my work. These days I work entirely for myself, abstract being the phase I'm going through now. I am completely free to make what shapes I like and to invent what colour I like, not being bound by any visual image.

Since I started writing this letter a week ago I have been through one of those horrible blank periods, torn between making myself paint a still life in the representational manner or carrying on with the fight and flogging myself until I squeeze out another abstract. Started off with a still life this morning but could not stand the sight of it and finished up composing an abstract using the still life as the germ . . .[11]

We must not forget that at this time Frost very much admired Victor Pasmore, who was undergoing his own transition from figurative paintings. Pasmore went through a brief period of what one might call abstract pointillism and this led to his abstract-geometric paintings, which in turn led directly to his coloured constructions.

7. From interview with David Lewis, July 1993, and the Milburn-Foster interview, see page 238

8. From interview with David Lewis, July 1993, as above

9. From letter written from London in 1948–49 to Yan Kel Feather

10. From letter to Yan Kel Feather, as above

11. From letter to Yan Kel Feather, as above

I would go up to Blackheath to see Victor; I was among the privileged few. I saw him making constructions for the first time. Suddenly what he was doing I saw to be linked with Ben Nicholson and his white reliefs and with Gabo and the Constructivists. I was so excited by all the possibilities which we hadn't had before. Painting a portrait or a flowerpiece – though there's nothing wrong with that at all – seemed then to be a limitation on conception and optimism. Everything suddenly began to open up.[12]

In addition to Adrian Heath, Terry formed strong friendships with Anthony Hill, Kenneth and Mary Martin, and other artists who were moving into hard-edge geometric abstraction and construction. The writings of Matila Ghyka on geometrical composition,[13] Worringer's *Art & Empathy*, and Herbert Read's 1936 edition of T. E. Hulme's *Speculations* on the philosophy of art[14] in which Hulme drew a sharp distinction between the figurative and abstract languages of art, were basic readings. Herbert Read and others were instrumental in founding the Institute of Contemporary Arts in Dover Street in London: the ICA gave public legitimacy to artists exploring the frontiers of visual art as well as providing a meeting place and forum for discussion. The work of the British Council and the Arts Council, both of which began to acquire avant-garde work by British artists, struck a positive note, encouraging acquisitions by other public collections, and various dealers' galleries began to take risks and show work by new and unknown artists.

It was all coming together for me. Victor came all the way to Battersea to see what I was doing. Minton, who later committed suicide, and Coldstream were at Camberwell at the time, but what they were doing there didn't interest me very much. All very nice people, but there was something stifling about it. Coldstream was god, but he seemed to put a straitjacket on my imagination. He came over to see one of my new paintings, and sat down in my chair and said, 'I think you should scrape it down and start again,' and that was the end of my crit from Bill Coldstream! The problem was that this was his attitude and he had his own way of producing art. It was right for him, but it became quite clear that this wasn't my way . . . I have no regrets at all. Rejection is every bit as important as appreciation, providing one has the confidence to withstand it.[15]

When Adrian Heath was writing his book on abstract art for Tiranti[16] I used to go and stay in his place in Fitzroy Street. You'd have all these things pinned up all round the kitchen: Kupka and all the early abstract painters, the Russian Constructivists – the whole thing was being discussed at breakfast and it was still being discussed at 2 o'clock the next morning. So although I didn't do history of art with any skill because I was never really interested in it, not dates and all that bullshit, I was lucky enough to listen to people talking about art and about painters and about what had happened. Of course I got absolutely sold on Russian Constructivism, which was just about the start of abstract painting as far as I was concerned. We had the Mondrian book, the Kandinsky book, all these things were around us. So I got involved with abstraction. The more I went to galleries, the more I looked at it, the more interested I became.[17]

12. From interview with David Lewis, December 1991, see page 238

13. Matila Ghyka, *A Practical Handbook of Geometrical Composition and Design*, Tiranti, London

14. T. E. Hulme, *Speculations*, ed. Herbert Read, Kegan Paul, London 1936

15. From interview with David Lewis, December 1991, as above

16. Adrian Heath, *Abstract Art, its origins and meanings*, Tiranti, London 1953

17. From interview with Sarah Fox-Pitt and David Lewis, 1981, see page 238

Madrigal
1949
oil on canvas,
28 × 36 in, 71 × 91.4 cm
(the artist)

St Ives 1950–54

While he was at Camberwell Terry Frost would hitchhike back and forth between London and St Ives. He would spend as much time as he could with his family in Cornwall. Sometimes Kath would visit him in London. In those days in St Ives there was a bookshop on Fore Street run by George Downing, with books in the front part of the shop and space for small exhibitions in the back. Lanyon, Wynter, Wells, Barns-Graham, Berlin, Leach, Hepworth, Nicholson, Denis Mitchell and others had exhibitions there, mostly of small things because the space was so restricted. In 1948 Terry had a show there of small paintings and drawings and Guido Morris printed the catalogue. Guido was a marvellous printer – the catalogues and the pamphlets of poetry printed and published by him are now rare collector's items. Somewhat like a mediaeval printer, he did everything by hand in his old fishing loft which he called The Latin Press, lay-out, typesetting in Bembo, rolling, and printing on exquisite handmade papers. He would always leave his jobs to the last possible minute and he hadn't even started on Terry's catalogue by closing time at the Castle Inn the night before the show. But by 2 pm the following day, there he was, looking pale, stained and ragged, with the catalogues, boxed, and tied with a red ribbon, three hours before the exhibition opened!

In 1948 a block of thirteen Porthmeor studios was bought by the Arts Council to be amortised by rentals from artists. They were large spaces with high ceilings and several had huge north windows overlooking the sea. Barns-Graham had No. 2; in 1949 Ben Nicholson obtained No. 5. In 1950, Nicholson interceded with Philip James, head of the Arts Council, to get No. 4, next door to his own, for Terry. At that time Terry had no studio and was still working at St Christopher's. James had stayed there and had bought a little painting of Porthmeor Beach 'for a fiver, and that made my month'.

In St Ives, Terry Frost began to develop the abstraction begun with 'Madrigal', with two related themes, known today as the 'Movement' and 'Walk Along the Quay' paintings. He was still living at 12 Quay Street, and his oldest son Adrian was about two. Every morning at first light he would take Adrian for a saunter around the harbour. St Ives was still a working fishing port in those days. Sometimes the tide would be out so far that the harbour was a sloping sandy floor with ropes draped across it in all directions, and stranded boats and masts were tilted at angles. In section they were semicircles with the lines of the masts acting as diameters, and the ropes were lines also but much thinner and longer, some

Walk Along the Quay
1950
oil on canvas,
60 × 22 in, 152.5 × 56 cm
(private collection, on loan to
the Graves Art Gallery, Sheffield)

taut, and some slack and writhing like snakes against the texture and ivory colour of the sand. Here and there were patches of wet, which glistened silver in the early light. Usually the hulls of the boats were black with green at the waterline, and a sharp red trim along the bulwarks. There were hand-painted buoys, and ropes, and folded brown nets; and from the masts came cable stays, and more ropes, and booms with furled canvas sails the colour of rust.

At other times the tide would be in, and all the boats would be upright, and their decks would be just below the level of the quay. Ropes lay below the surface as well as above, and the reflections of the hulls were upside down semicircles below the surface – reflections which shimmered when there was an early morning stirring of sea breeze. The floor of the harbour would no longer be ivory sand, but turquoise and sage green. The ropes above the water cast reflections, and the ropes below the water looped in great arcs so you couldn't always tell exactly which was below and which was above. Sometimes when the wind was high and fresh and sea swells were running in the bay, the boats and their masts would rock at their moorings, and they would stretch the ropes and release them, and the masts and riggings would describe arcs moving back and forth against grey rain-sodden skies.

'Walk Along the Quay' was a kind of revelation for me, having gone through the academic mill of perspective, tone, composition etc. Abstraction had taught me to recognise the flat surface at least. Things like physical shape and imaginative 'shapes', illusionistic things, all these things became more real once the penny had dropped for me. It's all right reading books and listening to different arguments but for me at any rate I always had to actually experience and discover for myself. So the walk along the quay was a genuine discovery. How was I to paint the experiences I was having in this locked harbour? I knew a bit about art from what was fashionable in the art school and from books. What I didn't want to do then was imitate Picasso, Braque etc. I really did think there was a chance of making something happen in an analogous way on a flat surface, flat surface being the vital important start. From understanding that, you can move into colour and what it does by intensity, proportion, overlap etc. Colour for feeling, to do with imagination and reverie, inspired by actual visual experience. This plus the training to use a concept causes a great deal of difficulty. Anyway, 'Walk Along the Quay' came from a true walk, a regular morning stroll and the constant movement always (without deep 'art' thought, always the killer of

Women in Quay Street
c.1949–50
drawing, pencil,
$4 \times 7\frac{1}{4}$ in, 10.2 × 18.4 cm
(the artist)

painting, oil on board,
$17 \times 29\frac{1}{4}$ in, 43.2 × 74.3 cm
(Belgrave Gallery)

inspiration and imagination) intrigued me. Intrigue is too strong a word. Really I just enjoyed the scene first, then I could not help 'seeing' all that was going on. If you walk along the quay, in fact, it is a hard under-foot experience. Things were happening to my right and beneath – my feet felt and saw all the shapes of boats tied up and either preparing to go out or unloading. The strange feeling of looking on top of boats at high tide and at the same boats tied up and resting on their support posts when the tide's out. It is a difference so great, like a silence and a bomb. Low water gives static shape, more smell, more detail of ropes, huge floats etc, high water gives in addition to colour an ever-changing form with a never-known movement, or always something new – reflection, colour, movement, nothing static or fixed, just surprise. The surprise of not knowing what is coming next. So after all this I had no problem in finding out how to paint 'Walk Along the Quay'. The size of the canvas was suggested to me by one I happened to have. It had to conform to my idea, the walk, so it was long, like the quay (the Pier past Smeaton's Lighthouse) and narrow. Everything was happening below me so I think for the first time I managed to paint up the canvas or along the canvas, like I walked along the quay, in fact I just walked up the canvas with paint.[1]

The studies for 'Walk Along the Quay' were done before Terry had a studio. They and finally the big painting were painted in his bedroom with the tall canvas propped up on a chair in the corner. Of showing that painting to Ben Nicholson, Terry said:

He sat in front of 'Walk Along the Quay' and he had a sandwich. He sat for what seemed like a couple of hours but it couldn't have been. He looked and looked, then he left without saying anything. And he never did say anything about it. But afterwards he arranged to have the painting put into the 1951 Artists International Association's Abstract Art show done in London in connection with the Festival of Britain, and he brought Peter [E.C.] Gregory to see it and Peter bought it. That was the kind of chap Ben was.[2]

Perhaps what Ben saw in 'Walk Along the Quay' was something of Constable's physical directness or something of Turner's poetic subjectivity. Perhaps he saw, in the flattened internal space of the painting, a new and vigorous aspect of Cubism. Or perhaps he saw what he said he saw, those references to a familiar natural world of hulls and ropes and flurried water in which this painting of Terry's abounds – not described, but transmitted to us through the action of brushstrokes and quality of paint.

Boats and Houses
c.1950–52
pencil,
9 × 8 in, 22.8 × 20.3 cm
(the artist)

Fishing Boat
1948
pencil,
$3\frac{1}{2}$ × 5 in, 8.9 × 12.7 cm
(the artist)

Grey and White Seascape
1952
(whereabouts unknown)

1. From Terry Frost's notes on the St Ives years

2. From interview with David Lewis, December 1989, see page 238

49

Black and White Movement
1952
oil on board,
70 × 40 in, 177.8 × 101.6 cm
(Tate Gallery)

▷ *Green, Black and White Movement*
1951
oil on canvas,
43 × 33½ in, 109.2 × 85 cm
(Tate Gallery)

But I believe that what he saw was all of these elements at once, and that they formed the beginning of what he used often to refer to as an 'idea' – that curious alchemy, which musicians understand so well, of coalescing many strands of thought and perception into a thematic and plastic language of rich potential development, and that Terry had a lifetime as a painter ahead of him to pursue the theme. For what Terry was beginning to do in that series of paintings was to take elements from the natural world around him, and develop from them an abstract vocabulary from which to construct a wholly new reality.

A painter of marked architectonic virtue, Frost only began to paint after the recent war. A pupil of Pasmore, his 'brush-touch' still resembles Pasmore's. But Frost's concern with space *behind* the *canvas, and with a landscape subject-matter from which he derives his forms, alienates him from the Pasmore of today. The limpid, swift clarity of the scissoring banana-forms in '*Movement in Green, Black and White*', 1951, evokes the bobbing of moored rowing-boats in St Ives Harbour. Even without colour, one feels the water surface (which now admits the eye deep down into submarine gloom, and now rebuts it, keeping it* at *the surface) implied throughout the surface of this picture. All the shapes stop the eye, as a bat stops a ball, cleanly and finally at a given depth in the imagined space in the painting.*[3]

When I visited Terry Frost in his Porthmeor studio, we could hear Ben Nicholson moving around next door in No. 5. He would listen to jazz on a little radio he had, then we would hear scraping sounds as he prepared the textures of his boards or canvases, which he referred to as 'grounds'. Then suddenly the radio would click off, and we would know that he was painting. 'He would always blow his nose before he drew a circle', Terry recalls. And he would ask either of us into his studio, but never both of us at once, to see new paintings as he completed them.

He would say, 'What do you think of that, Terry?', and he'd always give me a cork-tipped Craven A and a glass of sherry. That was big, coming from Ben. Well I was quite innocent, and in many ways he was an ordinary little bloke, and then I'd think, my God, this is Ben asking me. But I'd be perfectly frank. 'I don't think you've got the balance quite right there, Ben!' And he'd send me away. Then the next day, knock, knock, knock. 'Will you come and have a look, Terry. You were quite right. I think I've got it now!' And then he'd come into my studio to have a look at what I was doing, and he'd move everything out of the way so that he could look

at one piece of work at a time without anything to disturb him, and he'd say, 'you've got something there', or sometimes he'd say 'well, I don't think that's quite working,' and I'd ask him what I should do. 'My dear chap,' he'd say, 'that's up to you!' Or he'd say, 'I like the *idea*; but you haven't given it enough *authority*'.[4]

Ben had that diamond painting over his damp patch on the wall at Carbis Bay. I think it was 1926, a very early painting and he swapped it with me for my painting[5] with the boat shapes which the Tate have got now. We shook hands on it. I was very pleased. But Philip James had been down and I got a letter the next day from old man Brown of the Leicester Galleries and it said 'we would like your green and black and white painting, your pink one and your grey one'. He listed the three that Philip James had seen so I had to go round to Ben and say 'I've had this letter from the Leicester Galleries . . .'. Ben said 'do you more good to have a show in London', so we re-shook hands and he released me from the deal. The pink one I'd scraped off the night before (I used to work at night then when the children were quiet) so I had to bloody sit down and repaint it. They sold the three of them and that was my first start, the Leicester Galleries, so Ben was quite right, it did do more good, but I missed that one of his.[6]

But all was not well in the artists' community in St Ives. Several artists, including all the 'moderns', decided in 1949 to secede from the St Ives Society, and to form a new group, the Penwith Society, which would be inclusive of all the arts, including crafts. A wonderful space – an old potato loft – was rented, and Peter Lanyon, Terry, Denis Mitchell and I spent our spare hours scrubbing the floors and painting the walls white so that it could become a gallery. Herbert Read was elected its president. To ensure fair jurying of works submitted for group exhibitions, the Society decided to create three categories, A = figurative, B = non-figurative, C = crafts. The artist making the submission should choose the category (and thus the jury) best suited to the work. But several members thought that art should not be categorised, and resigned. Among those artists who left were Berlin, Lanyon and Guido Morris. The debate grew bitter. I don't think the wounds ever healed.

In an attempt to stabilise things I became the curator of the Penwith in 1951. I also became Hepworth's part-time secretary, researching and cataloguing work from her early days as a sculptor onwards. This formed the basis for Herbert Read's monograph on her work, published in 1952, and also for her exhibition in the British Pavilion at the Venice Biennale for which I wrote

3. From Patrick Heron, 'Space in Colour: Notes on nine British Painters', *Arts Digest* (New York), 15 March 1955, pp.8–11

4. From interview with David Lewis, December 1991, see page 238

5. This was 'Green, Black and White Movement', 1951, see page 51

6. From interview with David Lewis, April 1979, see page 238

Collage
1950
oil, charcoal and collage on board,
16 × 29½ in, 40.5 × 75 cm
(Pier Gallery, Stromness, Orkney)

Terry Frost in St Peter's Loft, c.1952, annotated on the back by Peter Lanyon: 'Erectivism: the beginnings'

Photograph by Roger Mayne, a corner in 12 Quay Street, showing works from the very early 1950s including the lithograph 'Blue Moon', see page 209 the introduction. Working at the Penwith and for Barbara enabled me to give up working at Rose's.

Barbara Hepworth was commissioned to carve a large stone piece for the 1951 Festival of Britain. She chose to do, not one piece, but two standing sculptures as a single composition, 'Contrapuntal Forms', in blue limestone, each ten feet high and weighing several tons. She took on Denis Mitchell as her full-time assistant, along with a young sculptor, Owen Broughton, who had previously been an assistant to Henry Moore. Terry Frost joined them on a part-time basis, allowing him to provide for his family as well as to continue painting.

Barbara offered me a job at eighteen shillings a day, one day a week. At first all she'd allow me to do was move sand in a wheelbarrow and clean up the yard; and then one day ten tons of Connemara limestone arrived on a big low-loader. It wasn't easy, manoeuvring that low-loader into position at the back door in that narrow lane, all on a hillside. Denis and I had to erect the gear to hold ten tons of stone upright, but we did it, and got the stones into position on the stand. The great thing I learned from Denis was to take our time and never rush because you cannot make a mistake with heavy stones like that. You had to move each one a little bit at a time and adjust it with wedges, then move it another little bit, until you got it in position; it took a long time.

So Barbara put me to roughing out along with Owen and Denis; we had to stand on scaffolds. It made quite a change in the way the local people around Quay Street and Back Road West looked at me. There I was, a father with kids, apparently no job, and now I was coming home covered in white dust, with my knuckles in elastoplast, and I'd been *working*, not just painting those silly pictures.[7]

. . . I have been working for Barbara Hepworth since before Christmas so have managed to creep through winter. I have of course learnt quite a lot about sculpture while there and have in fact almost completed my first carving.

I have a chance of showing in London in May with a small group of abstract painters and sculptors headed by Victor Pasmore, Ben Nicholson, Robert Adams etc. If I get into this show I really shall be wide open to the critics. If they notice my work, even if only to heave strings of derogative tripe at it, that will be better than complete silence. Sales of course are practically non-existent for the unknown abstract painter. I did sell my second abstract in twelve months last week, my total earnings from sales being £45 including sales of most of

my best Camberwell drawings and a couple of straight-up-and-down paintings.[8]

It was a Godsend to me, living on that corner on Quay Street. I'd wake up in the morning and there's a bucket of crabs on the doorstep, and not a word from anyone about it. So you suddenly realise that you're not alone any more, even though you're foreigners, or 'furriners' as the Cornish used to say. Or a neighbour comes up and says 'I've just done some washing, m'dear, and here's some hot soapy water if you can use 'n' – at a time when soap was rationed and very scarce. I'm trying to explain about the reticence and generosity of people for whom life is very tough. You see, the fishermen's life was dangerous, out there on the sea every night when gales spring up out of nowhere.[9]

The great thing was to experience how Barbara worked. She knew what she wanted. It was a reductive process. You went inwards . . . .. But Barbara didn't start off with drawings of what she was going to do, she started with high points which she marked in blue, and then we'd go in around those high points. Then she'd come in with a claw chisel and she could turn the form this way and that way with the same cut, so she would take off from nothing to half an inch and make it work in all directions. Then she would describe that turn with the claw and Denis and I would carve it for a couple of weeks while she was working on another part. She was relating all these cuts to the one side and then to the other side and top and bottom all the time; she could actually 'see' the other side when she was on this side and I could never understand how she could do that.

It stopped me painting for a bit. Here I was making something actual at Barbara's – and my painting seemed to rely, not on the actual, but on illusion. So I started making constructions and mobiles. It took me about nine months to get over the effect.[10]

I turned to constructions and collage because they were the opposite of carving. Carving is reductive; construction is building up. I began with a white board on a white board, white on white, related perhaps to Ben's white reliefs, but more to Malevich. I had seen a lot of Peter Lanyon's constructions in his studio earlier but paid little attention to them. He didn't talk to me about Gabo very much. I heard a lot about the Russian Suprem
atists and Constructivists and Gabo from Adrian Heath and Anthony Hill; and we talked a lot about Duchamp-Villon, Kupka, and Lissitzky. I was very moved by how early on Kupka was making pure abstract paintings in colour theory in vertical and disks.

Black and White Movement
1953
oil on canvas,
30 × 20 in, 76.2 × 50.8 cm
(private collection)

▷ *Pink Painting*
1953
oil on board,
24 × 16½ in, 61 × 42 cm
(private collection)

7. From interview with David Lewis, December 1991, see page 238

8. From a letter to Yan Kel Feather from 12 Quay Street, early 1951

9. From interview with David Lewis, October 1993, see page 238

10. From interview with David Lewis, October 1993, as above

I saw a Lissitzky at the Leicester Galleries that knocked me out, white, black and ochre, clear shapes, and including the letters CCCP with an exclamation mark, a big vertical and a big dot! It was a period when art and social commitment came together. I also read a lot about the relation of organic forms to universal geometries in *On Growth and Form*. From constructions I went back to collages, and this helped me get back into painting.[11]

While *Contrapuntal Forms* was being made in Hepworth's studio the composer Priaulx Rainier was laying out the garden at Trewyn with pathways, pools and rock gardens, and planting it with trees, shrubs and flowers, many of which were sub-tropical, as settings for outdoor sculptures in stone and bronze. To me that garden (which visitors to the Hepworth Museum enjoy so much today) is an image of her music, at once intense and gentle, in which every note and every silence strike their own clear sound.

I was particularly interested in the way she would talk about her music in painting terms; she would talk about the colour of a sound, and the shape of a sound, and the spaces between sounds, and the rhythms that connected them.[12]

The years 1951 and 1952 were particulary important for Terry. He showed with Adrian Heath, Pasmore, Anthony Hill, the Martins, Eduardo Paolozzi, Robert Adams and Terence Conran in Adrian's studio in Fitzroy Street. Pasmore, William Scott, Lynn Chadwick, Kenneth Armitage, Anthony Hill, Constant Niewenhuys (of the COBRA Group), Adrian Heath and Robert Adams were among the artists who visited St Ives. Pasmore sat on the rocks at Porthgwidden and made drawings of waves which were forerunners of his spiral paintings. Michael Tippett came to work with Barbara Hepworth on the stage sets and costumes she was designing for Sophocles' *Electra*, for which he was doing the music, and the white marble maquettes were carved by Denis Mitchell and Terry Frost.

With Mitchell and Frost, I edited a series of broad-

11. From interview with David Lewis, October 1993, see page 238. *On Growth and Form* refers to D'Arcy Thompson's book, 1942, and to the exhibition at the ICA, 1951. The symposium papers, by scientists, philosophers and art-historians, were published as *Aspects of Form*, ed. Lancelot Law Whyte, Lund Humphries 1951 (revised edition 1968)

12. From interview with David Lewis, October 1993, see page 238

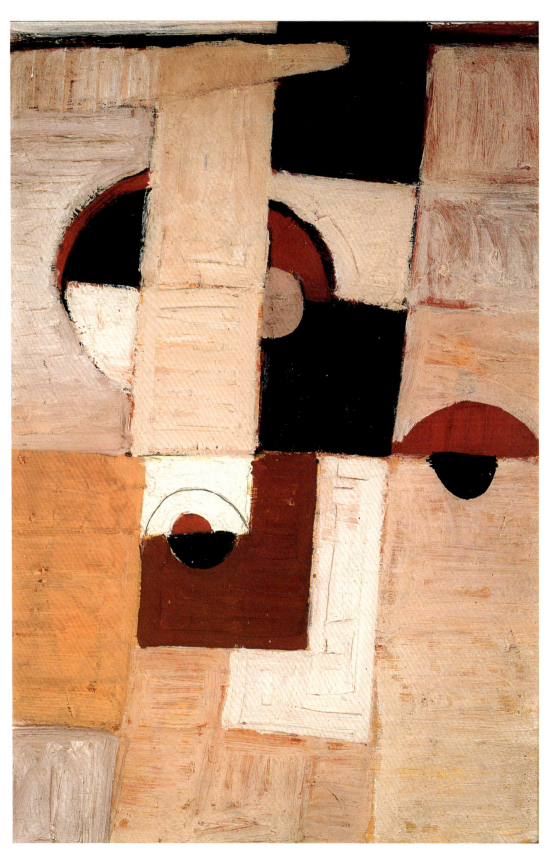

sheets published through the Penwith. Willie Sandberg, Director of the Stedelijk Museum in Amsterdam, David Baxendall of the National Gallery of Scotland, Lillian Somerville from the British Council, George Dix from the Durlacher Gallery in New York, and Charles Gimpel from London were among those who visited St Ives at this time. They saw the studios of the younger artists as well as those of Ben and Barbara and the regular Penwith Society exhibitions.

We had a little show of abstract art at the AIA in 1951 and that's where I met Roger Hilton. I introduced him to Ben outside the AIA because Roger had an old taxi for sale and Ben wanted a car but Ben wanted a sporty car to go with his cap! Roger was still doing landscapes and had seen one of my paintings: he had just met Constant and various people from the COBRA Group, and that led me to meet Pat Heron. Pat came and spent a long time with me; he was very good to me. Altogether I had one of the best trainings anyone could get, because I met people who each in their own way were genuinely trying to do something.[13]

Among the exhibitions Frost participated in, in addition to 'Abstract Art' and 'Abstract Paintings, Sculptures and Mobiles', both put on by the Artists' International Association, were 'Danish, British and American Abstract Art' at the Riverside Museum in New York, 'British Abstract Art' at Gimpel Fils in London, 'Seventeen Collectors' organised by the Contemporary Art Society and exhibited at the Tate in London, 'British Abstract Art' at the Galerie de France in Paris, and 'The Mirror and the Square' at the New Burlington Galleries in London. Frost had his first one-man exhibition at the Leicester Galleries in London in 1952.

Most of Terry Frost's paintings in these exhibitions derived from the theme of boats and ropes – semicircular or new moon shapes rocking back and forth down the canvas with rhythms orchestrated by diagonal or slanting lines and spirals. They were painted with broad expressive brushstrokes and thick impasto within a roughly geometric framework. Some of the paintings were black, white and grey; others were in bright, sometimes primary colours. A few paintings done in that transitional period when he was working for Hepworth incorporated collage; this was still extremely rare at that early date for works on canvas. One of these was 'Blue and Yellow Collage', 1951.[14] It was

One of the first of the very pure abstracts that I ever did, but related, nevertheless, to the visual experiences that were around me, the geometry of the area, and associated with the 'Walk Along the Quay' series.

There was always a strong blue light at the end of the quay in those days.[15]

It's to do with blue evenings. In twilight blue lasts so much longer than any other colour, it's like a note on a cello the way it just slowly disappears, trailing away, and as the blue is gradually disappearing into blackness (black, after all, contains all the other colours), then suddenly that blue light at the end of the pier gives you a sharp prick – and to have the structure to hang it all on gives one the rhythm.[16]

In recounting his memory of that blue, Terry talked of being haunted all his life by certain poems which evoke colour, particularly those of the Spanish poet Federico Garcia Lorca[17] and the poetry of D. H. Lawrence, and Terry reminded me of Lawrence's 'Bavarian Gentians':

> *. . . Bavarian gentians, big and dark, only dark*
> *darkening the day-time torch-like with the smoking*
>   *blueness of Pluto's gloom,*
> *ribbed and torch-like, with their blaze of darkness spread*
>   *blue*
> *down flattening into points, flattened under the sweep*
>   *white day*
> *torch-flower of the blue-smoking darkness, Pluto's dark-*
>   *blue daze . . ..*[18]

One of the weekend exhibitions in Adrian Heath's Fitzroy Street studio, May 1952; dark vertical painting by Terry Frost on the left, other works are by Pasmore, Adams, Hill and Kenneth Martin; for an account of these important showings see Alistair Grieve, 'A Group of Abstract Artists in London 1951–55', *The Burlington Magazine*, November 1990, pp.773–781

13. From interview with David Lewis, October 1993, see page 238

14. See page 169

15. From interview with David Lewis, December 1991, see page 238

16. From notes for the catalogue, Belgrave Gallery exhibition 1989

17. See pages 216–224

18. From 'Bavarian Gentians' by D. H. Lawrence, courtesy of Faber & Faber.

Corsham 1952–54

In 1951 Peter Lanyon and Bryan Wynter began teaching at the Bath Academy of Art in Corsham. Terry Frost joined them in 1952. Concurrently he accepted a part-time post at Willesden Art School in Dollis Hill, teaching anatomy to daytime students and painting to evening classes. These two commitments allowed him to leave Hepworth's studio. He commuted to Corsham from St Ives but on the days he taught at Willesden he stayed with Adrian Heath in Charlotte Street, always returning to his home in St Ives and to work at 4 Porthmeor Studios.

Teaching now became an activity of great importance to Terry Frost, not because it was foil to his work as a painter or a respite from it, but for precisely the opposite reason. Teaching became a means of creative discovery, an integral part of painting. Corsham and Willesden were extensions of his studio. But they were something else as well. They gave him a sense of freedom, of being his own man. He was teaching now and the days of being a student and an apprentice were behind him. He found himself accepted as an equal by his peers, a member of what he called 'the greatest trades union of all'.[1] William Scott had been to Terry's studio in St Ives, 'to look at my drawings, but being a painter he looked at my paintings. He said "they make me look rather old fashioned".'[2] Corsham spurred Terry to new ideas, and because he so enthusiastically relished the opportunity to test out new ideas, he became a lively and inspiring teacher.

Corsham Court, where Bath Academy of Art was housed, belonged to Lord Methuen, who was a painter too; the grounds had been laid out by Capability Brown. The Academy was residential, which meant that the students and faculty were there 'to work twenty-four hours a day, no messing around'.[3] There were activities almost every evening, lectures, poetry, music, theatre. One of the painters who taught there was Peter Potworowski: 'Peter knew Satie, and for the first time I heard Satie's music and I also heard how lovely the spaces are between his notes.'[4]

Besides the fine art faculty there were resident musicians and poets. Terry particularly responded to the poet James Kirkup, partly because he had always been drawn to poetry, but also because

James was such a flamboyant charater, flaming red hair, bright waistcoats and braces, and a glorious vocabulary which he loved to enunciate in a voice clear and round. I shall never forget one harvest festival when he came to read poetry in flowing sleeves and a straw codpiece.[5]

Harbour
1951
oil on canvas,
14 × 18 in, 35.5 × 45.7 cm
(Phipps & Co)

Terry Frost with students at Corsham Court

1, 2, 3. All three quotes from interview with David Lewis, December 1991, see page 238

4. From interview with David Lewis, October 1993, see page 238

5. From interview with David Lewis, October 1993, as above

Clifford Ellis was the Principal of Corsham and he'd opened up a marvellous school, but it didn't quite conform with the expectations of the people who'd provided the money. The students had to take the exams whether the teachers liked it or not, because that was how the school could get its backing, and he needed a teacher who could get the students to pass the drawing and Intermediate exams.

So I was called in to teach life drawing, which I did, and the next year the students all passed, simple as that. I was known as 'plumb-line Frost' . . . I remember sending Ben a note about how I was doing it. I used coloured cotton to link from the person drawing to an easel and to the nude and to various places in the room, so that I could render the spaces as planes and develop a sense of volumes in depth. Ben thought that it was a brilliant idea. I learned a lot in the process and the students learned a lot. Lanyon, of course, was teaching painting. He'd smash a cup and his students would have to paint all the bits, concave and convex, and space; so we had a very good school of painting.

DL : One important aspect of Corsham seems to have been that all the teachers became colleagues, involved in each other's art. I can remember the energy and inspiration you all drew from being there together, particularly Peter.

Absolutely. Potworowski, William Scott, Kenneth Armitage, Bernard Meadows, Jack Smith, they all used to come there periodically. There was a wonderful exchange of ideas, we had a school of teachers with a range of ideas, from Potworowski who was a very classical painter to Peter who was a romantic, and then you had William Scott, and then Bryan who was always a bit of a Surrealist.[6]

Harbour
c.1952–54
oil on canvas,
$18\frac{1}{2} \times 22$ in, 47×55.9 cm
(private collection)

6. From interview with David Lewis, December 1991,
   see page 238

Yellow Painting
1952
oil and collage on board,
$69\frac{1}{2} \times 48$ in, 176.5 × 122 cm
(private collection)
also known as 'Yellow and Black Painting',
'Yellow and Black Movement'

From 'Nine Abstract Artists'

. . . In answering the question 'Why do I paint as I do?'
. . . the most significant and the simplest approach is by
way of example: I have recently completed a 'blue
movement' painting. I had spent a number of evenings
looking out over the harbour at St Ives in Cornwall.
Although I had been observing a multiplicity of movement during those evenings, they all evoked a common
emotion or mood – a state of delight in front of nature.
On one particular blue twilit evening, I was watching
what I can only describe as a synthesis of movement and
counter-movement. That is to say the rise and fall of the
boats, the space drawing of the mastheads, the oppos-
ing movements of the incoming sea and outblowing off-
shore wind – all this plus the predominant feel of blue
in the evening and the static brown of the foreshore
generated an emotional state which was to find
expression in the painting 'Blue Movement'.

In this painting I was trying to give expression to my
total experience of that particular evening. I was not
portraying the boats, the sand, the horizon or any
other subject-matter, but concentrating on the emotion engendered by what I saw. The subject-matter is
in fact the sensation evoked by the movements and the
colour in the harbour. What I have painted is an
arrangement of form and colour which evokes for me
a similar feeling.

The process of painting this picture was not as swift
and decisive as my description might imply. Its first
form was that of a pencil drawing, then a monotone,
then one-, two- and three-colour lino-cuts, a small
painting of similar proportions and finally 'Blue Movement' itself. These progressive stages helped me to
clarify my ideas, to adjust the various forms to a state
of dynamic equilibrium, and to arrive at a final proportion for the canvas . . .

Seeing is a matter of looking and feeling, for things
do not look exactly like you think they do. To look
with preconceived notions of visual experience is to
destroy the possibility of creating again that experience
in paint. If you know before you look, then you cannot
see for knowing.

Lawrence Alloway (ed.), *Nine Abstract Artists, their work and
theory* Tiranti, 1954. The texts from each artist were in fact
heavily edited or rewritten by Alloway. Besides Terry Frost, the
artists were Robert Adams, Adrian Heath, Anthony Hill, Roger
Hilton, Kenneth and Mary Martin, Victor Pasmore and William
Scott. Terry worked hard on his text but 'Micky Lloyd, Adrian
Heath's brother-in-law and a really good logical positivist,
tortured me into re-writing it'.

◁ *Corsham Black, Silver and White*
1953   oil on canvas, $43\frac{3}{4} \times 30$ in, 111×76.2 cm
(private collection)

also known as 'Corsham Blue and Silver', 'Corsham
Silver and White'; painted after a walk at night, ice
crunching underfoot, tall trees and a blue moon.

Blue Movement
1953   oil on canvas, 43×48 in, 109.2×122 cm
(Vancouver Art Gallery, gift of the Contemporary Art Society)
Bought by the C.A.S. in 1953

The Leeds connection

Ronnie Duncan

Terry Frost was at the heart of something remarkable that happened in Leeds in the 1950s. The mainspring was undoubtedly the Gregory Fellowships at the University. Established by Peter Gregory in 1950 as a pioneering experiment to bring artists onto the campus, they produced an upsurge of activity in poetry, painting and sculpture whose impact reached far beyond the University and the City itself. Leeds became an exciting and vibrant place for the arts during the best part of a decade and not the least remarkable feature was the cross-fertilisation of activities and interests: academics, politicians, architects, businessmen, critics and artists all coming together as a community to share in a ferment of creativity.

Just how far the Fellowships were the catalyst for this phenomenon is hard to gauge but their success certainly surpassed their founder's expectations. And with Bonamy Dobrée and Herbert Read advising Peter Gregory on the choice of artists a first-rate succession was assured: poets, painters and sculptors, mostly at a formative time in their careers, brought together within the University, which itself was then at a stage of explosive growth. Many of the Gregory Fellows were later to achieve fame: Reg Butler, Kenneth Armitage and Hubert Dalwood among the sculptors; Terry himself, Alan Davie and Trevor Bell among the painters; Jon Silkin, Geoffrey Hill and Thomas Blackburn among the poets. The critic Norbert Lynton taught at the School of Architecture and Derry Jeffares was Professor of English. The appreciation of new and innovative art was encouraged and in Bill Oliver of the Yorkshire Post *these activities found a keen and perceptive spokesman.*

Peter Gregory's idea was a straightforward one of mutual benefit. For the University, the stimulating presence of creative artists on the campus. For the artist, a roof over his head, a studio and a small stipend: freedom from material worry so he could get on with his work. From the University's point of view the benefit plainly depended on the contribution the artist was willing or able to make. In a man of Terry's warm outgiving personality and compelling enthusiasm the choice – quite apart from the claims of his talent as a painter – proved ideal. On his side the appointment could hardly have been more timely, not just creatively but because of his circumstances. Terry arrived in Leeds in 1954 with a large and growing family and without private means to support them. As an artist he was poised at the threshold of his career. Now for the first time he had the material freedom to develop creatively and he made full use of the opportunity. Terry has always acknowledged this formative

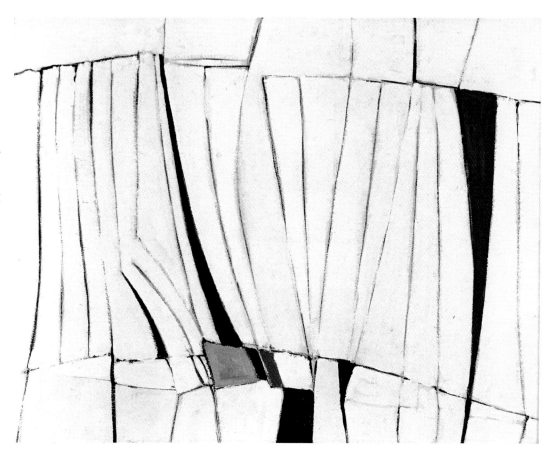

Red, Black and White
1955–56
oil on canvas,
$27\frac{1}{2} \times 36\frac{5}{8}$ in, 70×90.5 cm
(Pier Gallery, Stromness, Orkney)

Red, Black and White, Leeds
1955
oil on board,
48 × 72 in, 122 × 182.8 cm
(private collection)

period with gratitude. Those three years of breathing-space were probably crucial to his development into a major abstract artist. But the benefits were far from being one-sided. With characteristic gusto Terry entered into the cultural and social life of both the University and the City of Leeds and it was not long before his house-cum-studio became a powerhouse of ideas and a meeting place for congenial friends.

The cross-fertilisation of interests and disciplines took many forms. In the University's Department of Botany, for example, Professor Irene Manton, an enthusiast for Terry's work, hung abstract paintings alongside blown-up microscope photographs of the cells of plants.[1] The Gillinsons, business people involved in the arts, mounted exhibitions of new work in their factory canteen. Poets read their poems in private houses, people from varying walks of life began to support emerging artists in the most effective of all ways – by buying their work. Social life brought together seemingly improbable assemblies of academics, politicians, professionals, businessmen and journalists.

It was an exciting and enjoyable time. It was also great fun. Terry's enthusiasm and irrepressible spirits ensured entertainment for everyone in his company. I recall his rescue of an unusually heavy party for artists and politicians given by a Leeds business couple. Hugh Gaitskell was there, surrounded by earnest students. Solemn music played throughout the evening, until Terry found a demonstration disc among the classical records. Pop music suddenly blared out, to the horror of our hosts, but too late: Gaitskell had already seized the prettiest girl in the room and was dancing with abandon . . .

The most important and enduring cross-fertilisation involved the City's College of Art under the tutelage of Harry Thubron, whose revolutionary methods of teaching were to become legendary nationwide. Thubron welcomed the arrival of these creative artists at the University with open arms and quickly prevailed on them to take part in his classes. During one exceptional spell Alan Davie, Hubert Dalwood and Terry himself all worked together at the College of Art.

But there was a further dimension to Terry's time in Leeds, one of incalculable significance to him creatively. He has himself called this 'the true experience of black and white in Yorkshire'. It arose from the impact made upon him by the bleak sparseness of the North, the landscape of the Wolds and the Dales and especially the high Pennines with limestone outcrops intersected by drystone walls running vertically over the contours of the hills. He has described one such transforming experience. He was visiting Herbert Read at his home at Stonegrave in the Wolds and they took a walk together:

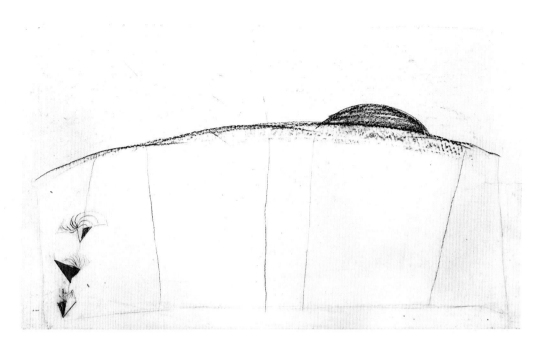

Yorkshire Study
c.1955–56
charcoal,
$16 \times 27\frac{3}{4}$ in, 40.6×70.5 cm
(Andrew Usiskin Contemporary Art)

1. See her letter on page 68

Sheet of Studies
1956
watercolour, gouache and pencil,
22 × 30 in, 55.9 × 76.2 cm
(private collection)
Studies for a decorative screen for a factory canteen

I drove through the snow and had lunch with Herbert Read at his house at Stonegrave. After lunch we went for a walk. Herbert lent me wellingtons and we struggled through the snow, so deep it came over the tops of the wellingtons; the angle of the hill seemed about 45 degrees and we had to lean to walk and counter the slope. It was a clear bright day and I looked up and saw the white sun spinning on the top of a copse. Afterwards and now I recall that I thought I saw a naples yellow blinding circle spinning on top of black verticals. The sensation was true. I was spellbound and, of course, when I tried to look again 'it' had gone, just a sun and a copse on the brow of a hill covered in snow.

I do remember my heart almost stopped at the experience and it was gone. So I came back and painted *Red, Black and White 1956*. I didn't come back and just paint the picture. I never was able to do that. I never wished to do that. I always have to absorb the moments and then let them go, for I have to make the idea, the discovery. Sometimes I go for a couple of years before I can get clean as it were and discover the moment again in paint.[2]

This early encounter with a strong black and white environment led to a series of paintings exploring its possibilities in taut geometric shapes. These included the hexagon, often locked into black verticals, derived from seeing shafts of sunlight within a wood.

I have long maintained that Terry Frost uses black with uncanny authority and with the ability to evoke more colour from it than any other artist of our time, including Kline and Motherwell. (No wonder his favourite quotation from Rochester is 'All colours are contained in black'). The Yorkshire experience of landscape, whilst adding to his vocabulary of shapes – the arcs, wedges, circles and chevrons evoked by the sea and by the shapes of bobbing crafts – honed and simplified his painting. It also led in a direct line and nearly 40 years on to the recent Duende *series of coloured etchings where Frost explores the mystic significance of black for the poet Lorca and for his native Spain. It continues still to the present day. On a visit to Terry a few months ago in his sun-filled house high above Newlyn I was delighted to see a series of crisp new paintings in red, black and white, works of arresting power and simplicity. Here was the artist in his mid-seventies still producing work of undiminished vigour and with all the old magic and inventiveness.*

In 1958 Terry went back with his family to St Ives. That fertile breathing space of his time in Yorkshire was to lead to the most productive phase of his whole career. On his return to Cornwall he found his St Ives contemporaries – Hilton, Wynter, Lanyon and Heron – all working at full creative stretch. For a span of this rich period Terry's work became a kind of dialogue with that of the greatest of his peers, Roger Hilton.

For many people fortunate enough to have known him in Leeds the bonus of the Frost connection only began with his departure. For me, an interested businessman spectator, it led to my collecting his work: also that of his contemporaries in the wider world of the constellation of sculptors, artists and potters associated with St Ives. My first visit there in 1958 was especially memorable for meeting in Terry's company the poet W.S. Graham, beginning a friendship with that marvellous and scandalously underrated poet lasting until his death in 1986. I shall also record, since it concerns Terry, the only cricketing triumph of my life, when I bowled him out in revenge for not choosing me for his side at one of the annual Cricket Matches between the Farmers of Zennor and the Artists of St Ives. The memory is still sweet of dismissing the martinet skipper of the Artists' Team . . . .

I owe to Terry Frost the awakening of an interest in abstract art that has become a lifelong involvement. The seriousness of his dedication to painting together with his no-nonsense directness of approach gave me access to abstract art which otherwise might never have taken place. I warmed to his painting credo – 'A state of delight in front of Nature' – and found that living with examples of his work brought me a lasting share in that delight. As for the man himself, my admiration has grown for his courage, a quality that is mirrored in his work. Terry's achievement is extraordinary for an artist who came late to art and with no background in it, for despite the pressures of family responsibilities and the hostility or indifference of the general public to abstraction he has never compromised his integrity, never succumbed to the temptation to repeat a success. Terry has always been fluent about his own work. It may be abstract but it is essentially outgoing in direction and exhilarating in its impact. His paintings are affirmative and joyful, in the spirit of his own favourite expression: 'Life is just a bowl of cherries'. Like their maker, Terry's paintings have a generosity about them, also a daring and impulsive quality. The best of them will endure because in his search for that equivalence in paint of the emotion the visible world arouses in him he has always had the courage to take risks, to dare to make things in a new and fresh way.

For me, that credo of art as 'A state of delight in front of Nature' has resonated ever since those heady days when Terry Frost came to Leeds.

2. From a notebook c.1975

Red, Black and White
1956
oil on board,
48 × 37 in, 122 × 94 cm
(private collection)
This painting was illustrated in the 'Critics Choice' exhibition catalogue, Tooth's 1956; Terry Frost had been Herbert Read's choice

Irene Manton

In response to a question from the curator of the newly established gallery at Lancaster University, to which her paintings were bequeathed, Professor Irene Manton wrote of the interest Terry Frost inspired:

This interest arose as an incidental consequence of an early meeting with Terry Frost, the painter. He had come to Leeds in the early 1950s as a Gregory Fellow. This fellowship had been set up by a wealthy philanthropist in order to bring a practising artist or musician into residence in Leeds, feeling that this would rub off beneficially onto students. Whether it had that effect I do not know but it had a very profound effect on me, at that time a fairly junior member of the University staff. My attention had been attracted by a show of Terry Frost's paintings that had been set up in the entrance hall of the University and my first reaction to see-ing abstract art for the first time was to feel how different this was from the Chinese painting in which I was already interested. Feeling that I would like to have a photograph of some kind to record the exhibition, I made enquiries about the artist, about whom I knew nothing, not having previously given special attention to the appointment of a Gregory Fellow. Having failed to find him I was at last approached by my research assistant who was at that time a sub-warden in one of our halls of residence – Tetley Hall – who told me that the Gregory Fellow was living next door and would I like her to invite him to coffee to meet me. This was done, but I was horrified by the mental state of Terry. His own show had been on display for two weeks but nobody had said a word to him about it. He had been used to abuse of various kinds in London, where modern art is not always treated with respect, but he had never before been totally ignored. He thought we were hopeless barbarians and I was so shocked by this that I went to the Vice-Chancellor about it. I then learnt, with surprise, that the founders of the fellowship had felt that the Fellows themselves would be put off by contact with the University staff and elaborate precautions had been made to prevent this. I thereupon took steps myself to try to salve the wounds of the Fellows. My first step was to buy a picture, choosing one of those exhibited. I hung this in the dining room of Tetley Hall, but in order to make quite clear to students that this was not just a throw-away device for dealing with a fairly large, unwanted picture, I was at pains to visit Terry Frost in his studio in order to buy another one of his pictures to hang opposite the larger one I had already bought. This device worked well in more ways than one. I discovered, with surprise, how much more you get out of a picture hanging in one's room or house compared with the initial effect in a gallery, and this is where my purchase of pictures began. The ones I chose to buy were never merely those that I liked, because I felt and feel that you like what you understand and you understand what you know. I bought only if I had a feeling that there was something in a painting that I might understand.

Collage
1956
collage and charcoal,
15 × 11 in, 38 × 28 cm
(private collection)

Notes for a talk by Terry Frost to the students at Leeds, 1954

I suppose the easiest way for me to have tackled this talk would have been to have collected some slides of my contemporaries and to have talked about their paintings. However, I gathered there were quite a few people up here who preferred me to talk about my own approach to painting. A much trickier problem, of course, because talking about painting and actually creating a painting provoke a completely different set of questions and answers.

As I practise painting and not lecturing or writing I am in rather a strange position. So if I should digress a bit at times, or dry up, it will be because I am working in a comparatively new medium. I hope, however, that some of you may be able to get some benefit from what I say about my kind of painting.

It ought to be easier for me to tell you something about what I have actually experienced, rather than the alternative of looking up lots of books and then giving a lecture. I shall try to talk to you about my approach to painting, the manner in which I get my ideas and the way I try to carry them out. But you must bear in mind that what I say refers to pictures that have gone, are past. I am now involved in the next set of problems, so what I say may only have been the experience for one particular picture and have no connection at all with the painting I shall work on next. Each picture has to contain some discovery or otherwise it would be dead – or just repetitive and dead.

You see, when I am involved with painting I don't think coldly like this at all. Thought, painting, everything becomes one, and time just ceases until one has got what is wanted, or is defeated. And of course the painting has to stand, or fall, by itself. I don't make a habit of going round talking publicly to people about what I am doing. As Sickert once said, 'Never judge a painter by his patter. It's the work that counts.'

I had better give you an idea of how I led up to this way of painting. First of all I was self taught, and worked painting POW friends' portraits, still life, landscape, etc. A very exacting task; if the portrait wasn't liked, then I heard about it in much stronger terms of abuse than the critics dare use now. Good training that was. The sunsets, pines, pinetrees, frost, every blade of grass I looked at intensely. Certainly I learnt how to see the things around me for the first time. The things that

were given free of charge. I am sure that was the best education I could have had before becoming a professional painter. Well, after three years of that I came back home determined to paint, and by various means I have managed to keep on painting. I know when I came back and went on my first visit to the Bond Street Galleries, accompanied by Adrian Heath who was a POW friend of mine and who had taught me quite a lot about the technique of painting, I was pretty sceptical about this modern stuff . . . for I hadn't got further than Van Gogh and certainly had never seen an Old Master. However, by familiarising myself with Old Masters and Modern Painters I gradually began to think and could tell which was a good one, and vice versa.

I went to St Ives. I had to get a long way from my parents, because although at this time I was still painting in the traditional manner they found it hard to understand why I should want to give up a good job for painting pictures. While at St Ives I managed to obtain an ex-Service grant which took me to Camberwell, where I came under the influence of Coldstream, Rogers, Pasmore, Seabrooke and Martin in the main. Pasmore became my particular influence during those days and he advised me to spend no time at all at the art school but to visit the National Gallery and modern galleries and see what was going on, as well as what had gone on before.

It wasn't long before I became dissatisfied with the way I was painting. I think it was mainly brought about by the copying of various Old Masters and the intense analysing of their compositions, which was rampant at Camberwell amongst a few of us at that time. Not all of course felt the need to try to make things from the abstract angle, but we did all learn to respect our areas and to design right through the area to the edges. We learnt about contrast in colour, and light and shade, and in drawing, and what we didn't learn was that the Old Masters and the best of the Moderns knew how to divide their rectangle geometrically with as much spontaneity as the average man knows his ABC.

Well, I am still interested in the same things today and am always concerned with the two-dimensional structure first, to see that it involves the whole area right up to and including the four edges. You may think that everybody does that, but I couldn't agree. Certainly all good works of art have that positive structure underlying the result, whatever the subject. But too many painters rely upon the interest of the subject, and on the effect of the colour or texture in a surface manner, and do not go deeper than that.

Leeds Painting
1954–56
oil on canvas,
66 × 72 in, 167.6 × 182.9 cm
(private collection)

Abstract with Red Verticals
c.1956
oil on canvas, 25 × 30 in, 63.5 × 76 cm
(private collection)

Leeds letters

Believe me Roger, I am at rock bottom. I'm sad and fed up for it seems that I'm too English a painter. Not sad and fed up because I am an English painter, but because I shan't get the easy money that these boys are pulling in from the States. I did so want to give up teaching.[1]

We haven't got a fucking painter in this country who really makes a bloody straightforward paint shape statement. They are all eclectic or chi-chi and too bloody limited for words. . . . It makes me weep that no-one in this country can get dealer or any kind of support to help them gain the certitude that comes with doing nothing but painting . . .[2]

You must realise that there are two different planes of activity, two different levels, two worlds, within this world, which do not meet and which have no connection. To think of one in terms of the other is the greatest mistake. I have just been reading a book by Maritain called Creative Intuition in Art and Poetry *which isn't at all bad and shows a certain insight into the creative process.*

You must realise that any work which is of real value will not come to be appreciated by a large public until many years later. The question of how the artist is supported doesn't matter. If you are a painter you are committed. You will automatically adjust your output to your span of life. An artist is not an artist for nothing. The circumstances of your life and the circumstances of your art are two different things. On one plane you are but a poor animal who must be sustained as best he may, on the other you are in touch with something much vaster and more mysterious – the creative process itself. The difference between the artist and others is that he has access to these creative sources inside himself. His life in fact consists very largely in keeping a sort of inner score – the matrix where these things go on . . .

I think your trouble may be the confusion which has been caused in our minds about painting, owing to our misinterpretation of the abstract or non-figurative thing. Don't worry any more about architecture or construction. For myself I have decided it is all nonsense. The adventure of painting is far from finished. Painting must be given back its soul. In this respect your painting is an object lesson to all of us. I have always believed so strongly in you as a painter that I have never really bothered to tell you so . . .

If people are not buying you it may be because they feel instinctively that there is more to come. Let the bastard starve for a bit and then when he is all but dead from his effort to survive and bring forth we will hope to get the best things cheap. Let him bring forth in the wilderness and then

when he is safely forgotten about we can go down and fling a few pounds to his widow and get everything in his studio. Then you will see the books appearing and the prices soaring up. . . .[3]

Exhibition at Leeds College of Art, c.1955; Terry Frost in braces, Norbert Lynton centre in white shirt and Ricky Atkinson next to him, Harry Thubron far right; works by Barns-Graham, Pasmore and others were shown alongside first year students' work

Press photograph for *The Yorkshire Post*, c.1954

1. From a letter to Roger Hilton written in Leeds (Tate Archive)

2. From a letter to Roger Hilton, as above

3. From a letter written to Terry Frost in Leeds by Roger Hilton (Tate Archive)

Leeds 1954–57

As things turned out the three years Terry Frost spent as Gregory Fellow in Leeds were pivotal. For the first time he was truly on his own as an artist. More importantly, he experienced in the Yorkshire Dales an upland and bare landscape which bore a formal relationship to the familiar upland moors of Cornwall, but which demanded a vocabulary utterly different from the rocking boats of Cornish harbours.

When I get a new idea, it may take two years before it becomes a language in my mind and in paintings to convey that idea.

Thinking about the Frost paintings which came out of those Leeds years, my mind goes back to a painting he had done in about 1951–52, 'Yellow Day'.

It was a very hot summer with heat which seemed to vibrate off the earth and the granite rocks. The air was very still; even sound seemed to vibrate. One couldn't copy what one saw. Could I find colours to convey the idea? I had been studying Analytical Cubism, so I began working in panels. This enabled me to paint flat within each area. Yellow and red and black are strong together. The black lines between the areas began to vibrate. I got the rhythm of the light and the hot feeling of sunlight moving round until we get to the magical places of dry heat. This is how one arrives at a reality no one else knows anything about until that person *experiences* the force of the painting itself in its colour, its form, its tactile surfaces, and its scale.[1]

In place of the rocking semicircles of the Cornwall period, attenuated rectangular panels or trapeziums, separated by black lines, predominate in the paintings of the Leeds period. Some of these are known as the 'washing line' paintings because the black lines soar upwards to a horizon at the top of the canvas.

Some of the canvases inspired by the Dales are hot dry summer paintings in brilliant orange and red with powerful black lines. Others are winter paintings in which the snow colours are cold and wet.

Just sitting in a Land Rover with Kenneth Armitage and being in a vast cape of white and cold but brilliant space, the sharp air and smooth folds of white snow resting on fields, hanging on black lines . . .. Things like the Land Rover freezing up were useful because we had to walk to a farm and ask, quite early on a Sunday morning, for some warm water, and the walking was good because I went down and the white came up all around and yet it never touched me, so I was a black

Yellow Day
c.1951–52
oil on canvas,
18 × 24 in, 45.7 × 60.9 cm
(private collection)

1. From interview with David Lewis, July 1993,
   see page 238

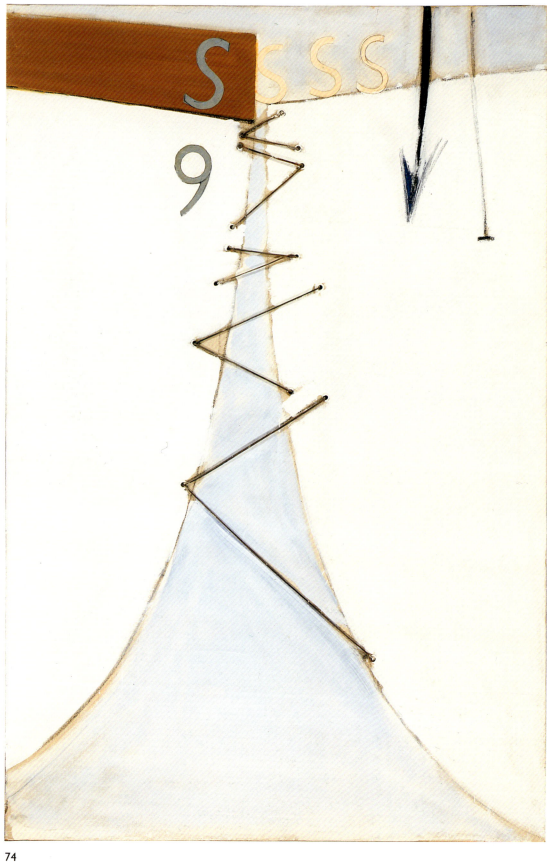

SS9
1962–63
oil and collage on canvas,
60 × 40 in, 152.5 × 101.5 cm
(private collection)

Night Black and Green
1962
oil on canvas,
76 × 48 in, 193 × 122 cm
(private collection)

thing in a funnel of white with no space that I knew. I could not touch the sides, the space and silence went with me as I walked, and I was so small.[2]

Parallel with these developments in his paintings, Frost found himself drawn into an unexpected and rapidly evolving educational milieu. Under the direction of Harry Thubron a basic course in art education was taking shape in 1955 at the Leeds College of Art. Recognising not only rapid technological change in the scientific world but the need to reinforce the inner territories of perception and values in each individual, the impetus of Thubron's initiative was not to teach the known but to discover and extend the unknown. Its origins lay partly in the Bauhaus and in the teaching principles of Johannes Itten and Lazlo Moholy-Nagy but it drew strength particularly from the presence in Yorkshire of Herbert Read and Victor Pasmore. Herbert was living at Stonegrave to the east of us, and was deeply involved with Bertrand Russell, Canon Collins and others in the nuclear disarmament movement. Several of us, including the builder/developer Peter Stead who ran the Symon Quinn Gallery in Huddersfield, participated in the early Aldermaston marches, and we saw the movement swell from a couple of hundred people to national and international proportions. The University, which was up the road from the College of Art, had its activists too, people like Asa Briggs, Fernando Rodriguez, Alasdair MacIntyre and John Rex. As might be imagined, we as students made little distinction between our political enthusiasms and our work in the classroom: the basic course was infected with strong ethical and social commitments. Following his period of building constructions, Pasmore was a member of the architectural team working on Peterlee New Town. He called for 'the development of new foundations in art training, on a scientific basis' in the following words:

A modern 'basic course' should assume a relative outlook in which only the beginning is defined and not the end. Thus the student is asked to embark, not on a static imitative system, but on a dynamic voyage of discovery the means of which are empirical, on the one hand, and analytical on the other . . . A foundation course of this kind can no longer be divided into the separate departments of painting, sculpture and architecture. On the contrary each category is carried out in all three forms by the same student. An exercise in the partitioning of space, for instance, begins in the division of two-dimensional areas (drawing) and develops into actual three-dimensional structures (architecture). Similarly a project in shape making and in shape relationship begins in two dimensions (drawing and painting) and ends in three dimensions (sculpture or construction). This unitary and

integrated principle of development makes possible a form of study which can be established in a school of art or technology which deals with visual art in any form.[3]

I had enrolled as a first-year student of architecture in the basic course at the Leeds College of Art in 1956. It was a unique and exciting time. I found myself with sixty other students in architecture, painting, sculpture, interior design and product design. There was no differentiation between us. Terry Frost's tenure as a Gregory Fellow overlapped with those of two further Gregory Fellows, the painter Alan Davie and the sculptor Hubert Dalwood. All three taught in the basic course. We were all jammed into one large studio room with long tables. The noise was overwhelming. To get some peace to do my work, I used to retreat under the tables. From that vantage point I could always recognise who was in the room from their feet: Thubron wore huge hiking boots with soles like rubber teeth, Frost wore sloppy oversize soft brown shoes, and Herbert Read's neat little brown shoes were always highly polished and laced with precision.

To us as students in Leeds the most important aspect which Terry Frost and the other Gregory Fellows represented was not that there was agreement among them. Quite the contrary. The most important principles were exploration and discovery. You made one mark on a paper and immediately the paper itself became a shape and a scale. You made a second mark and a complex discipline of form, space and scale began to assert itself, demanding further action. These were your own marks, your own commitment. Even if the marks were imitative, for example a drawing of a hand or a tree, it was the marks which took over, creating their own criteria of discipline and freedom. As a student of architecture, I began to see drawing, the making of a sequence of marks – the latest mark in relation to the previous marks in the shape of the paper – as a metaphor for taking action in the inherited context of a city, in which each action taken sets up the threshold and discipline for the next.

It was exciting to us as students to hear Terry talk about such simple things as the sun and seeds, lorries and clouds, and walking in the Dales, experiencing the almost vertical fields on each side rising to the brilliance of a white sky, or his description of Kath in a bathing suit laced up the back sitting on a rock beside a rushing stream in Nidderdale, as the starting points of a series of paintings, a series which would – although none of us knew it at the time – continue for a decade to come. Years later I would clearly see the connection between Terry's words about the magic of sun and water and hills and the words of Louis Kahn, the American architect, when he

Stays
1962
oil and collage on canvas,
72 × 72 in, 182.9 × 182.9 cm
(Tate Gallery)

2. From interview with David Lewis, July 1993, see page 238

3. In 1959 an exhibition and catalogue, 'The Developing Process', set out the radical ideas behind the Leeds and Newcastle courses, see page 85

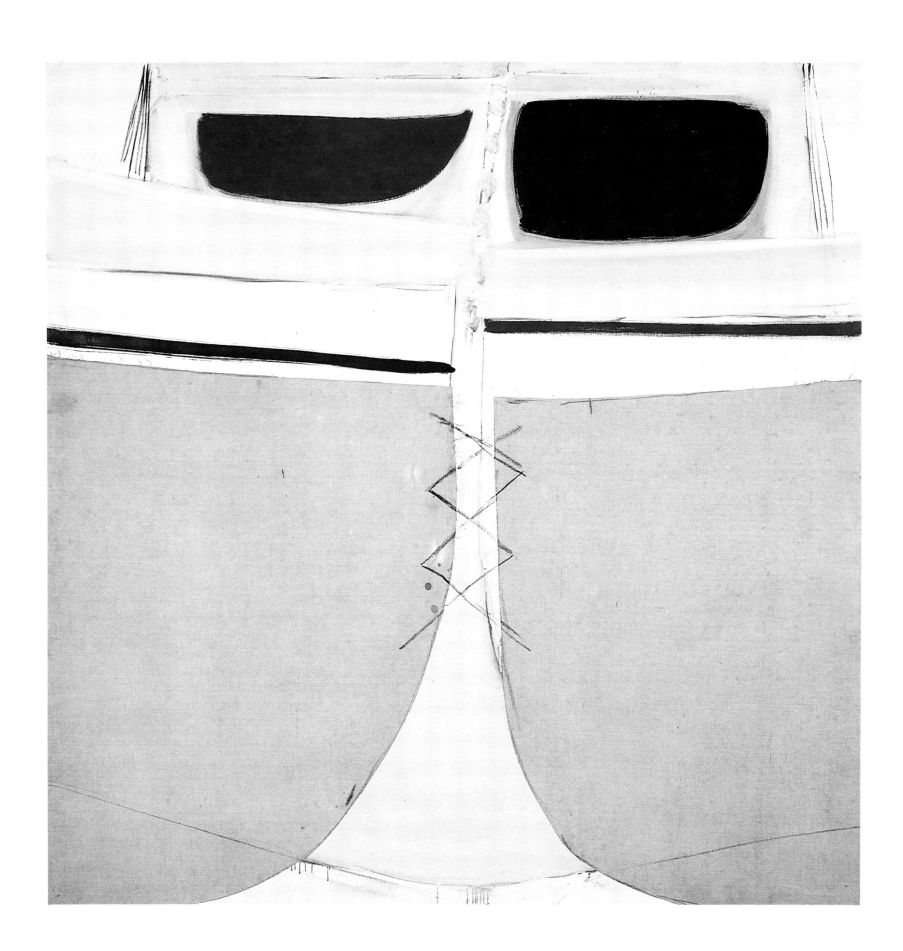

would talk about the power of sunlight, shadow and stone in bringing the quality of mass and surface and texture of buildings to magical life.

I made a drawing of Kath from behind as she was sitting with her feet in the cold rushing water of the stream, and there were these two semicircles of her buttocks coming in from the side of the paper with the crisscross of the lacing of her bathing suit, tied in a bow, in black charcoal – and that simple drawing had a lot of meanings for me. I remember as a kid I used to have to lace up my grandmother in the ivory-coloured stays, and how she had a bit of red flannel in the front where her cleavage was. And I remembered how Ben used to talk about 'tightening up the form' as though he was talking about a spanner. And then when I looked at those semi-circular shapes in my drawing my mind went back to the boats, and I thought about how the brown mizzen sails at the stern are laced taut to keep the boat into the wind. So I glued two raw hessian shapes onto a canvas and I thought I could pull them tight by knocking holes through and lacing the forms with leather Army bootlaces. That was 'SS9'. I wasn't very happy with the lacing so the next time I got the proper tools for punching holes and grommets so the laces wouldn't tear up the canvas, and then as I was lacing up my shoes I saw that the trick was the triangular slit which you draw together when you tighten the laces; and all these things led to a series of paintings, collages and lithographs all with laces. Well, I took one of them up to London to show Leslie Waddington, and he said, 'Terry it's too sexy, it's like a chastity belt'; then he bought it for himself, so I knew it was OK. All of this led to the dyed banners I made in sailcloth, and paintings with hanging forms.[4]

The presence of so much creative ferment at the Leeds College of Art and at the University had its impact on the community. Very soon a whole group of people were stimulated by what was going on. Exhibitions were organised, not just in galleries but even in pubs; new collectors such as Bernard Gillinson, Irene Manton and Ronnie Duncan began purchasing paintings and sculptures; recitals of the work of modern composers were organised; lectures on contemporary art were given; events occurred at the three City Art Galleries, Leeds, Bradford and Wakefield, and the inevitable controversies heated up. The one extraordinarily valiant private gallery, the Symon Quinn run by Peter Stead, showed avant-garde paintings and sculptures by artists still relatively unknown to the broader British public, among them Terry Frost, Adrian Heath and Roger Hilton.

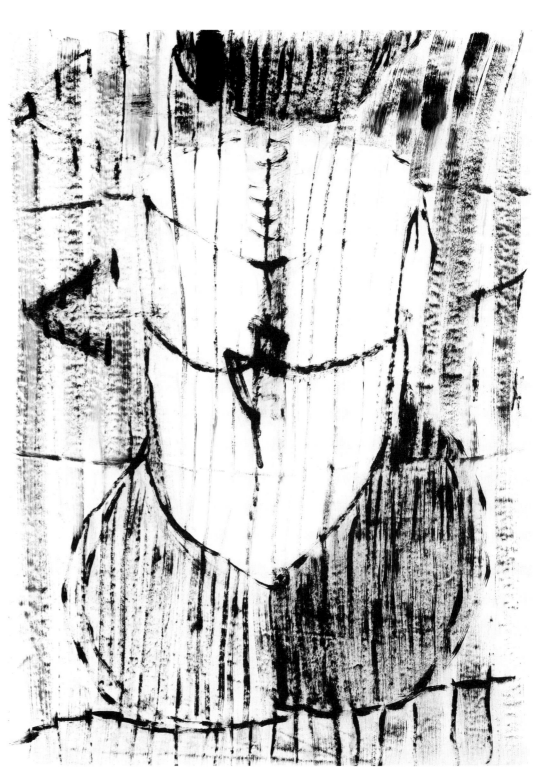

Figure, River Nidd
1955
oil on paper,
30 × 22 in, 76.2 × 55.9 cm
(private collection)

4. From interview with David Lewis, July 1993, see page 238

Photographs by Roger Mayne

Over the years, Roger Mayne has made a number of visits to photograph Terry Frost's work, his studio and his family: several of his photographs appear in this book. These six prints are from a series taken in the Frosts' flat in Leeds in 1956.

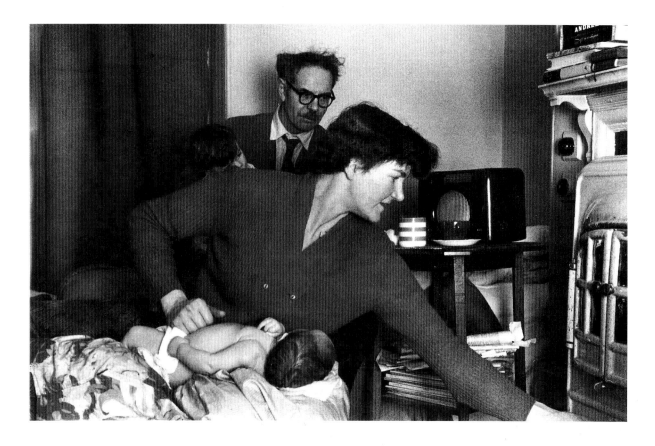

St Ives 1958–63

In 1957 Terry Frost returned to Cornwall to work full-time in St Ives, at 4 Porthmeor Studios. By then Roger Hilton was working part of each year in Newlyn. Barbara Hepworth, Bernard Leach, Peter Lanyon, Patrick Heron and the other artists living in St Ives continued to be magnets for international visitors, including the American critic Clement Greenberg, the painters Mark Rothko, John Hultberg and Jack Bush, and New York art dealer Martha Jackson. In 1958 Terry had his third one-man exhibition at the Leicester Galleries in London, and was represented for the second time at the Carnegie International in Pittsburgh. In 1960 he had his first one-man exhibition in New York at the Bertha Schaeffer Gallery.

In New York they all came to my exhibition, de Kooning, Rothko, Kline, Newman, Motherwell. I was staying with Larry Rivers. Newman and Motherwell took me to their studios. I accepted it all as normal and they accepted me. They were all painters struggling to get somewhere like I was. They worked hard; they would sleep until noon, do eight or nine hours in the studio, and then starting at eleven at night proceeded to drink me under the table! Then we'd go at four in the morning and have breakfast at a Chinese restaurant.[1]

Terry Frost and Michael Snow (see page 186)

Terry Frost and Patrick Heron at the Leicester Galleries one-man show, 1958, photographs by Roger Mayne

1. From interview with David Lewis, October 1993, see page 238

Colour Analysis from Nature

In 1959, an exhibition, 'The Developing Process', at the Institute of Contemporary Arts, with an accompanying catalogue, set out to show the new methods of art teaching developed by Harry Thubron, Victor Pasmore, Richard Hamilton and Tom Hudson in association with Hubert Dalwood, Alan Davie, and Terry Frost. The colleges concerned were Leeds College of Art and the Fine Art Department at King's College, Durham University, Newcastle upon Tyne (usually referred to as 'Newcastle').[1] The artists each contributed a page to the catalogue. Terry Frost's was as follows:

It is a very good starting point for 1st Year students to study colour. In colour analysis students are faced with the fundamentals of colour related to form. The basic problem of alerting people's senses to colour can be demonstrated by using a flower for an example. The students are free to analyse and to synthesise as they will, and in so doing, they come to grips with certain basic problems:

The grammar of colour mixing gives an analogy in paint on paper of the colour of the flower.

Objective drawing: a description of the particular proportions and shape of the colour. The drawing (constructed) and the colour (felt) are both put into one's grasp at the same time.

The training of the eye in selection.

The training of the hand.

Training in seeing the part in relation to the whole.

The being involved to such a degree that one's senses are continually aware of colour and its relationship to a particular form at all times . . .

All of our students have found that with sufficient effort (I want to emphasise that it does not have to be the talented student only) the rhythm of growth can easily be observed, understood, and put down on the flat with the medium. This in turn enables the student to tackle the various problems of construction in any department of the School of Art. At the same time it gives them a sound foundation for their own creative ideas, and they can make their own work grow, as in nature.

A student given, say, a 'thesis in yellow' will discover with complete freedom within yellow organisation, harmony, and discord all allied to proportion and form, which would be very difficult to come by from the study of colour-theory alone. Simple things are noted like the differing greens on leaves or stalks which come with each differing yellow. The amount of yellow or orange to blue and purple in a pansy. The cool and warm of colour. All these things are covered in an objective way in colour analysis, plus the surprise and reward of personal discovery.

. . . My mood has been one of deep depression and I'm still in a very shaky and queer state. I have not been working well for some time and I think I have become confused. It's partly due to my selling paintings regularly for twelve months, a thing I've never done before and it's very worrying. Not half as nice as worrying about not selling them. Can't explain this better, but certainly I don't like it. I can't see any point in just painting pictures for sale. I didn't start off with that idea and it is so difficult to keep one's integrity and to refrain from doing that which you know you can do. I only hope that I can get used to this professionalism, for if I don't I'm a finished man and I might as well do some other job.

You must forgive me for this depressing letter, but here I sit in the doldrums. I expect once I lift a brush it will be alright but I'm empty right now.[2]

Obviously the place is suiting you (or they have you under lock and key) otherwise you would have been around in London disrupting the lives of the weak and polite. I trust you have been turning out a few odd bits of work, for I hear you are neck and neck in it with Davie for the Biennale next year. I hope you make it! I must say I have felt very tempted to come out and join you but I haven't the temperament to enable me to clear off just when I feel like it . . .

I'm thinking of moving back to the Midlands and cutting right out of the art world. I don't think I shall ever recover from the procrastinating and off-hand way in which I was treated by Waddingtons when they thought that I really was going to buy a house in London. This has bitten into me deeply as a lack of confidence on their part in my work. The lesson has been learned though. I know whatever happens from now on will have to be by my own making . . .[3]

1. See also page 76

2. From letter to Yan Kel Feather written on 1 March 1960

3. From letter to Roger Hilton (in Paris) written on 2 October 1962 (Tate Archive)

Yellow Triptych
1957–59
oil on board,
90 × 144 in, 228.5 × 365.8 cm
(Tate Gallery)

Drowning Blue
1960–61
oil on canvas,
$48 \times 65\frac{1}{2}$ in, 122×166.3 cm
(whereabouts unknown)

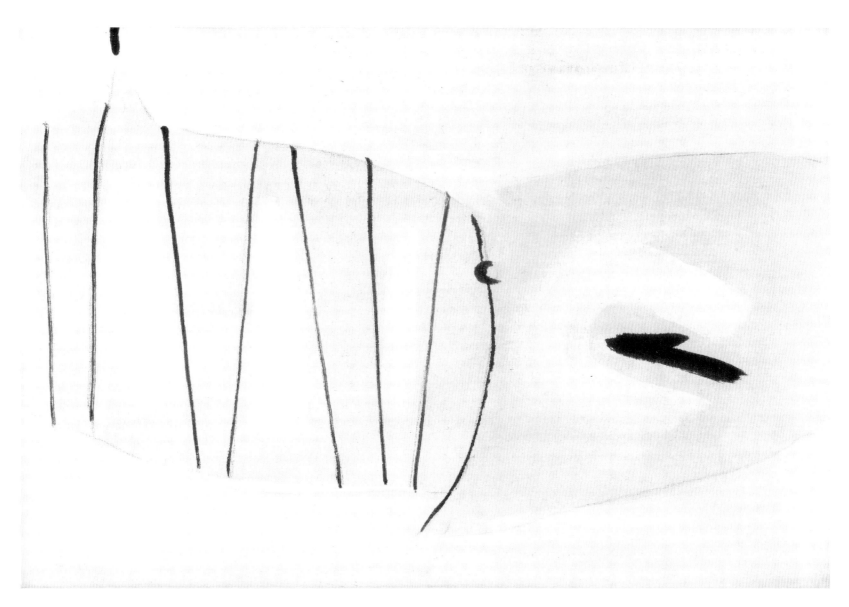

White Painting
c.1958
oil on canvas,
20 × 24 in, 50.8 × 61 cm
(private collection)

Untitled (Verticals)
1958
oil on canvas,
30 × 25 in, 76.2 × 63.5 cm
(Anthony Frost)

Umber and Grey
1960
oil on canvas,
72 × 52 in, 182.9 × 132 cm
(private collection)

Linen Blue and Yellow
1960
oil and collage on canvas,
76 × 48 in, 193 × 122 cm
(Austin-Desmond Fine Art/Mayor Gallery)

Figure, October 1962
1962
oil and collage on canvas,
68 × 87 in, 172.7 × 221 cm
(private collection)

Study for Figure   ◁ *Grey Entry*
1962   1962
oil on paper,   oil on canvas,
9 × 11½ in, 22.9 × 29.2 cm   72 × 78 in, 182.9 × 198 cm
(the artist)   (private collection)

Lunch at Kerris with Peter Lanyon, back left, and next to Terry Frost, Mark and Mell Rothko; photograph by Paul Feiler

Collage Christmas card from Peter Lanyon, late 1950s; left to right Frost, Wynter, Lanyon, Hilton, Heron

Terry Frost and family at 12 Quay Street, 1961,
photograph by Roger Mayne

Terry Frost's studio in St Ives, about 1960

The Three Graces

The Three Graces has been a recurring theme throughout Terry Frost's work since he studied Rubens' painting
in the National Gallery when he was a student at
Camberwell. He has exploited the mysterious drama set
up by three figures, three forms, first seen in the
dynamics of Rubens' composition with glances and colours interacting across the canvas. For him, the idea of
the three graces was allied to the idea of a sensuous figure
of love, as in Gwennor, goddess of love, who appears out
of the sea-fret wet and glistening, and unwary fishermen
drown in love.

Blue and Brown Figure
c.1959
oil on canvas,
30 × 60 in, 76.2 × 152.4 cm
(the artist)

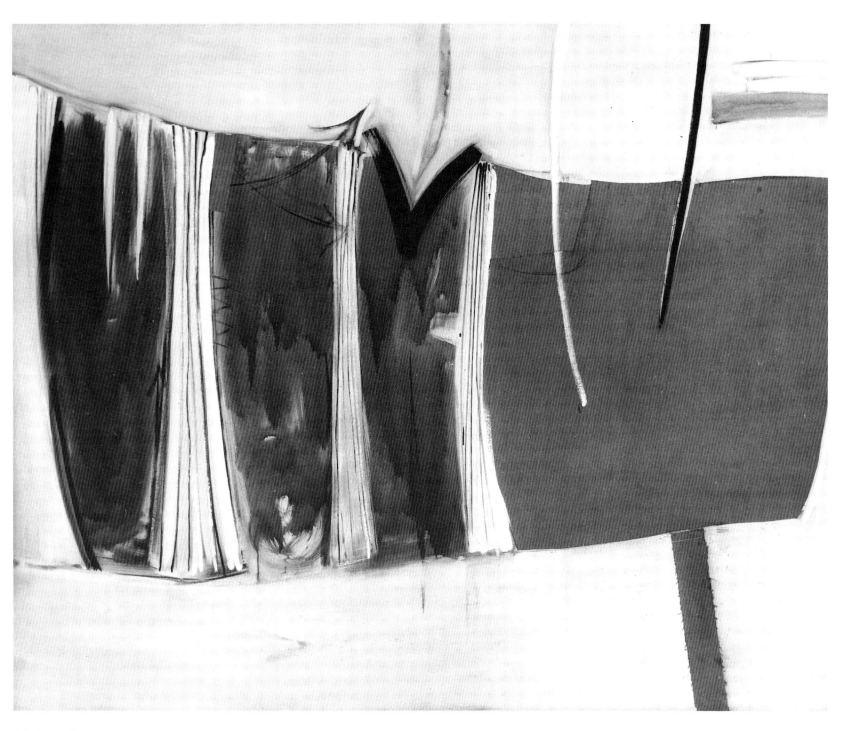

The Three Graces
1960
oil and collage on canvas,
78 × 96 in, 198 × 243.8 cm
(Bristol City Museum and Art Gallery)

Blue and White Figure
1959
oil and charcoal on canvas,
48 × 29 in, 122 × 73.7 cm
(Gillian Jason Gallery)
This is a version of Gwennor, goddess of love.

◁ *Terre Verte and White Figure*
1959
oil on canvas,
20 × 30 in, 50.8 × 76.2 cm
(Wakefield Museums and Galleries)

Ochre, Black and White Figure
c.1956–57
oil on canvas,
25 × 30 in, 63.5 × 76.2 cm
(whereabouts unknown)

Banbury 1963

Am writing in haste as I do not have any time to even think. Screaming children, burst pipes, all building up to the biggest and blackest depression. And yet I also like the place and feel the challenge, and know damn well I shall outlive the blackness of this thaw . . . the boiler split, towel rail split, as well as numerous bursts, one of which made a shocking mess of the room we had chosen to live in. Had a letter from the solicitor yesterday in which he said no insurance company ever insures against bursts in empty property. So there we are. I know you will have a little chuckle at my baptism into house ownership.

We feel better today as it's milder, the birds are singing. The green grass is showing and lots of bulbs have pushed well through. Today is the first time we have seen the garden for up till now it has been a white layer of ice and snow . . .[1]

Terry Frost had been feeling that he had to make a move away from Cornwall; 'the steam had slightly run out for me'. In 1961 he had a successful exhibition at Waddington's in London and found a house in Richmond for £7,000; but it wasn't that easy. When he admitted to the mortgage company official that he was an artist, he was informed abruptly that 'artists are rogues and vagabonds'. He then found a house in Fulham, only to be told by a surveyor that 'you've chosen the whitest elephant in London!'[2] His spirits dampened, he did nothing until the following year when he and Kath were on their way to visit Terry's mother in Leamington. They heard of a house in Banbury, and on a whim stopped to see it. Kath fell in love with it. It was a big square house with large rooms and high ceilings, and a lovely garden. The fact that it was only an hour from London by train was a big factor in its favour. Somehow it didn't matter that the house faced north. To pay for it Terry needed work. He wrote to William Scott, who put him in touch with an art school in Coventry. There he got two days a week before taking a post as Visiting Lecturer in Fine Art at Reading University in 1965 – where he was to remain until he retired as a full Professor in 1981. And so the Frosts came almost back home.

Shortly after settling in at Banbury, Terry met Lord Bearstead, who had been his captain in the Warwickshire Yeomanry in Palestine, and who invited him over to Upton House:

Marvellous paintings, Titians and Rembrandts, and ceramics; and there in the dining room was a splendid

Stubbs. The whole area is so historic, it's hard to think of the Battle of Edge Hill in the Civil War being fought among these beautiful and gentle steep hills with steel windmills and country villages which are still real villages, hollyhocks in the gardens and peach trees trained round the doors, and village churches whose bells ring out over the fields. Everywhere you turn is at once a surprise and a confirmation, hedgerows which are blue in the winter and cold pale blue mists rising from the valleys.

When I first went to Banbury, another magical discovery was going to Compton Wynyates, the Marquis of Northampton's place. There was a Cromwellian upholstered chair with a blue seat, it was the unforgettable blue of that seat with the black wood of the chair, and the space between the legs: it was a piece of sculpture. Then when I went across to the little chapel which stood out there on its own, there were the flags which had been carried into the Edge Hill battle, and one of them had black chevrons with blue circles all round, blue and black again, so fragile it was like a spider's web; I knew that if I blew, the whole thing would have disintegrated. You might not think it's very important but standing alone in that chapel with that chevron and the blue olives all round it, was a moment I've treasured. I don't know if I've thought of all the possibilities of a chevron but I've certainly used it a lot. As I was walking out I saw that someone had started to peel layers of plaster off the walls and a blue full moon was right there in the wall. These experiences were so moving they have affected my paintings ever since. I came home and painted a grey, mixing my oils in such a way that I could get a black craze, and then I ran that blue through it; it had to be a single wet stroke and absolutely accurate; and there it was. What I had experienced gave a whole new meaning to chevrons for me, and new meanings for circles as well.[3]

Banbury turned into a period of settled maturity for Terry Frost. Although it was essential for Terry to teach to bring a steady income to his large family, teaching was also something he took very seriously. It became an extension of his boundless enthusiasm and creativity. Sometimes he would drive to Reading; at other times he would travel by train, and stay overnight, sleeping in the studio he had in the school. And whether he went by train or drove, the landscapes were a perpetual source of inspiration and pleasure. On sharp winter mornings the rimy frost would make blue patterns on the hedges; and coming back in the evenings he would come around the same corner in the road and there between the hedges was the sun, sometimes red, sometimes golden, sometimes

The house in Old Parr Road

Terry and Kathleen Frost with Leslie Waddington at the 1963 one-man show

1. From a letter to Jane and Denis Mitchell on Terry Frost's arrival in Banbury, spring 1963

2. From interview with David Lewis, July 1993, see page 238

3. From interview with David Lewis, July 1993, as above

lemon yellow, always the same and never the same. And on the train he would see on his way the church steeples of Oxford and the towers of the colleges against the rain saturated sky, with rain drops on the train's windows tracing diagonal silver paths in perpetual motion.

Gleaming the steel lines
Slipping behind the window
My lovely train-riding sun
Bouncing your head on six willows
Preparing to land your container of gold
In cleared lilac above the green fold.
Stop and sit at King's Sutton Halt
Just to my left
And now to my right
Come with me to Banbury.

Rain soaked green of old England
Pruned willows and chopped down trees
Green of England and buffet cheese
Coated oaks and hedgerows of bread and cheese
Raindrops moving
In uncharted ease on the
Window of seeing.
Cuttings, and caravans to let,
Blue coaches, yellow and brown
Shades of the old G W R
Towers cooling and tall chimneys of Didcot
Steeped in grey rain.

Go with the rain and see
Undisturbed people in cemeteries
What agony or happiness do they contain,
Grey wet tombstones of quiet security.
Oxford; yellow cabs and passengers
Connect up to the mail.

Spend the night, and will you
Trudge for days behind the grey?
Or have you a return ticket for the day?
You travel in space and touch
Everything once.
Meander; race up and down,
Under and over, through and beyond
Giving new colour with every movement
Until the night screen descends
And gives your light farewell.
Old currant bun of delight,
A travelling companion with a heart of gold.

'Reading to Banbury', also known as 'Oxford to Banbury', this, like many of Terry's poems, was written on the train.

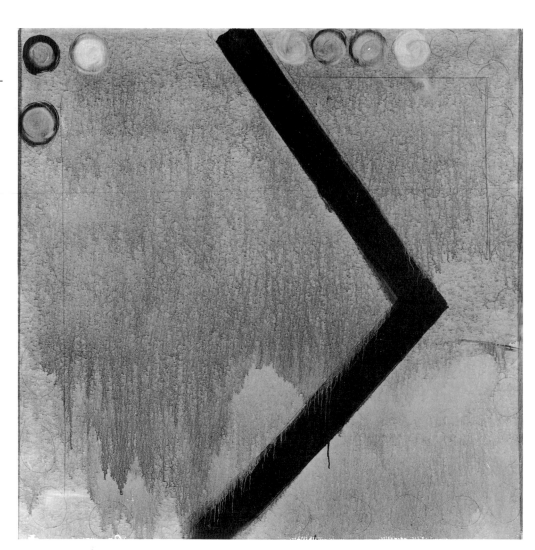

Chevron for Compton
1963
oil on canvas,
48 × 48 in, 122 × 122 cm
(private collection)

▷ *Untitled (Two Chevrons)*
1964
oil on canvas,
48 × 48 in, 121.9 × 121.9 cm
(private collection)

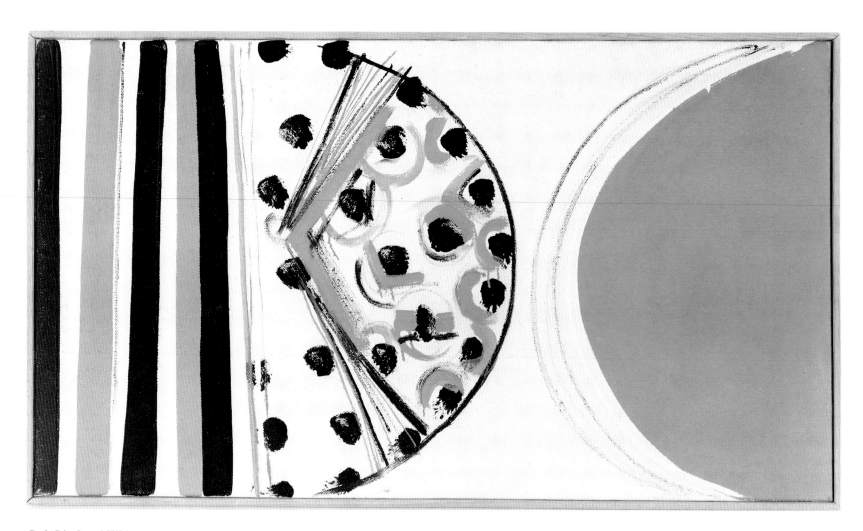

Red, Black and White
1962
oil on canvas,
20 × 36 in, 50.8 × 91.4 cm
(private collection)

Harvest Moons
1962
oil on canvas,
50 × 60 in, 127 × 152.4 cm
(Redfern Gallery)

Lorries and road signs

Although lorries were one of the things Terry Frost had always been looking at with particular interest, it was in Banbury that he began to make drawings of them. He photographed them and he photographed the road signs that irritated him so much in Banbury's traffic system. The town was crowded and busy, especially on market days and it was suffering disruption on a large scale from the beginnings of new development.

Somehow the heraldic imagery inspired by the Compton Wynyates banner and the commanding brashness of road signs were brought together in new, harsher shapes and colours in paintings of the early 1960s. The Midlands were already exerting an influence towards broader, more open and at the same time more rigorously simplified paintings, before his visit to San José in 1964 led Terry Frost towards the greater freedom of gesture and scale of his mid-1960s paintings.

◁ *M 17, October 1962*
1962
oil on canvas,
72 × 72 in, 182.9 × 182.9 cm
(British Council)

Road Sign Study
c.1964–66
crayon,
$8\frac{5}{8}$ × 11 in, 21.8 × 28 cm
(the artist)

Lorry Study
c.mid-1960s
crayon,
$9\frac{7}{8} \times 6$ in, 25.1 × 15.4 cm
(the artist)

Photograph by Terry Frost

Trader
1967
drypoint,
$11 \times 8\frac{1}{2}$ in, 27.8 × 21.2 cm
(the artist)
The Ford Trader reminded Terry Frost
of a Degas portrait with rétroussée nose.

The mid-1960s and San José

Meanwhile Terry Frost's fame was spreading. His position among Britain's leading artists was more firmly consolidated each succeeding year. In 1963, 1966 and 1969 he had a series of one-man exhibitions at the Waddington Gallery in London. A steady stream of British Council exhibitions in the United States, Europe and Canada brought international attention to his work. In 1964 recent paintings and works on paper were shown at a one-man exhibition in Zurich at the Galerie Charles Leinhard and an exhibition of paintings from the Bertha Schaeffer Gallery in New York was shown at the California Palace of the Legion of Honor in San Francisco in 1964. The same year a summer of teaching at the University of California in San José exposed him to new and totally different experiences. A fully equipped studio was put at his disposal. For the first time he was introduced to water-based acrylics, a medium which, because of its bright matt quality, accentuated what he was already referring to as the 'heraldic' character of his paintings of that period. But even more telling were the hot dry colours of Southern California and the vastness of American space. He was driven into the desert and was amazed to find not the barrenness he had expected from seeing Wild West movies but an incredible richness and variety of colours and textures, the rocks, the cacti, the wild flowers, and vast differentiations of scale, from mountains to petals.

Terry Frost working in San José, 1964

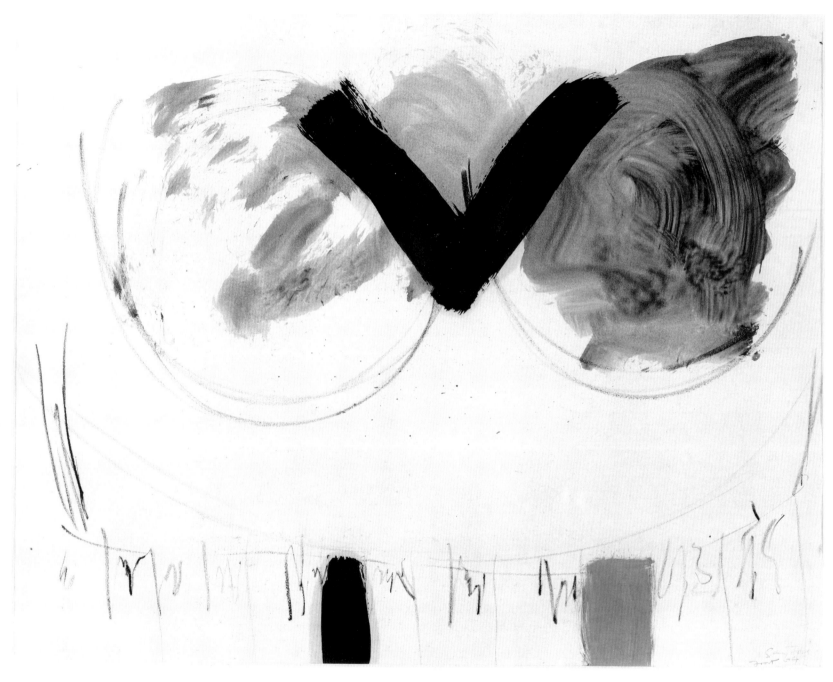

Black Chevron
1964
oil and charcoal on paper
18¾ × 24 in, 47.6 × 61 cm
(the artist)

▷ *Untitled*
1964
gouache and watercolour,
21 × 15 in, 53.3 × 38.1 cm
(private collection)

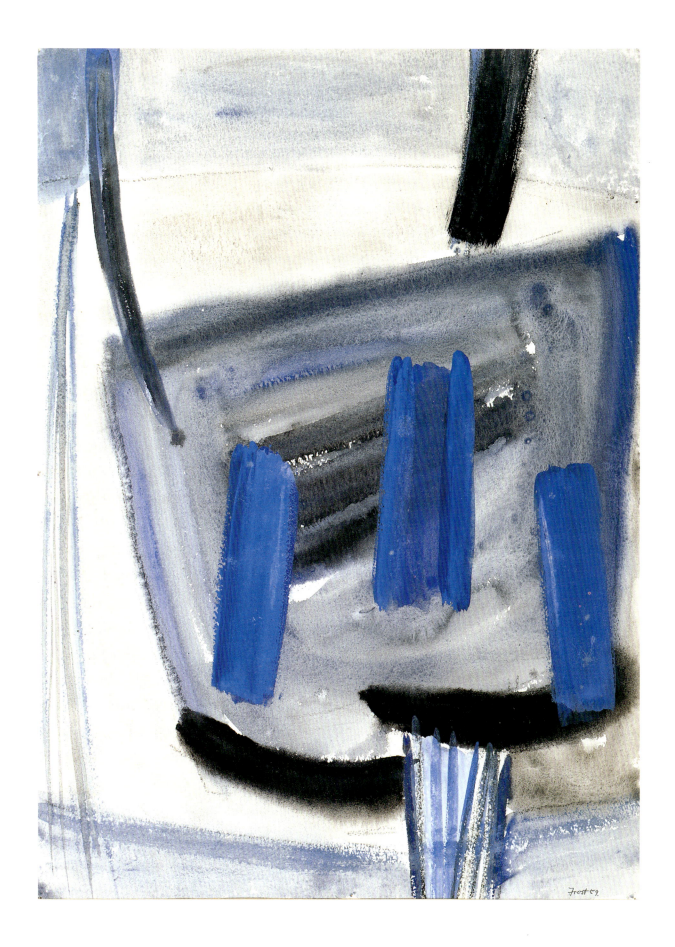

Untitled
1964
oil and charcoal on paper,
$18\frac{7}{8} \times 24$ in, 48×61 cm
(the artist)

The late 1960s

Although C- and D-shapes had been part of his vocabulary since the abstracts of 1950–51, by the late 1960s they were taking on new roles. As part of his exploration of the possibilities opened up by his work with colour mixed from red, yellow and blue[1] Terry Frost found himself using repeated series of D-shapes to carry colour across the canvas. He was also intrigued by the intervening shapes and the rhythms they set up. Two large-scale D-shapes, almost touching, and pairs of large tilted quadrants – both reminiscent of the boat-like shapes of earlier work and also related to the bikini images – had appeared before but now they were transformed, enlarged and sharpened: harder-edged, harder-coloured.

You can do so much with the curves. You can make them full or thin, slow or fast. The tension brings vitality to the white space around them – they ooze authority and life.

It seems that nowadays everything has slipped back to some horrible kind of poor painters' figuration, saved only by the literary side. Your kind of decorative sexy figuration is too nice, and I'm in the soup because I have got lonely and my paintings have become more isolated and I've got frightened and run myself into a corner and so far I don't know how to paint myself out of it. I'm sure you enjoy your situation in a strange way. I'm windy of not having contact with people like yourself, although everyone who did anything in painting while I was getting to know about painting have disappeared like you.[2]

. . . the glorious warmth of sunshine and noise-free air of the camp in the Gorges du Tarn, the often attractive wiggle of the other circle of warmth and delight . . . then that arena at Nimes comes bursting back into the picture and I'm again high up on that massive Roman structure which is so superb an oval, and each stone of such immensity, cut to slot together, not only to support and hold up tons of stone, but to turn and make a longing curve in all directions. The form of a semicircle down to the centre ╲‿╱ at the same time the oval ◎ . And the funny part of this struggle with wonder and amazement in the heat of the midday sun was to come out, walk round and come face to face with the refrigeration plant which was building up ice for a performance of something on skates . . .[3]

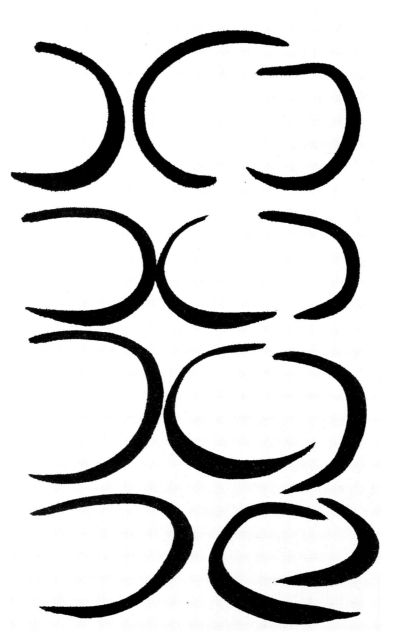

Study
c. late 1960s
ink,
$8 \times 4\frac{7}{8}$ in, 20.3 × 12.4 cm
(the artist)

1. See page 186

2. From a letter of 5 March 1967 to Rogert Hilton, who had moved to a cottage in Cornwall in 1965

3. From a letter to Claude Rogers written after a family camping holiday in Anduze, 1969

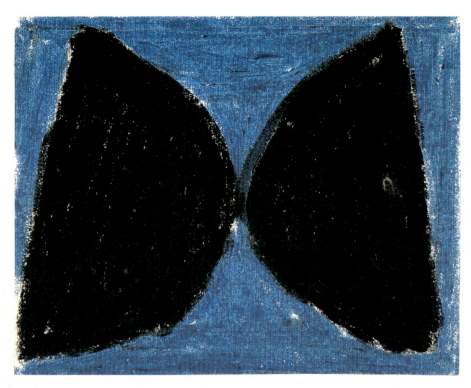

Study
c.1966–67
crayon,
$3\frac{7}{8} \times 5$ in, 9.8×12 cm
(the artist)

Red, Black and White
1967
acrylic on canvas,
78 × 102 in, 198 × 259 cm
(the artist)

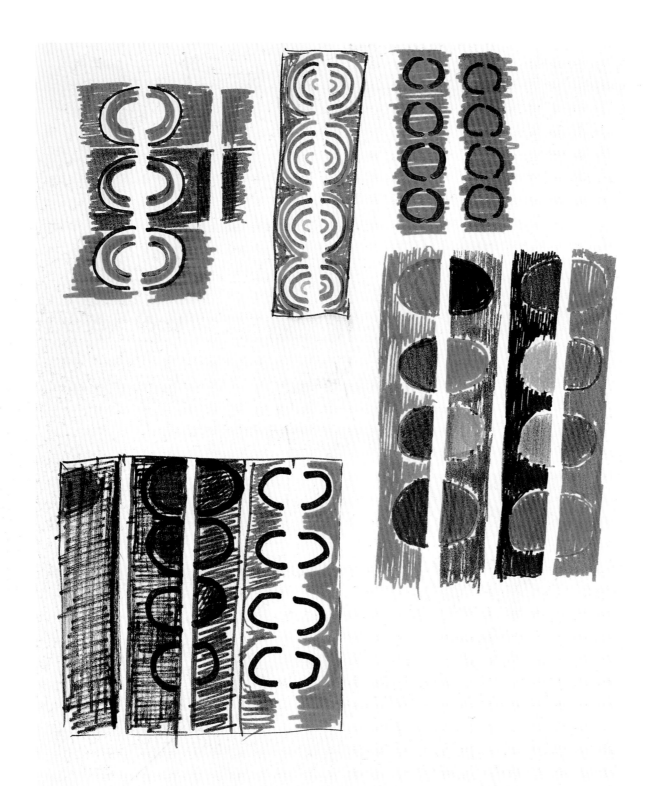

Sheet of Studies
c. early 1970s
marker pen,
$12\frac{1}{2} \times 7\frac{3}{4}$ in, 31.7×19.7 cm
(the artist)

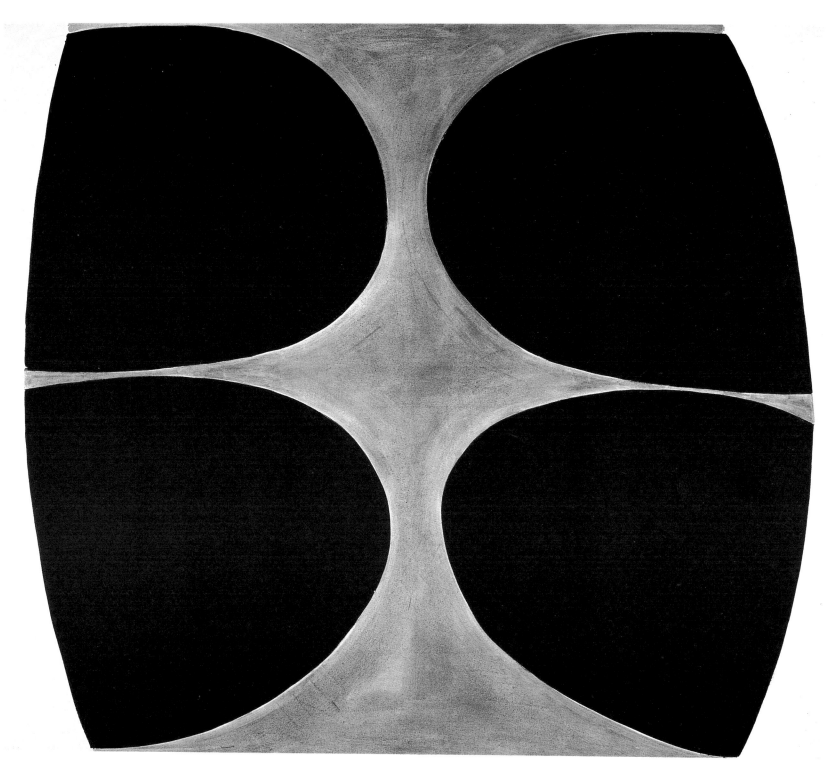

Untitled, January 1969
1969
acrylic on canvas,
77 × 85 in, 195.6 × 216 cm
(the artist)

Untitled
1966
oil on canvas,
78 × 96 in, 198.1 × 243.8 cm
(the artist)

'Twelve Artists' exhibition organised by Tom Cross
at Reading Art Gallery, 1968; also visible, works by
Tom Cross, Carole Hodgson and Alan Plummer.

Summer Blue
1974
oil and collage on canvas,
$51 \times 61\frac{1}{2}$ in, 129.5 × 156.2 cm
(Robert Blunden)

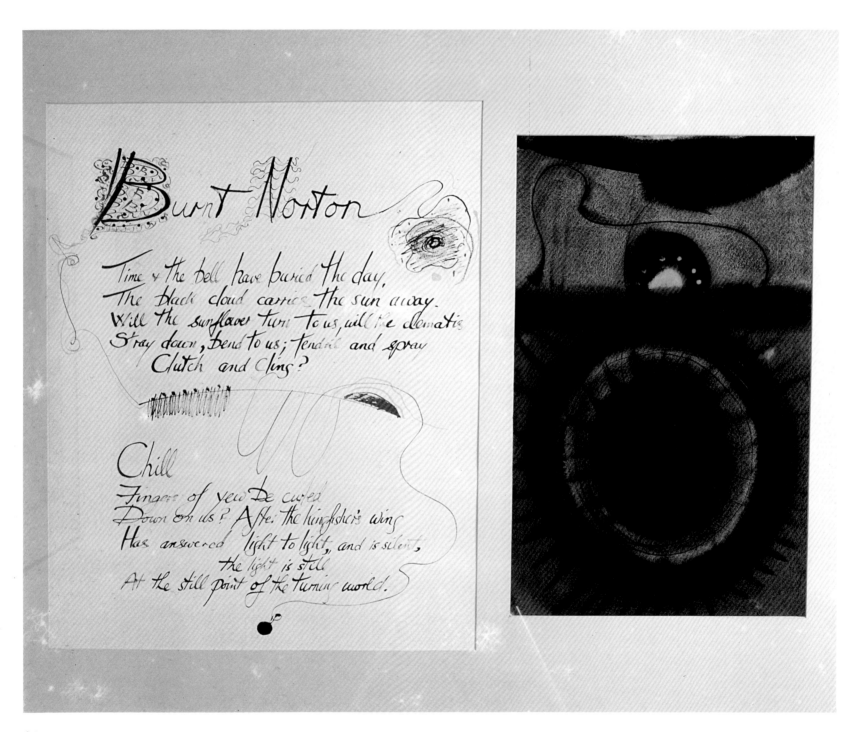

Burnt Norton
1974
gouache and collage with ink calligraphy,
21½ × 14 in, 54.6 × 35.5 cm
(Manchester Education Authority)

The Game of Chess

Terry Frost's presence brought a stream of artists, dealers and intellectuals to the house in Banbury: Roger Hilton, Robert Adams, Joe Tilson, David Hockney, Hubert Dalwood, Alan Wood, among many others. Ann Hartree opened the Prescote Gallery in a converted stable on Richard Crossman's nearby farm. 'It became quite a centre and people came from everywhere to join in those lovely days.' Alan Freer from the Manchester Education Committee paid a visit and commissioned Terry to make ten works on paper based on poems. They included Ezra Pound's poem, 'The Game of Chess'. Subtitled 'theme for a series of pictures', the poem was so rich in colours and images that Pound's words spurred Terry to make a 'game board' of 32 spaces for 32 pieces of collage, and a whole series of collages and paintings ensued.

Red knights, brown bishops, bright queens
Striking the board, falling in strong L's of colour,
Reaching and striking in angles,
*   holding lines in one colour:*
This board is alive with light
These pieces are living in form,
*   Their moves break and reform the pattern:*
Luminous green from the rooks,
*   Clashing with 'X's of queens,*
*   Looped with the knight-leaps...*
'Y' pawns, cleaving, embanking, ..[1]

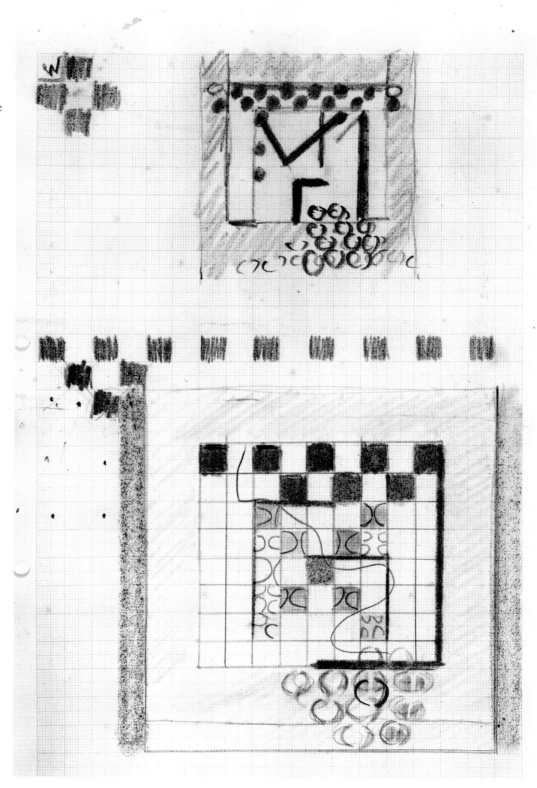

Studies for The Game of Chess
c.1974
pencil and crayon on graph paper,
$11\frac{1}{8} \times 7\frac{7}{8}$ in, 28.2 × 20 cm
(the artist)

1. From Ezra Pound 'The Game of Chess', also known as 'Dogmatic statement on the Game and Play of Chess – Theme for a series of pictures', courtesy of Faber & Faber

The Game of Chess
1974
gouache and collage,
$21\frac{1}{2} \times 14\frac{1}{2}$ in, 54.6 × 36.8 cm
(Manchester Education Authority)

Suspended forms

Pursuing ways of making colour act, of holding colour without a hard structure so that it could be free to express only itself, Terry Frost developed the idea of suspended forms. The sharp and shallow horizontal D-shapes of earlier work were ranged together in overlapping series, as in the 20 feet banner made in 1969, but they also became sagging curves and pendulous loops in a long and productive series of paintings, collages, constructions and soft sculpture from the late 1960s, into the 1970s, even emerging again in the early 1980s.

The problem of colour and suspended forms became a central preoccupation. Notebooks filled with a rush of ideas and new colour ranges emerged, as if breaking out from the rigorous explorations of hue in the 'Through' paintings, into looser overlapping shapes. It was almost as if the soft strokes of a brush had become coloured forms although it was the cut curves of collage that had created the shapes.

I did a whole series of 'Suspended Forms' paintings, which eventually I developed into collages and then into the shapes themselves, cut out and suspended on each other to make one large suspended form, without a stretcher.

Also, I did a whole series of filled canvas tubes, which I was able to suspend to bring out any curve I wished. I put six or seven together and made a bundle of circles which I called 'Bundle of Sunsets'. It was shown at the Bear Lane Gallery, Oxford.[1]

I painted paper with gouache and cut it to make collages of suspended forms. I then put them into a perspex cover and mounted the forms on a perspex backing so that the forms were able to look free. The idea was to try and get the suspended forms as free as possible. They really don't need a backing, except that I thought of all the different colour walls they might have to hang on, so the way they are mounted is a compromise.[2]

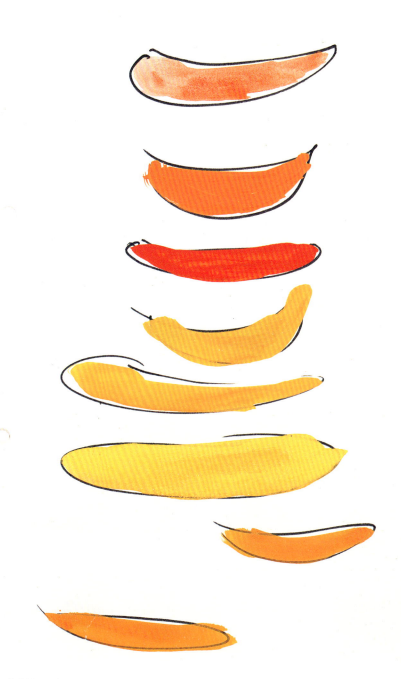

Suspended Forms Study
c.1966–69
watercolour and ink,
10 × 8 in, 25.4 × 20.3 cm
(the artist)

1. See page 202

2. From notebooks c. early 1970s

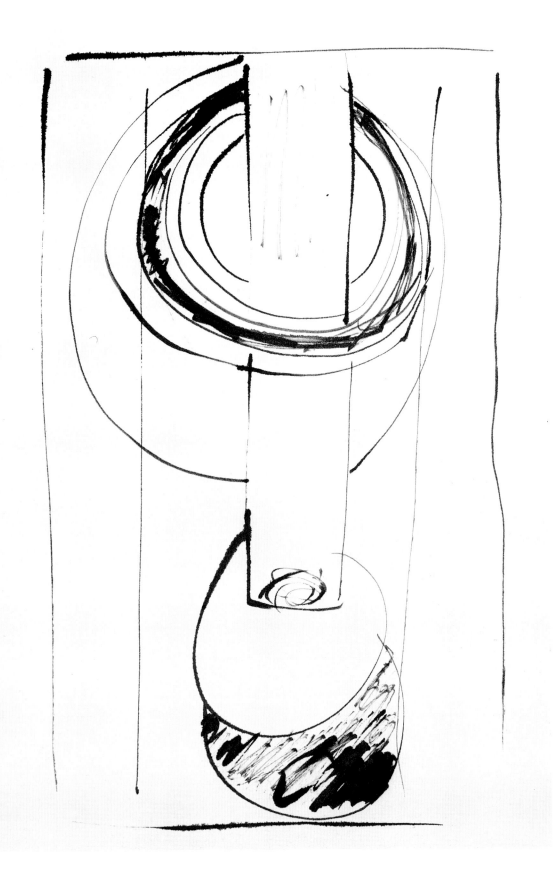

Pisa Study
c.1978
ink,
11 × 8in, 28 × 20.4 cm
(the artist)

Suspended Forms
1971
acrylic on canvas,
65 × 32 in, 165.1 × 81.3 cm
(the artist)

Photograph of the 20 feet long 'Suspended Forms' banner hanging out of the window in Banbury

Stacked Colours
1981
acrylic on canvas,
60 × 36 in, 152.4 × 91.4 cm
(the artist)

Terry Frost reports that after a trip to Pisa everything started to lean to the right.

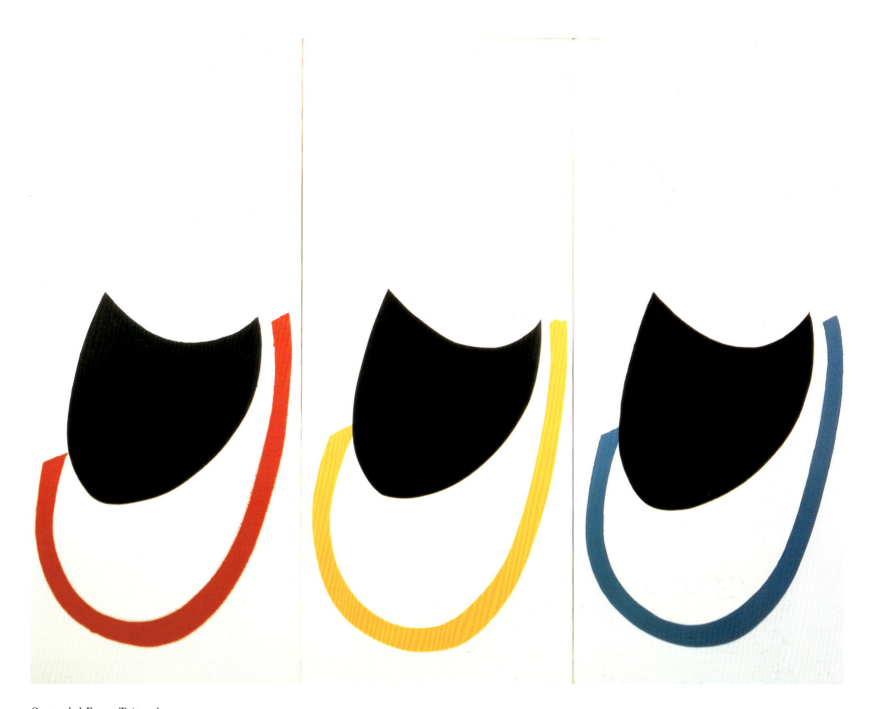

*Suspended Forms Triptych
(Red, Yellow and Blue)*
1986
acrylic and collage on canvas,
56 × 72 in, 142.2 × 182.9 cm
(the artist)

Newlyn 1974

Give me a day of my own time
Time of my own
Own day of my time
Dream, sleep, live, die,
Wake in your own time.
Sleep and your own time brings complete fulfilment.
In your own time travel to anywhere,
Everywhere is possible.
In your own time you can feel the blue of time and
    space
or feel the sucking grey day,
Wind-blown leaves and sawn-down beech
(thirty-two maisonettes are going
Where the beech has stood for sixty years).
In your own time of freedom
Red bricks and demolition
Dust your dieseled nostrils
Passing the crib.

Exhibition at the Serpentine Gallery, 1976, photograph by Jorge Lewinski

I think the thing is to put everything back into a painting now. I don't mind if it's got tone, or perspective, or anything. I don't care two hoots now. I mean I've got over those days when I was being pedantic and obstinately believing in this, that or the other. Now, I do anything I want to do. I suppose that comes with age.[1]

During the last two or three years of living in Banbury Frost visited Cornwall from time to time, often staying with Bryan and Monica Wynter. Gradually the idea that he might like to return to Cornwall to live began to take shape in his mind but he didn't want to be in St Ives. Every year the town was relying more and more on tourism. In the summer the narrow streets around the harbour were churning with holiday-makers and the residential streets on the hillsides above were jammed by coaches and cars in search of parking areas. The artistic integrity of the town had begun to suffer. Peter Lanyon had died after a gliding accident in 1968; Nicholson had moved to Switzerland; Sven Berlin and Guido Morris had left; W. Barns-Graham was spending at least half the year in Scotland. Bryan Wynter and Denis Mitchell each began to look for a house for Frost elsewhere than in St Ives. Several possibilities were turned up but nothing was quite right. Then Mitchell found a house in Newlyn, at the corner of Tredavoe Lane, but liked it so much he bought it for himself.

It was not long after that that Frost found the house

Untitled poem, 19 December 1973

Photographs by David Lewis

1. From a talk given at Plymouth Art Gallery in 1976

at the top of Tredavoe Lane. It had belonged to two artists, Charles Breaker and Eric Hillier. In what is now Frost's studio they had run a small summer school for watercolourists in collaboration with Marjorie Mort. When Hillier died, the family trust decided to sell and Frost promptly made an offer, though he had no cash for the deposit. Fortunately, John Hoskin and Adrian Heath were able to answer the call 'just like that', with cheques for £5,000 each, and the house was his. The house in Banbury was put on the market and sold in six weeks, enabling Frost to pay back the deposit, and so the move was complete.

As the move to Banbury had been, buying a house in Newlyn was also in a sense a return home for Terry Frost as a number of his St Ives friends now lived on the Penzance side of the peninsula. John Wells and Denis Mitchell had their studios in Trewarveneth Street, halfway down the hill towards the harbour in Newlyn. W. S. Graham and Nessie Dunsmuir lived in Madron, a little village about two miles away; Bryan and Monica Wynter lived at St Buryan, a few miles in the opposite direction. Sheila, Peter Lanyon's widow, moved to Chywoone Hill in Newlyn shortly after the Frosts' arrival.

Claude Rogers, head of the School of Art at Reading University, invited Terry Frost to continue as a resident artist with a studio, and to be there for two or three days a week. This arrangement had a number of advantages. The long train rides gave him precious time to write letters, to think and make entries in his notebooks. From the train window he saw the same landscapes and the same towns and villages, but always differently and his letters to me were always full of observations as though he were discovering these places for the first time, finding ideas and images for new paintings. At Reading, he was still able to treat teaching as an extension of his studio and he was close to London, for visits to galleries and friends.

In 1976 the Arts Council and South West Arts organised a retrospective exhibition which went to a number of cities including Newcastle, Bristol, Leeds, Chester, Birmingham and Plymouth as well as being shown at the Serpentine Gallery in London. It included paintings, drawings and collages and there was a catalogue essay by David Brown. In 1977 Frost was included in the survey show of 'British Painting 1952–77' at the Royal Academy and that year a fifty-minute documentary about him, made by John Hooper, was broadcast on BBC1 television. In fact, the number and range of Frost's exhibitions were undiminished and in 1978 he had three one-man shows including the last he was to have at Waddington's, and those at the Compass Gallery, Glasgow and the Oxford Gallery, Oxford.

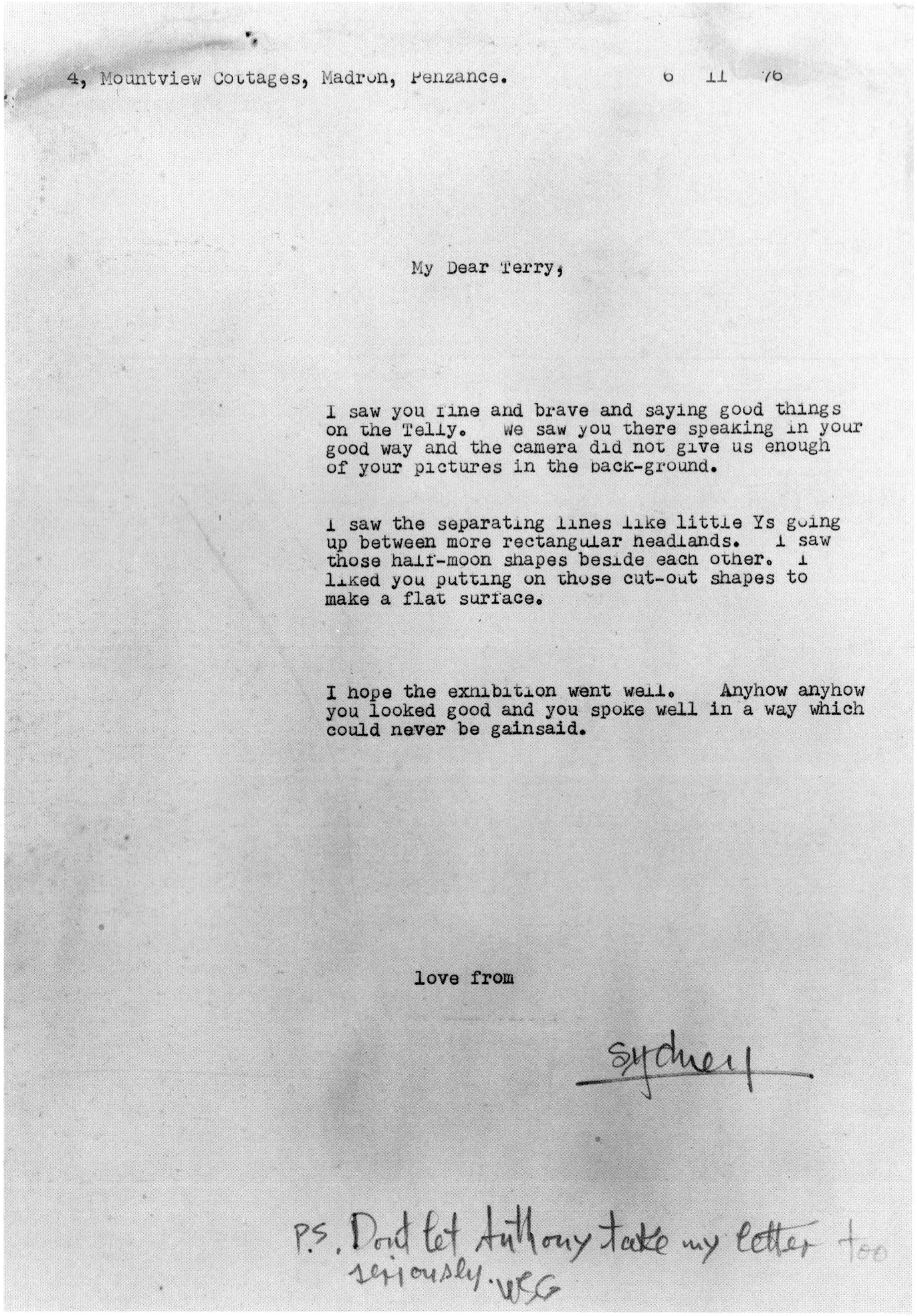

4, Mountview Cottages, Madron, Penzance.   6 11 76

My Dear Terry,

I saw you fine and brave and saying good things
on the Telly.   We saw you there speaking in your
good way and the camera did not give us enough
of your pictures in the back-ground.

I saw the separating lines like little Ys going
up between more rectangular headlands.   I saw
those half-moon shapes beside each other.   I
liked you putting on those cut-out shapes to
make a flat surface.

I hope the exhibition went well.   Anyhow anyhow
you looked good and you spoke well in a way which
could never be gainsaid.

love from

Sydney.

P.S. Don't let Anthony take my letter too
seriously. WSG

Letter from W. S. Graham, dated 6 November 1976

Newlyn Rhythms
1981–88
acrylic and collage on 20 canvases,
88 × 110 in, 223.5 × 279.5 cm
(the artist; at present on loan to County Hall, Truro)

Photograph by Terry Frost,
taken in Newlyn, 1987

Photograph by Terry Frost,
taken in Banbury, 1972

Photograph by Terry Frost,
taken in Santa Fe, 1983

Canada and white

Networks of friends have always been a way of life for Terry Frost. One of the artists with whom he taught at the Leeds College of Art was Eric (Ricky) Atkinson. Ricky followed Harry Thubron as head of the painting school at Leeds, and then in 1969 he emigrated to Canada with his wife Muriel and their two children, to become head of the Art Department at Fanshawe College in London, Ontario. He brought a number of British and American artists and writers to the College, including Victor Pasmore and W. S. Graham. Terry responded to Ricky's repeated invitations for teaching visits, in 1975 and 1976. It is characteristic of Terry that an experience which for most people would be dreary and eminently forgettable was magical for him. On one of these visits to Ontario, he

experienced that marvellous drive to Stratford and it was raining the whole way. I saw all the greys, which were imaginative originally, but I saw them all in reality on that drive. It is important to have imagination and to get confirmation of imagination, to make marks which keep other people's imagination alive.[1]

He was thinking of the 'Through Greys' paintings. There is something emotionally soothing about grey and these were wonderfully calming paintings; Terry referred to 'the soft sleep of greys'.

On another drive he was caught in a snowstorm between London and Toronto. The storm was so severe that visibility was less than twenty feet. The car was enclosed in a swirling soft cocoon of white. The only way the car could move forward was for Atkinson's son Sean to lean out of the passenger side window and guide them forward. This experience led Terry to the series of paintings referred to as 'Through Whites' and 'White Outs' – the Canadian term for wind-driven blizzards: 'I would never have done such a white painting if I hadn't got into a "white out" in Canada.'[2]

Looking at the 'White Out' paintings of this period it seems as though they incorporate many experiences simultaneously, the looping, swirling movements of line and texture of wind-swirls, but also the boat movements of earlier paintings, and even of the movements of bodies trudging through snow and plunging downhill head first on toboggans. Here is a poem written by Terry in Leeds:

Breasts in the dark.
Wind in the wool.
Crisp formed buttocks
The elements caress
the forms
The snow redefines
their shapes.
See and touch
Together, brings
a magic of living.
The sternum is pressured
at the thought.
The beat of the heart
goes mad at the sight
and touch of sun and snow
and thought of form forever there.
Imaginative imagery can travel
a million toboggan rides
but a hand on form
is a nipple hard fact. So action follows,
A love, a poem, a painting.
Are they *all* the same creative act?
Moments of black and white
truth are rare.
The sun spins and the
issues get
dizzy. Lay back on
the calm again. Lay on
the breast of pure form (permanence)
and let the elements
sweep their black whiteness
over again.
Peace of the long black
line of journey
into whiteness.
Black the permanent way
of discovery.
The line to everywhere
following the form through
in and out, up and under,
held to the breast of form. The landscape
suckles the black and white.

1. From interview with David Lewis, December 1991, see page 238

2. From interview with David Lewis, as above.

Poem, written in Leeds, c.1955, after snow in the Dales and a tobogganing session in Roundhay Park in which Terry Frost careered helplessly down a steep slope.

Canada Whites
1985–86
triptych, acrylic on canvas,
60 × 90 in, 152.4 × 228.6 cm
(the artist)

◁ *Through Whites*
1981
oil and acrylic on canvas,
48 × 48 in, 122 × 122 cm
(private collection)
For other 'Through' paintings see page 189

The Mediterranean and the Sun

The brightness of the Mediterranean had a profound effect upon Terry Frost. He began the first of several visits to Cyprus in 1977 when he was invited by the British Council to be a judge, with Professor Gramadopulos of Athens, of a painting competition in Nicosia, and to stay to teach summer studio in the art school founded by the painter Stass Paraskos. Terry loved the creative spirit and generosity of the Cypriots.

It's a land of painters and poets, every person and every child is doing something in art or music or dance, beautiful slow classical rhythms involving all the parts of the body, and the gods and goddesses are real.

He visited monasteries and saw bearded priests restoring ancient icons. He drove with the sculptor George Savides to Platres up winding mountain roads with landscapes far below reaching out towards the sea.

. . . five hours' driving on a precipitous road. You were looking down on the foliage of the trees and the sun, which was gold, when we started, became blood red. It was on one side one minute and the other the next, up there, down there as the road twisted and turned up the mountains.

Moon me your blue
Over gold and Cyprus green
Lean on the cut
Of blue and gold.
Our Peugeot rides high
On the rose
Of the night
Gold warm air
Pressed by the
Car headlights
As blue mountain
Dark descends.
A convoy of trees
Support a blue of space
For your moon-white face,
Windows wound up
And warming red light
Seals our differences.

A vast grey quarry scoured into the landscape between olive groves and patches of intense cultivation appealed to his sensibility; the colours he found had an aridity and

a depth that seemed to belong to ancient rhythms of the earth, markedly different from Cornwall and Yorkshire; this was not a landscape of wind-scoured granite saturated with rain. In the heat of the Cyprus day the dry redness of the soil and the white arid rocks seemed to absorb and hold captive the power of the sun; at night the moon over the sea was a milky blue and at dawn it shared the pale cerulean sky with a lemon white sun.

These experiences are only exciting when they have the power of being absolutely new; after you've seen them you can't experience the same thing in the same way again.

From the late 1970s and through the 1980s Terry Frost made a series of paintings incorporating Cyprus suns with black olives and the legendary goddess of love, Aphrodite. A bottle of ouzo, a check tablecloth and the explosion on his tongue of black olives hot from the oven were fused in his memory with the white gold glare of the sun. In some of the paintings mosaic medallions from Knossos become further versions of The Three Graces, a triumvirate Aphrodite.

Terry Frost first went to Spain with Tony Johnson in the late 1950s but in the late 1960s he began to get to know it better. He found there a deep echo of his own love of black as well as of brilliant sunlit colour. In Ronda he found himself

. . . drowning in a valley of sage green, standing on a bridge between an orange sun and blue moon – a heart-stopping moment between two gods.

Then the sun is setting beyond the mountains and there is just a moment when the sun becomes a vast red circle, then a semicircle, then a quarter circle, and all the time you can see, in your mind's eye, that full red circle and its hot redness, even though it's gone, and gradually the red and then the green are getting darker.

The sun has been perhaps the most enduring of Terry Frost's themes. Whether in the Mediterranean or out over the Atlantic, its rising, its blazing, black glare and its many shades of setting have been a rich source of imagery.

Big bright red
Among vast blue heavy lead
Above a moving weight
Of cold deep heavy water

Sunset over Porthmeor

Moving completely to a
Perfect semicircle of love

Photograph by Terry Frost, taken in Spain, 1968

'Climbing to Platres' poem by Terry Frost, c.1973–75

All quotations from interview with David Lewis, April 1979, see page 238

Photograph by Terry Frost,
taken in Spain, 1968

Church, Cyprus
c.1977
biro,
$11\frac{1}{2} \times 9$ in, 29.2 × 22.8 cm
(the artist)

Sun-up, Cyprus Series
1986
acrylic on canvas,
48 × 25 in, 122 × 63.5 cm
(the artist)

◁ *Cyprus Blue*
1987
acrylic on canvas,
60 × 48 in, 152.4 × 121.9 cm
(the artist)

Between two gods
1986
acrylic on paper,
18 × 14¾ in, 45·7 × 37·5 cm
(the artist)

Summer Rhythm
1986
crayon, gouache and collage,
$23\frac{1}{2} \times 16\frac{1}{2}$ in, 59.7 × 41.9 cm
(private collection)

Orange and Red
1973
acrylic and collage on canvas,
56 × 72 in, 142.2 × 182.8 cm
(the artist)

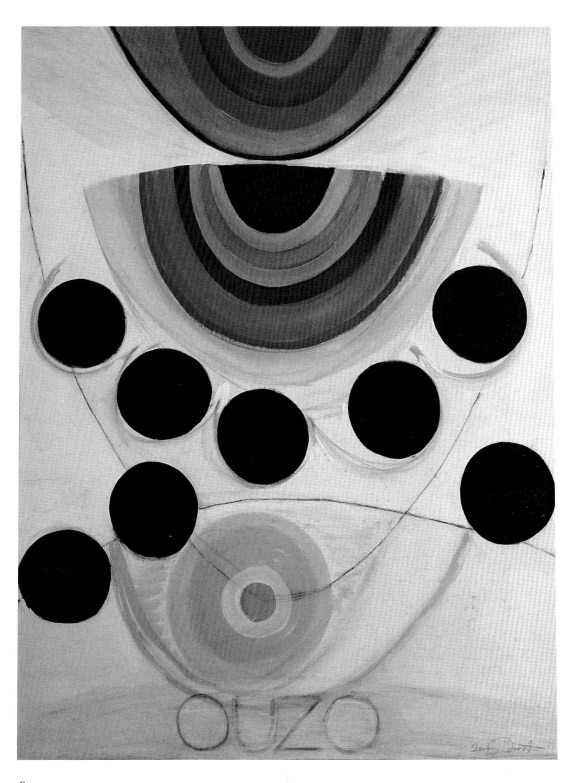

Ouzo
c.1987
acrylic on canvas,
60 × 42 in, 152.4 × 106.7 cm
(private collection)

Pelican and Olives for Paphos
1986–89
oil and acrylic on canvas,
51 × 66 in, 129.5 × 167.6 cm
(the artist)

▷ *Sun Necklace*
1987
acrylic on canvas,
24 × 20 in, 61 × 50.8 cm
(private collection)
'putting a necklace of olives round the sun is like
making contact with the gods'

1980—1994

On his visits to Canada, Terry Frost would drop down to Pittsburgh to see me. I would go to the airport to meet him, and then we'd have a great party. On one visit he brought Kath. On another, in 1980, he arrived in deep financial depression. He had travelled to Vancouver for an exhibition there of works on canvas and on paper at the Frans Wynan Gallery. But when he got to Vancouver he found that the gallery was itself facing financial difficulties. By the time he arrived in Pittsburgh he was exhausted and in despair; he didn't even have enough money for his air ticket home. But he had brought with him a portfolio of the large painted collages on paper which had been destined for Vancouver. On the morning after his arrival, while he was still sleeping, I took his portfolio to my office and rallied my architect friends, clients, and two or three art collectors I knew. It was a morning of feverish activity. I wanted desperately to sell at least two or three before Terry turned up for lunch. But by lunch time everything in the portfolio was sold! Terry was able to buy his ticket and fly home with money in his pocket.

In the early 1980s interest in his earlier paintings helped Terry Frost financially, but it had its depressing downside; it seemed to him like a vote of no confidence in his recent work. I had frequent letters from him about it but felt powerless to help. I was an architect, not a dealer or a gallery owner. He sent me a huge flat package with a dozen recent paintings on paper and collages in it. In contrast with his dark mood, these works on paper were bright and joyful and full of radiant energy. I persuaded a Pittsburgh gallery, Concept, to show them. Over a period of a year they were sold, but it wasn't as easy as before. Some we bought ourselves. With others, we found ourselves negotiating prices downwards to close a sale.

It's been a strange old going on the last three years or so. One got lifted up several times only to be socked down again, but after all the anguish of the Inland Revenue, the gallery dropping me in the financial soup and the appalling lack of sales I think I am adjusting to a different set of expectations. I don't think I understood the change of atmosphere, fashion, circumstance or what have you. If Roger H had still been around I might have got the message, for he twigged well in advance and would not allow anything (but drink) to change his attitude. I have been soft and compromising. I should be as obstinate with these shamateur figurative painters as I possibly can, not that I am against any one painter or what they believe in. After all, that is what

we both do. But the swelter of fashion, of decorative pattern abstract which has arrived on the scene – plus the agonised semi-political, pseudo-sociological figurative painting – has momentarily killed the life of the art scene, of painting, at any rate.

. . . a show I saw recently . . . an artist painting in the manner of Rembrandt and around Velasquez, ideas beautifully done, skilled handling of thick juicy oil paint. But always in every stroke looking back not to go forward but to be safe in the arms of the past, and of course he has cried all the way to the bank. God damn it, it makes me weep. I wish I had saved you a particular cutting in which the critic used every name including Goya, Velasquez, Rembrandt etc etc while filling two columns avoiding talking about the actual paintings. Incidentally I got one line: 'Frost makes it all look so easy with his vibrant colour'. I only sold one painting which is the worst I've done in thirty years. You see critics over here fall over backwards to write pages of waffle once there is the slightest figurative element. Even Leslie Waddington said to me it's what the people want. I don't think Kandinsky, Mondrian, Malevich etc painted what people think they want. There have always been people making a good living doing just that but one doesn't rate them as creative artists . . .[1]

I find myself becoming more and more confused by the reality of the world I live in. In this I do not mean the world in the widest sense, ie Red Brigades, Tasmanian aborigines etc but selfishly my confusion is with my own life. Not with my painting; it is no more confused than it has ever been and I feel optimistic. But time and peace of mind to paint seem very hard to come by. My teaching, which I love, has once again become my main source of income. This is a big disappointment to me. I would prefer my painting to keep me and my teaching to be allowed to be my pleasure. Debts to Waddington plus an inquisition by the Inland Revenue have almost brought my heart to a standstill. I really see no way out, and I begin to despair that I will ever have the strength to survive the cruel financial situation. I am not frightened of going bankrupt or being broke; that is the 'I' of me but the 'me' of me is not on a good wicket at all. My anxiety to lead a peaceful painting life is being rubbed out by my feeling of hopeless despair. I look or feel as if I could destroy the funny belief everyone must have built up about me. If only I could explain simply that unless there is a miracle we will not be able to carry on even as we do now in 1980. I must get the figures worked out in large black type. Income and expenditure. I know that at present my expenditure is

1. Letter to Duncan de Kergommeux in Ontario, written very early in 1980

at least £1,000 more than I earn. If I could provide
enough money for my family I would go and live
in one room just to exist. I wish I knew how to cope.
I think I have been carried along by the art scene to the
detriment of my home life. So much so that life is
becoming increasingly touchy and fragile. I do not
remember things. I constantly lose my keys, glasses,
pens, letters. I am now a dead loss, a loser, a nuisance.
My worries have eaten into me and I think it would be
better for everyone if I disappeared.[2]

Parallel with agonising over his personal matters. Terry
Frost felt anguished over the state of the world, the Cold
War, the rising tide of violence in Northern Ireland,
Middle East terrorism, and the soaring interest rates of
the time. Many of his letters of this period, written on
the train on his way between Cornwall and Reading,
referred to the latest international situation. In some his
mood was sombre. It was as if his own blood was shed,
his own soul was imprisoned. In one or two, he had
clearly lost political hope. Then from the window he
would watch the familiar landscape, and his mood would
shift; he would draw sustenance from fleeting permu-
tations of colour and light, and from the permanence of
hills and valleys. 'The moment is as long as you are in
contact.' he wrote in one place. In another: 'I paint
because I can't help it, it's part of my life. My thoughts
are ever on it.'

I became aware that in his paintings he re-established
contact with exuberance and joy. It was through nature
and landscape, which he would distil into a radiant sign
language of colour and rhythm and form, that he was able
to reaffirm a perpetual and ongoing renewal of life. With
colour and form and rhythm he transformed his spontaneous sense of discovery and wonder in nature into an art
in which immediacy and spontaneity are held within a
formal holism of interrelationships. In these years, as
though to compensate for his anxieties, his work grew
more vibrant, more assertive, more radiant.

The studio in the house, with mobiles made c.1991;
photograph by the Royal Commission on Historic
Monuments, 1993

2. From a notebook, 1980

Black Sun, Newlyn
1983
oil and acrylic on canvas,
84 × 72 in, 213.4 × 182.9 cm
(the artist)

Blue for Newlyn
1989
oil and acrylic on canvas,
89 × 55 in, 226 × 139.7 cm
(the artist)

Heart and Spiral
1990
acrylic, crayon and collage,
12×8 in, 30.5×20.3 cm
(the artist)

◁ *Blue Heart*
1989
gouache,
$8\frac{1}{8} \times 8\frac{3}{8}$ in, 20.5×21.3 cm
(the artist)

Squeeze Collage
1993
acrylic and collage on board,
$13 \times 26\frac{1}{2}$ in, 33×67.3 cm
(private collection)

Red, Black and White Squeeze
1993
acrylic and collage on canvas on board,
$24 \times 41\frac{3}{4}$ in, 61×106 cm
(the artist)

Dawn
1987
oil, acrylic and collage on canvas,
72 × 60 in, 182.9 × 152.4 cm
(Belgrave Gallery)

Exhibition at the Mayor Gallery, 1990

Untitled
1992
diptych, acrylic and collage on card,
10½ × 15 in, 26.7 × 38.1 cm
(Belgrave Gallery)

▷ *White Hot*
1993
acrylic, oil and collage on canvas,
42 × 42 in, 106.7 × 106.7 cm
(the artist)

Photograph by Roger Mayne, 1990

Thinking and working

. . . People who want to paint are always different and odd simply because they have so much of value inside to protect and I think one must sometimes be difficult in order to defend oneself. One has to hate or appear to hate things outside to give strength to the real which is within. It's a difficult thing I am trying to say, but you might grasp what I mean, for both you and I know from our own experiences of life that we alone have to make art in order to do our real work and no such thing as a fairy godmother can help. If we threw away our responsibility to ourselves then we would become one of the maddening crowd . . .

. . . I have to fight harder now than ever to retain a little bit of myself. The odds here are all pitted against me. But I know that I must make the effort to outwit the odds . . .

. . . I am fighting hard between my long bouts of lethargy. God, they worry me: lethargy, conscience, economics are just painful sores to be creamed up and healed, and wiped out with the change of the weather. But the art conscience remains a permanent growth in the guts, ignoring economics, world crises and the like.[1]

I am not here
I am not here
At two o'clock in the morning just for fun
I am not here for something[2]

. . . which brings me on to the business of my imagery. Adrian,[3] says is it memory or imagination? I think if I really knew the answer to that I wouldn't be able to find the image in paint. Of course I have a memory. My memory frightens me because it is not good enough and it seems that it only remembers tiny facets of the past – in fact what it wants to remember. But it has a big battle with my tendency to have a crowd of ideas and images rushing through my head, which almost takes my breath away and wears me out for I have to slow them down and try to come to a decision on which one I can take up. This involves so many things before a decision can be taken. Do I really feel like tackling the idea in my head? Is it worth it, this continual battle with art, life, society, politics, envy and so on? Why not stop completely? Why not give up? Is there a canvas ready? Should I do a doodle? Should I do a collage, a crayon drawing? Usually I end up doing them all until I make a final move. My imagination is more like reverie – when I can get alone, but in company, ie on a train,

I can Walter Mitty my way to the most wonderful ideas. The landscape talks to me in a poetical way, whites stand out against greys, red soil and green grass are more than just that. It is a secret cell that sparkles in the head and heart. This is true, it's not made up – and it's a wonderful contact with all that you have learned and all that you can see and feel in one moment. The moment of truth. Really not explainable. But it's all to do with what you have been trying to do; it doesn't come by chance. You have to want to be carried away to the main idea. The real problem is then with you, sorting it all out to find the particular and find a simple way of saying it.[4]

Being interested in abstraction, in Constructivism, and in the experience of being in and around St Ives, led me on to deal with painting which was the result of walking, going somewhere else, going to another bit of the landscape. Peter Lanyon took me out and we would walk over it, gaze at it, breathe the air and lie flat on our backs in it; he called it being intimate with the landscape. That was very important to me, as well as what I saw and experienced in the town, the harbour, the streets, the rooftops. I had not set out with the intention of working like that but it became mixed up with geometrical division, space, movement and so on. Then Roger Hilton and I became friends in 1951, and Roger, who had been involved with COBRA and all that gang, he and I were both struggling to flatten things out, to paint on a flat surface, to accept that we were working on flat surface. We didn't want any illusionism, none of that nonsense. We wanted just flat shapes and the colour had to work out from the canvas. We were determined to use colour and get out of the trap of having to use perspective. If you keep a colour flat then you've got to find a shape that will hold it flat, therefore you are involved with proportion and relationship to the next colour you put on. So that was a really good training, probably no better than the objective drawing of the Coldstream Guards and the Euston Road, but it was all part of my training.

Later, when we used to correspond, Roger wrote and said it's time we took the cork out of the bottles and put everything in. He was starting to put the figure in and I was very cross with him but the point is that I also then began to put a little bit of the old sex thing into paintings. It was almost copulation at times with those blacks and whites but it was very loveable. It was done with poetic licence to make something lovely so that the fact that the black went into the white gave some kind of sensuous situation.[5]

1. From letter to Yan Kel Feather, written in Leeds, c.1954

2. W. S. Graham, Stanza 72, from 'Implements in their Places', published in the collection of the same title, Faber & Faber 1977

3. Adrian Heath

4. From a notebook, c.1980

5. From interview with Sarah Fox-Pitt and David Lewis, see page 238

Untitled
1962
watercolour,
$22\frac{1}{2} \times 15$ in, 57×38 cm
(private collection)

Circle of Love
1975–79
acrylic and collage on canvas,
61½ × 56 in, 156.2 × 142.2 cm
(the artist)

It's a question of whether you are prepared to give to the primal spirit, whether you are not afraid to appreciate a sound, a colour, and to stand up and say so. Like going to Wells Cathedral, a great experience. There is an inverted arch which holds the building up to God in the heavens, holds the whole vast structure up. It is really superb. I walked around and up the steps to the Chapter House. You turn through darkness, the steps slowly appearing, angled, worn, and turning, tilting you and transporting you through space that is trapped in time. It is very dim. Then suddenly you come out to be faced with a circle of light. You are bathed in a burst of light from the circle. It was an experience very much to do with colour, moving through different lights, moving through the form in a kind of architectured garden.

After five minutes to get your breath back you can begin to see the carved seats all round, with heads behind. Each face contains an expression, thought up by the lads who did the carving. Rather saucy, and you felt the whole humour of the period, but all done with beautifully manipulated light and space. That was a discovery, Wells Cathedral, because I didn't know what I was going to walk into.[6]

6. From interview with Sarah-Fox Pitt and David Lewis, as above

From 'Romantics': 1963

Terry Frost and Alan Davie are intuitive painters. Their work, that is, belongs to the romantic tradition as clarified in this century by Kandinsky, who argued for and tried to produce, an art of 'inner necessity'. The tradition is so old and its programme so simple (not to say trite) that it may be asked whether it still has the seeds of life. The answer is that a totally subjective art cannot exist, and that this kind of artistic concern thrives because of the need to find viable compromise solutions. Intuition can be only one factor; external sources will have to supply formal elements through which intuition is to be expressed. However much a painter may claim to be working only out of his own personality and rejecting all else in order to protect the uniqueness of his art, he is influenced by countless external stimuli, including the entire world of art – not least the picture he himself painted last week.

Characteristically, Frost makes no claims of any sort, but his paintings assert his view of art, and never more clearly than in the works currently on show at the Waddington Galleries. His solution to the subjective-objective dichotomy is to familiarise himself with a narrow range of forms or images and then to improvise on them freely. His very familiarity with his themes diminishes the need for conscious decision and permits a relatively unfettered following of possibilities that come up in the act of painting. This solution has crystallised in the course of Frost's development without his having to invent it. The bobbing rhythm of the boats around St Ives and the quality of its landscape led him into an art that was three-quarters abstract and yet representational. The less flexible pattern of the pasture lands and the black stone walls of Yorkshire, the long months of snow in the Dales, taught him to see pictorial structure as the aim of abstraction and helped him towards a brusqueness of manner that has lasted to this day. His formal themes are now traffic signs and bikini tops (not boats), pretexts for a guileless display of personal warmth and vigour.

From Norbert Lynton, review of exhibitions by Terry Frost and Alan Davie, *New Statesman*, 22 November 1963; Terry Frost's was his second one-man show at the Waddington Galleries, October–November 1963

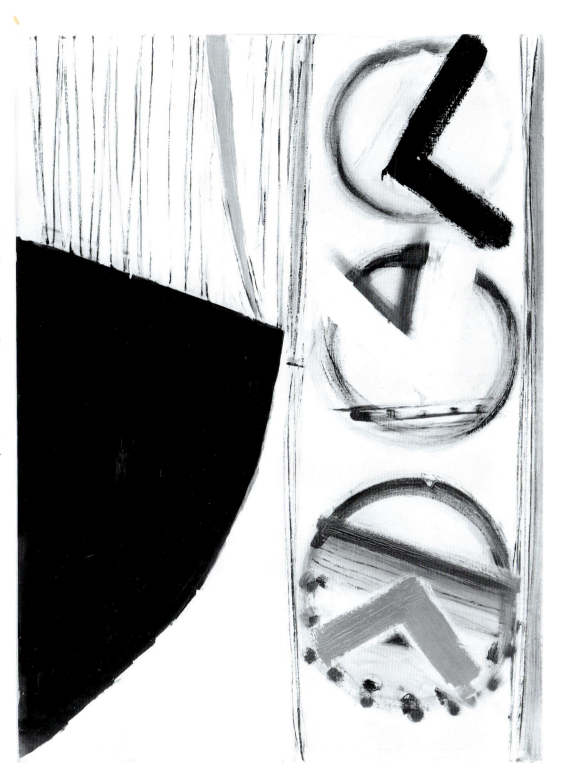

Black, White and Orange
1963
oil and collage on canvas
48 × 36 in, 121.9 × 91.4 cm
(Belgrave Gallery)

Forbidding Mourning
1991
oil and acrylic on canvas,
$29\frac{1}{2} \times 22$ in, 74.9×55.9 cm
(private collection)

Painted just after William
Desmond's funeral and
titled after the poem by
John Donne.

Abstraction and figuration

letters between Roger Hilton and Terry Frost

. . . I have been with abstraction sufficiently long now to feel the call of the wide open spaces and to feel that any return to an evocative, tasty kind of painting goes so much against the grain as to be impossible to contemplate. One finds oneself in a position where the last thing to do with a canvas is to cover it with a good smooth coat of some good strong colour. When you have got to this stage your days of dabbling with paint on canvas may be said to be over. One has to ask oneself how these sheets of pure colour can be used. One has to realise I think that aesthetic evolution has speeded up like everything else and that old ideas die very hard. Also that it takes several people working intuitively along certain lines, roughly related, to produce something new. Let me say right out that of course I agree that eventually the artist must design the house or the town (not just add bits to it) and of course I see the insuperable objection to this at the moment. May I point out however that economically you can't very well base yourself on the sale of paintings anyway, though it does help. On the other hand if you lose interest in painting in the old sense you cannot continue to practise it. And another thing, you can only do what you believe in. . . .[1]

. . . still as for exploring of course one has to explore. At the moment I am not so concerned with the physical aspects of painting as the moral ones. What are we supposed to be doing? The mechanism of painting has to be harnessed to some idea. You have to be in other words representing something. Now we can expose a totally blank canvas and hardly an eyebrow will be raised. You can't go further than that. So we have to start again and paint something. What? It is the old question that led to non-representational painting in the first instance. What a relief one didn't have to paint anything. The main stumbling block was got over. Well we have had a lovely splash with it. But can we go on splashing blithely for ever. Some time there must be a meaning or a message. Greenberg in a letter to me said Rothko kept on talking about a message and how this irritated him. Greenberg. You've got to have something to hang your hat on. We have leaned heavily on various things but it doesn't seem adequate. It's the old story. Once you have learned to paint you've got to find something to paint about. On the contrary the pure abstraction I can do, that is why I seldom do it any more. One can't spend one's days turning out things like Ellsworth Kelly, or if you like [1953–55] Roger Hiltons. One hopes eventually to make a synthesis between the pure abstract and the personal quality of your drawings show for instance, but this will take time.[2]

. . . but as for a message, oh no. Figuration yes, but what message, to doodle one's life away, to reel and stumble after every impulse, to imitate the adventures of all extremists in an effort to gain recognition for something while alive. Isn't this to do with ego? (and on my part does it smell of sour grapes?) What message? Society has always been bent on destroying itself. But to fall in with that is to give up . . . then if you want to get involved [in moral problems] and take action, then I don't think you paint.

In any case I can't believe in the religious message put across in so-called religious paintings because they were done at a time when people feared religion and could not read or write. [I don't believe they] really had any religious content. Not unless the individual was deeply religious and could transfer his religious feeling to the painting and back. If the message was really there with potency it would still be there today. For me, I like the painting or I don't, irrespective of when or why it was done. I don't think I am alone. Goya for instance in his [war] etchings didn't make me feel ill because I think I was too busy admiring the work. So you see your message idea is phoney to me, and not moral.

Take Monet's 'Water lilies' and the big painting in the Orangerie. Take Goya's 'Marchioness de G' we saw in the Louvre. Carpaccio's paintings in the Accademia in Venice. Rubens' 'Three Graces'. Mondrian's 'Boogie-Woogie', Canaletto's 'Stonemason's Yard' in the National Gallery. I only quote works I've seen and like. Works which have a great and religious feeling, only I don't know really what religious means, [it's] more a magic. No message in the sense of the [ban the] bomb campaign or socialism or the Kruschev line. Please define message, religion; figuration I understand, abstract I understand. And I think I can recognise and sense a work that has what today I will call magic and demands reverence, respect, worship, me to raise my hat and bow. What the hell has this got to do with message. Write a book, or take a dog collar, but don't paint. As for having done abstract art in 1955, well you know the answer to that one.[3]

1. From a letter from Roger Hilton, early 1950s, written at the time when Pasmore, Heath, the Martins and others were promulgating collaboration between artists and architects towards new forms of abstract constructivist art. All the letters to Terry Frost from Roger Hilton quoted here are in the Tate Archive.

2. From a letter from Roger Hilton, c.1963

3. From a notebook, evidently a draft of Terry Frost's reply to the Hilton letter above

It is disconcerting not knowing whether my next show will be of chaste abstracts or violent figuration but in any case it will be one or the other. If abstracts they will be very chaste. Spiritual. Calm. If figurative they will be fulgurant. Demonic. Tragic, expressionistic, violent, wanton and destructive. It seems to me that it is the nature of the time we live in with untold possibilities of destruction, untold possibilities of building a new world. In a way I feel there is too much starting from the canvas. There is nothing innately wrong about figuration. It is the technique for carrying it out that is difficult. Abstraction of the neo-plastic kind is based on the square. It can't I think ever lead to figuration. The other as practised by the Americans has apparently led to some sort of figuration. One gets tired of smooth, well-ordered surfaces and longs for loose, broken-up, pulpy ones. At the same time I have to admit that such things are outside the current development of thought. I would not know how to set about them. I admit I like something ordered and under control. Ultimately I suppose the nature of one's work is limited by one's powers. We are not free to do what we want. We have to do what we can. . . .[4]

As for being mithered or whatever the expression was that you used about painting – aren't we all? Isn't the whole thing in a jam? Don't we have to paint DESPITE the impossibility of seeing a way out? You will be able to keep your freshness long after the rest of us have dried up and the silly world will follow as soon as they think it's the thing to do. Hang on to ALL your pictures and one day you will make a fortune. . . .[5]

. . . As regards drawing and painting one is lucky if one can slip a bit in when nobody is looking. One can imagine the world going up in flames and THEN perhaps as the brushes and paints began to frizzle at last one would be free and would paint knowing oneself and the picture would cease almost simultaneously. No wonder Nero fiddled while Rome burnt. Probably the best he ever produced. . . .

Well Frost you know I wish you all the best for your show and I'm sure it will look terrific.

I understand your troubles only too well and I'm still backing you. One has to bleed and keep on bleeding. . . .[6]

For Michael Milburn-Foster's film on Terry Frost, an interview was set up[7] with Adrian Heath and John Hoskin putting the questions. It included the following:

AH: *. . . people ask me what sort of painter I am and I say abstract, and I get exactly the same kind of reaction now as I did in the early fifties . . .*

TF: It's like taking an American to a cricket match. You have spent your life painting but the people who are the most critical, the most difficult to deal with, are people who haven't even bothered to take the time to look at paintings. I've often said to them, 'which painting do you like?' and they don't know the name of a single painting. I have been attacked by people who don't even try to learn or understand. If you want to receive you have got to give. It's no good people asking me stupid questions about what I paint pictures of, what image I use, if they're not prepared to learn and see, otherwise we're poles apart.

AH: *Let's take this person, say from the National Gallery; in most paintings from there there is an answer that is visible on the canvas and there is an answer behind that visibility . . .*

TF: Yes, well in the first place there is a story. Before I knew the 'Judgement of Paris' I didn't have that kind of classical education, I looked at the painting and the painting had to stand or fall by the painting. Now this is nothing to do with the story; the thing that fascinated me about that painting was that you've got the same figure used three times, side, back and front, so it makes a D-shaped turn. Three reds, one in the tree, one on the centre model, one on Paris, eye glance to make space; there is so much going on in that painting. The same things go on in 'modern art'.

AH: *The Three Graces have been painted in many different ways. You've talked about the formal interpretation but according to historians the content, which means the meaning of the picture, pre-existed, that is, the myth. Now, as an abstract artist, you don't look at Malevich or Mondrian and talk about myths. Myths have been made about them but you are stretching a point if you try and see a myth . . .*

TF: I think the great thing about being an artist is that you can stretch as many points as you want because if you don't stretch points, then you are landed with Gombrich. You can risk it, you can make your own myths. I know that my reaction to the sun and the moon is not to do with my reading but it's to do with my primitive reaction, to my feet being on the ground in a hollow when I saw those two, the sun and the moon, together. That gives me a moment of contact

4. From a letter from Roger Hilton, mid 1950s

5. From a letter from Roger Hilton, c.1963

6. From a letter from Roger Hilton, early 1960s

7. See page 238

with something which has gone on forever, and that is a myth. So the 'Gombrich' myth is used in one way to make a painting and the content of 'modern art' is as valid as that myth.

AH :   Myths were there before you or I or Gombrich.

TF: The artist is entitled to stretch words because he doesn't use words when he is painting. People have got to be prepared to go overboard if they want to understand what artists paint. Otherwise they don't deserve to know anything about art.

AH :   The implication of that phrase is that you do know what art is.

TF: That is the implication.

AH :   You are moving from public to private mythology . . .

TF: I've said you make your myth and paint it. My memory is what I rely on. A moment of discovery when I happen to be made aware, or aroused by something I discovered, by surprise : that goes in my store and that becomes my time and space and by the time I use it, it's myth that I'm working on. I apply all the things I've tried to learn about art, the grammar, the construction, the tightness, to hang my myth on. That's really why I often tell a story about how I got the idea and I know it's a true statement. What I don't really know, of course, what I can't explain, is how I get from the story, the memory, the myth, to what I actually make. It doesn't necessarily say to other people what that idea was, that I received at that particular moment and worked on two years later and produced this particular painting. The painting has to stand or fall by itself. Like I said about the Rubens, people have to appreciate the painting without knowing about the myth.

You can say it's presumptuous calling it myth but it doesn't matter what I call it, or what any painter calls it, if it is enough to get the confidence to do what they want to do.

AH :   It is important that your stimulus comes from – take Walk Along the Quay, *that was a walk, a time-based experience, something from which you have to make forms . . .*

TF: Yes, but I never thought about it at the time. I had been walking along the quay every morning with the children because the neighbours complained if they cried. There I saw those semicircles propped on a stick and I thought 'how the hell can I paint that?'. Then I happened to have a canvas 57 I think by 17 inches and I thought I had better walk up this, same as I do when I'm pushing the pram so it was just common sense to use that long shape ; I belted all these shapes up it and that was it.

Blue and Yellow Painting
1951
oil and collage on canvas,
20 × 24 in, 50.8 × 61 cm
(private collection)

I always tell stories about my experience and I don't think I exaggerate. If I was to describe the sun dipping into the mountain, when I'm standing on the bridge at Ronda in Spain: I'm standing in a bowl of sage green and the sun becomes that deep red, and it has a semicircle which I know is not there (and I don't know the scientific reason for it) but which is cutting into this sage green mountain, I'm sent. I don't need L S D, cocaine or anything. I still get a tremendous feeling just from telling it again.

I used that semicircle and the sun dipping – it is related to the sun on the Lizard too – in the Lorca, because there is a poem that deals with the sun dipping in the mountain and I had actually experienced it in Spain years before. I realise now I've used that dipping semicircle for quite a long time.

AH : Let's go back to the choice of colours because I know you have an interest in colour theory.[8] Do you use that consciously to colour your forms or do you use the colour of your inspiration?

TF : I think I use them all. I don't stop and decide to use colour theory and I don't say I'm going to use my emotional theory. It seems I decide the colour I want for the shape that has been related to the idea, and it may be quite different when it is put down on the flat canvas. It may be a very nice red in my imagination but when I come to put it down I might bring in my colour theory and say it is too yellow a red for my idea, so it has to become bluer, and that immediately affects the next colour. We must get the best of colours so it's good to know the theory but you can't stop to think about it.

AH : One uses the emotion to correct the rule or the rule to correct the emotion, but it's the metre that is there and you find the words for it or you abandon the metre.

TF : I think the problem is getting the best out of the idea because the material you are using can only exploit it so far.

For shapes I do lots and lots of doodles. For colour I paint on lots of paper. I make sure I have got at least 20 different yellows, 20 different blacks, 20 different reds, 20 different greens. If I've got an idea about black olives I've got to have a stack of black-painted paper for a start. I know I want to put them on a particular shape, a curve. I can't explain why I've always had the fascination for the curve. I suppose it's quite primitive. If you've done elementary biology you know a curve is one of the most important things and a split curve is most exciting. If you stick a black olive on that you're immediately aware of where you're going to put the

rest. The curve is something you can weight at one end so that it can take the weight of a black. A matt black at one end would be totally different to a black which was shiny and laid on thin, so that you would then swing your curve, drop it at the right; now all this would be related to my idea if I was dealing, as I have been dealing recently, with 'Aphrodite', or 'Paphos Delight'. 'Paphos Delight' comes from the experience of black olives, of suns and moons, strange smells, new country, the dance. All this is mixed up in these quite hedonistic paintings.

I think being able to look at a painting which gives you the opportunity to have solitude, to be yourself, to be able to wander into reverie is very important. I like to travel in time; to imagine and enjoy the spaces and shapes made by that colour is more than hedonistic, it is spiritual and that is a value, so I don't think words describe good painting.

AH : There is no reason why you can't reach a sound philosophical 'spiritual heaven' through joy as well as through the black side of life. But take Goya – nobody would say he only looked on the bright side of things.

TF : But I am looking at his black paintings, not on his philosophical approach to all the bullshit. When I saw the etchings in the Prado I got my nose right on them looking at that beautiful black and I wished I could do something like that, which is very mean of me but then I'm greedy and selfish. I thought he was magnificent.

The Russians, El Lissitzky, the photography of Rodchenko, they are my gods. It's the discipline of the work which affects me.

AH : You like the discipline of Goya?

TF : Artists are very strange people. They are most of them a bit wild, so I don't know about discipline. I'm using the word discipline but I think I had better bring it back to the word structure because structure in a painting is different to discipline in the individual. You can be the wildest, but you can put two things together tight on a flat surface and that's the discipline I'm talking about.

AH : The tightness, you mention very frequently and always have done, implies something that is rigid, tight . . .

TF : Rigid in two dimensions but not rigid spiritually, in the sense that it can be two shapes and two colours that move you in a particular manner. It is a time and spatial thing which different people will react to differently . . .

8. For instance, M. E. Chevreul, *The Laws of Contrast of Colour*, Routledge 1858, a particular favourite of Terry Frost's

White Figure, San José
1964
oil, gouache and charcoal on paper,
$18\frac{7}{8} \times 24$ in, 48×61 cm
(the artist)

Ride to Cordoba
1989
acrylic on canvas,
89 × 55 in, 226 × 139.7 cm
(private collection)
Also known as 'Black Olives For Lorca'

Desire, imagination and discipline

DESIRE: you can desire all kinds of things. Mine was concentrated on the sensation of satisfaction I felt when painting and later. Or, the full range of sensations, love, hate, delight, despair, exhaustion, vitality. Desire was always asking for more of the lovely feelings I got but time taught me that DISCIPLINE was a main ingredient to help obtain my desire. Discipline to contain my more emotional outbursts, discipline to make me think. Discipline to make my patient search for a colour which would relate to a form, which in turn would reach to the concept (the unknown in paint on a flat surface). Discipline to give me the courage to make the mark, the mark that I had never seen before – the unknown, innocence. Unknown – the Chapter House at Wells Cathedral, the Sun and Moon in Cyprus. Discipline to make contact between concept and image. IMAGINATION – clipping the wings of imagination might easily destroy the whole business: not knowing gives the opportunity to imagine.

There is no freedom without discipline.

Looking and seeing, escaping and imagination: action, image. If you look you can't see for looking. Looking for something to inspire you to work is an escape from taking action.

The decision to take action is the only way of seeing.

The imagination will throw up all possibilities. It's taking one of the ideas that makes the balloon go up. The image can so easily destroy what you saw.

If you look and look the tree becomes a tree and not a particular tree moment, the sun becomes the sun, any old sun, it's the contact via the imagination that touches the unknown and reveals possibilities.

Turn your back on looking and see.

If you must look, stand on your head to do it.

Experience the catalyst between theory and practice. Keep practice up with thinking. People who think themselves to a standstill often finish up as minor art historians (not scholars) and go round bludgeoning art students about dates and thirty-third-hand ideas about great paintings. Look at the works. Read the philosophers. Think and work as hard on the subjective as on the objective – one does not exist without the other, no matter what the logical positivists say. The National Gallery, Ethnological Museum, Tate, Wallace Collection, V & A etc are all available.

Reverie goes back to primal scenes, operating as a primitive soul – in spite of the triumphs of elaborated thought and against the very teachings of scientific experiment.

Concept and image – there's no cooperation between concept and image.

By asking a simple question about The Three Graces I found what concerned me was the, unknown to me, connection with the past, or as I prefer it, forever. Looking through many years' collection of slides I discovered that three shapes, three colours had been a very big part of my life, and this without a classical education, or, as far as I knew, it being pointed out to me as a magic number.

I could soon see that my unexpected concern with The Three Graces was leading me into a very serious line of research. The bait was very tempting and I have enjoyed the frightening reminder that there is so much to know. I needed discipline to extract myself from the temptation of deviation. Primitive instincts must exist in all of us, the forever constant surprise of something new – either in sound, smell or vision. New colour through technical means, camera, computers, new sounds, electronic noises – past knowledge and constants in the senses challenged by the new.

There's that quote from Karl Popper:

'. . . No matter how many instances of white swans we may have observed, this does not justify the conclusion that all swans are white.'[1]

Photograph by Terry Frost

All text from notebooks, late 1960s to early 1980s

1. Karl Popper, *The Logic of Scientific Discovery*, 1959, p. 27

'The Judgement of Paris', Peter Paul Rubens, National Gallery

Wall-painting from Knossos in the museum at Heraklion, Crete

'The Three Graces', mosaic in the National Museum, Naples

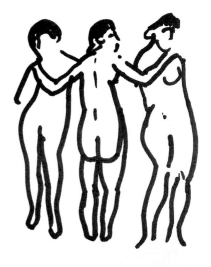

◁ *Life Studies*
  c.1952
  pencil,
  $15 \times 22\frac{1}{2}$ in, 38.1 × 57.2 cm
  (Andrew Usiskin)

◁ *The Three Graces*
  c. early 1970s
  ink,
  9×8 in, 22.8 × 20.3 cm
  (the artist)

  The Three Graces
  1956
  oil on board,
  48×72 in, 122 × 182.9 cm
  (private collection)

Teaching

Terry Frost began his teaching career early, with posts at Bath Academy of Art and Willesden School of Art in 1952. There were the fruitful years at Leeds and several short stints abroad provided particular and long-remembered inspiration, notably those in San José in 1964, Banff and London, Ontario in the middle 1970s and Cyprus in the late 1970s. He taught at Reading University from 1964 to 1981, during the last four of those years as Professor of Painting, and it was at Reading that his greatest contribution as a teacher was made.

Teaching was, for Terry Frost, an integral part of his creative life as an artist. He was a 'hands-on' teacher: he taught by doing. In an absolutely real sense the art school was his studio. No day went by without exploration, without the frontiers of ideas being pushed further by mind, eye and hand into territories uncharted by teacher and students alike. He taught his students through the excitement of his example to explore. Echoing Oscar Wilde he would often repeat that knowledge is good but imagination is better. Working with students forced Terry to order his ideas about his own work and to find ways of expressing them. Besides the words and admonitions he provided for teaching purposes from time to time, he also got into the habit of putting his private thoughts down as a way of clearing his head. Notes he made about teaching practices, art schools and art education in general show with absolute clarity that he was first and foremost on the side of the students and that he valued innovation far above orthodoxy.

A certain problem in art schools is to cope with a surfeit of ideas, some new, some old, and the pressures of other people's genuine beliefs and dogmas. The great problem is to sort out your own ideas. Practice is the answer, experience is the catalyst between theory and practice. Always try to make, or a great danger is that you could think yourself to a standstill. Take advantage of the offer of all techniques. Leave the school capable of using all the media, button up the grammar and stretch your awareness.

Don't just go paddling away, falling hook line and sinker into what is said to you. Follow up by going and looking at works, reading about different ideas. Don't get trapped into thinking that just painting and drawing day after day will make you a genius. Nose around, fidget around, get to talk to people whose work and work attitude you respect. Learn about how other people work and this may enable you to learn how you have to work to obtain the most out of your limitations.

Watch out for nostalgia (it takes too much time), the status quo (it stinks) and looking back (you trip up).

Take a gamble on looking forward into the unknown. Just watch that you keep your bootlaces done up otherwise you could trip yourself up and fall.

The artist wants to be free but tremendous discipline is needed to use that freedom. There is no freedom without discipline. If there is discipline and no freedom, that equals no art, only propaganda. I rely a lot on what has gone before. I am influenced strongly by all the wondrous works I've seen. They convinced me by the subjective sensations I experienced in front of them that art is a real part of our lives. Some people react more than others and to different interests. But to see something that takes you out of yourself into a moment of a new reality, a sensation far removed from our normal reality and all its problems, is a tonic and spirit-builder. One looks, sees and feels a good form.

Imagination works separately from reality. It belongs to us before reality. Reality isn't for long compared to imagination.

Image, before thought
    before narrative
    before emotion

Imagination thinks and suffers; it's primordial.

Teaching first-year students at Reading, 1966, photograph by Tom Cross

All from notebooks, early 1970s

Teaching at the University of California,
San José, 1964

Photograph by Roger Mayne, 1956

Colour

colour in acrylic
colour in oil
on flat
on round
in stripes
in verticals
in curves
in harmony
in discord
in contrast
through all intensities

Arrive at colour – a colour so organised and controlled as to be able to envelop you if you are willing to generate the mind and spirit. We all see and feel various effects from coming up against nature or man-made objects but always there is some colour somewhere which tempts, titillates or repels us, or leads us in and on, to a form and content and perhaps to something unknown to us.

The possibilities of a yellow walk
    a lying down sky
    a smiling black
    a soft black
    a tight black
    a fat black
    a mean black
    a blue black
    a red black

All these blacks are around us and they are a complete orchestra of magic (hence Black Magic chocolates, hard and soft).

The love of colour has to be real. In fact like love. And it must be concerned with reason, with the logical extension of a colour to its breaking point in order to discover the relations of colour and form, and together a final totality and authority.[1]

When I came home after the War, I hitch-hiked up to the Wirral to see a chap named Peters, who was a POW with me. When I got there it was a very posh house and I didn't even know which knife and fork to use, there were so many on the table. He took me into their garden, which was acres of gladioli – I'd never seen so many gladioli. Now, I didn't know much about painting at that time but I was knocked out by all these different colours. It was my first lesson in how, if one gladioli was a certain red it made the green look a certain colour and the earth look a certain colour. It was the same earth but it looked different if the flowers were different.[2]

Colour and structure and form : you could start from Ben Nicholson's window-box in Salubrious Place, seeing a crocus which is purple. It's got orange in the middle and it's a cup form with a positive shape sticking up in the middle which is contrast in form, the cup and the stamens, but also harmony. Then you get the angularity of the leaves, chevrons in blue-green making the soil look very brown, deep brown. So that's one, two, three, four things all in one flower.[3]

Photograph by Terry Frost, buoys outside the Trinity House Museum in Penzance

Photograph by Terry Frost, ship in Penzance harbour

1. From notebooks, late 1960s – late 1970s

2. From interview with Sarah Fox-Pitt and David Lewis, see page 238

3. From interview with Sarah Fox-Pitt and David Lewis, as above

Of people's choice of colour – great examples, boats or lorries. Certain colours do people's hearts good, other colours they dislike in various degrees. It is a question of reacting via the eyes through the heart and head for a full sensation. It is not a momentary sensation alone, for in my opinion, or rather, from my experience, I see better the next time. It's an additive experience; it's a sort of cleansing process, so that each colour builds up more of its own spiritual value, its own being. It doesn't necessarily have to be tied to a specific form. It can be a red which you recognise by its redness, not because it is attached to a rose or to lips. To recognise colour by itself is something we all do. How often have you heard people say 'what a lovely green' with no reference to the function of the green. 'What a lovely blue': this summer that's abstract and full of love.[4]

A shape is a shape, a flower is flower. A shape of red can contain as much content as the shape of a red flower. I don't see why one should have to have any association, nostalgia or evocation of any kind. It boils down to the value of the shape and the colour.

When we say red rose, which red?
Blue sea, blue sky, which blue?

If we travel through green blue to red blue there is a never-ending journey with each blue having its own value, its own colour, its own special working on the spirit. Each one is specific and it makes contact with the unknown. It turns into a moment of clarity.

. . . Just to think in terms of colour is enough to set the soul alight. This is colour without shape – in the spirit. Shapes are known to people by words but colour can make its own shape and exists in its own right.[5]

A red grey sea
On a snow day of grey
Moving wrinkles
Of gold sun saturated sea
Bow and stern
Clamped in the lap of loops
Of constant cold gold rhythm
Bob and bow of a boat
In the locked embrace
The cuddle of forever
Quick tempo of wriggling racing loops
Of red gold lines of sea
Reaching out to one step back
From saturated red ridged sand
Wet ridged red of white
Constant wrinkled wriggle
Of wet forever
Returning to its deep cold
Rhythm of stern and bow.
How does life complete
Its bobbing and weaving
With such certainty as sea,
Seeing us wrinkled forever
On the red tightrope of 'I'?
Fate is the cold slap
Below the dancing waterline.
The blue is where
The red should be now.

Lean on my moon of
Bright quartered lemon
Lean on my certainty of time
Spiral my colour
Yellow of moonset
Riding the blue
Weave of wet
Slipping
Never
Certain
Space

---

4. From a text done for students at Reading, late 1960s

5. From a text done for students at Reading

'Going through Exmouth', written in February 1978

Untitled poem, c.1980

Colour Down the Side of Blue
1969
acrylic on canvas,
60 × 50 in, 152.4 × 127 cm
(the artist)

All Over The Space
1969
acrylic and collage on canvas,
72 × 60 in, 182.9 × 152.4 cm
(the artist)

▷ *Black and Orange*
1959
oil on canvas,
17¾ × 19½ in, 45 × 50 cm
(Pier Gallery, Stromness, Orkney)

◁ *Three Forms*
1960
oil on canvas,
48 × 48 in, 122 × 122 cm
(Austin-Desmond Fine Art/Mayor Gallery)

Suspended Forms Study
c.1974–76
gouache,
(whereabouts unknown)

Yellows, 'Through' paintings and black

It was at Corsham in the early 1950s that Terry Frost first conceived the idea of teaching colour: not line, not form, not space, but colour – and allow form, space and line to follow.

A girl didn't know what to write her thesis on, and I was walking with her up the North Walk when we passed a bank of flowers, mainly daffodils, and I said, 'why don't you write it on yellow?' I suggested that she should look intently at all the different yellows we were seeing; and I realised that with each yellow there was a different green, and with each yellow there was a different structure – some were floppy, some were sharp, some were in perfect geometrical shapes. Someone could have written a book on that walk – and she had very little problem doing her thesis.[1]

On his return to St Ives he invited the painter Michael Snow to join him in making an investigation of yellows using cameras and notebooks along a stretch of some twenty-five miles of rugged coast from St Ives to Land's End, starting with the purple crocuses and their deep yellow throats in the window box at Ben Nicholson's house in Salubrious Place, and photographing lichens on granite rocks, the green yellow and red yellow of gorse flowers, a multitude of grasses, the iridescent fields of mustard, and ending with the lemon sun setting across the sea over the mist-shrouded Scilly Isles to the west. In his studio Terry made a catalogue of 365 yellows on two-inch squares 'until I ran out of paper', ranging between red, blue, white and black.

At Reading, Terry Frost asked sixty students to mix a black from red, yellow and blue. He wanted them to learn to mix oil colour cleanly and with a set aim in mind. Having mixed their different blacks, from the warm side until it broke to red and the same with blue, green and ochre, each student was asked to choose their mid-black, their blackest black. Terry was amazed at the resulting revelation of individual subjective choice – no two were the same. They made a mural of all the blacks ranged in order through from reddest, bluest, yellowest in to the true mid-blacks, so that everyone saw their own black take its place in the range of variations.

These experiments with the students led directly to a series of black paintings. In talking about the series,

Yellows, photographs by Michael Snow, taken in St Ives and near Zennor, c.1961

1. From an interview with Sarah Fox-Pitt and David Lewis, April 1981, see page 238

186

Terry recalls the words of the great gardener Gertrude Jekyll:

What a wonderful range of colour there is in black alone to the trained colour eye. There is the dull brown-black of soot, and the velvety brown-black of the bean-flower's blotch; to my own eye, I have never found anything so entirely black in a natural product as the patch on the lower petals of Iris Iberica. Is it not Ruskin who says of Velasquez, that there is more colour in his black than in many another painter's whole palette? The blotch on the bean-flower appears black at first, till you look at it close in the sunlight, and then you see its velvety texture, so nearly like some of the brown-velvet markings on butterflies' wings. And the same kind of rich colour and texture occurs again on some of the tough flat half-round fungusses, marked with shaded rings, that grow out of old posts and that I always enjoy as lessons of lovely colour-harmony of grey and brown and black.[2]

I learned to mix my colours, to mix red, yellow and blue make black, and if you do that you find there are as many blacks as there are yellows. A lot of people don't realise that; they think black is just black, but black, as the old poem says, is the container of all colour. The first colour to go now, as the light is going down, is red. Then different colours go at different speeds and then black contains them all. Black has got every colour. When you paint black, it must have colour.

. . . You see, it didn't matter how much colour theory you had studied. You can do colour theory and you can close the book. Then you can go out into nature and it's all there. Every colour is right, right for other colours, right for the form. It is after all what you have got to try and do in painting and it was such an eye-opener to me. Colour on granite, something hard, colour on grass, soft. It was a way of looking and with hindsight I know how valuable it was to me.[3]

It's the dialogue between your emotion and your passion and the colour that's at the end of the brush — because after all painting is language in the making . . . Colour is always something. There is no such thing as blue, not until it's a blue something. And that blue something has to be a totally new and discovered

Sonnet to Black by Edward Herbert, Lord Cherbury, 1582–1648, mss by Terry Frost

2. Chapter XVIII, *Wood and Garden*, Longman's, 1899

3. From an interview with Sarah Fox-Pitt and David Lewis, 1981, as above

● **Sonnet to Black** ●
Lord Herbert of
Cherbury

Thou Black wherein all colours
are composed
And unto which they all at last
return;
Thou colour of the sun where it
doth burn,
And shadow where it cools;
in thee is closed
Whatever nature can or hath
disposed
In any other hue, from thee
do rise
Those tempers & complexions
which disclosed as p... ...t of
thee,
do work as mysteries of that
hidden power;
When thou dost reign,
The characters of fate shine
in the skies.
And tell us what the heavens
do ordain:
But when earth's common light
shines to our eyes,
Thou so retir'st thyself
that they disdain,
All revelation unto
man denies.

experience in a painting. One thing blue can never be in a painting and that's a blue sea. Ben said, 'why should a painting imitate a rose when a rose never imitates a table?' One could cover a canvas entirely in dusty rose like Rothko and it's a rose painting. Someone asked Ben how he got a particular colour and he replied, 'if I knew how I got it I'd never be able to get it again'.[4]

'My students went out and wrapped the war memorial in black, and took me to a black meal. They blacked my face and blacked the room, and gave me black spaghetti and black wine. They read poetry about black and played black music. Since then I've done a series of grey paintings which are made of red, yellow and blue plus white.

Now there are those big black circles. I have always been a sun lover and a moon lover – not that I know anything about it psychologically – it's to do with the things that are always there in spite of our world's problems. If you look at the sun for a moment you experience black spots; if you go out in the cold the moon becomes blue; and in the heat the sun becomes black; and so in my paintings a big black circle is to do with the sun. In *Burnt Norton* T. S. Eliot wrote: 'Time and the bell have buried the day, The black cloud carries the sun away'.[5]

And yet the sun breaks out from the edges of the black cloud, something which everyone sees but doesn't notice, and I have tried to turn it into a compelling image.[6]

TF: . . . I wouldn't have painted the 'Through Blacks' or the 'Through Greys' if I hadn't insisted on the students finding out how many greys they could make or how many blacks, you see.

AF: But you never told the students that you can just chuck a bit of red in the black. They had to mix it all out of red, yellow and blue, but you can actually just use spectrum black and put some red in it, can't you?

TF: When you're in a bit of a hurry, that's OK. There are times when it's right to do that but it doesn't work in a poetic sense when you're trying to stretch your imagination and your mixture of colour together to get your concept out. It's a different thing. It's not to do with trying to write a poem in black and it took me bloody weeks, all those fifteen different blacks from red, yellow and blue. It's not quite the same thing . . .

. . . I've never left full abstraction. I couldn't paint the romantic paintings about the sun or the sea or any of those sensations unless I did the tight constructive abstraction – that is my structure. Unless I have that

certainty of structure, because I am a symmetrical painter, I've had it. I've got to have structure.

AF: But take the suns or the boat shapes – you use them in two entirely different ways. In the moorings paintings, which are meant to conjure up the moorings and the sun and the sea and space you use those shapes as completely abstract shapes with no reference to nature. I was just looking at that one upstairs, that little cracker where you tilt the pink boat shape, that segment on yellow. It's like a Matisse where he paints the table red on a red background and a red carpet – it's all red but he creates his own space and you've done it with that tilt. That's one where you've used the shapes in a completely abstract way.

TF: I've always made constructions too. People don't know that. Mine is a two-dimensional structure, tight to start off with, like a way of drawing, being certain about a shape. That's why I like 2H pencils instead of 2B because you have to make your mind up.

I reckon I've done my best painting when I've been trying to solve a problem, rather than things like the sun or the moon – they are only incidental – very important to me, but the real way of painting a painting for me is to be solving a problem: the yellows, the whites, the blacks, the greys – then you might do a decent painting because you're not trying to paint a picture. You're busy trying to solve a problem. There's tremendous commitment required to solve a problem . . .

'Nature is one thing and art another' – which of course Roger Hilton used to say.

And art must play a more elevated role than merely copying with abject servility the objects of nature, which are all right as they are, which are already beautiful enough, which cannot be copied. Art must not commit the folly of wishing to imitate the inimitable. The essential thing for the artist is to be found in the clash between his interior world and the exterior world.

This and what follows was written by a chap called Gasch:[7]

The artist should represent his own interior world, the visual counterpart of a poetic mythology. He argues that the interior is not pure fantasy because there is no such thing as pure imagination. It must feed on something, which is necessarily reality. The imagined world can become as real as the reality which kindled it. . . .[8]

4. From interview with Sarah Fox-Pitt and David Lewis, April 1981, see page 238

5. T. S. Eliot, 'Burnt Norton' from *Four Quartets*, Faber and Faber 1947; for Terry Frost's illustration see page 120

6. Interview with David Lewis, April 1979, see page 238

7. The Catalan art critic Sebastian Gasch, in an article on Lorca's drawings in *La Gaceta Literaria*, March 1928, quoted in Helen Oppenheimer, *Lorca, the Drawings*, Herbert Press 1986

8. From interview with Anthony Frost and Liz Knowles, March 1987, see page 238

Through Blacks
1972–73
acrylic and collage on canvas,
$84 \times 31\frac{1}{2}$ in, 213.4 × 80 cm
(private collection)
Another from this series is in the Tate Gallery

Thames Greys 2
1982
acrylic and collage on canvas,
48 × 80 in, 122 × 203.2 cm
(private collection)

▷ *Red Painting*
1970
acrylic on canvas,
59¾ × 60 in, 151.6 × 152 cm
(the artist)
Also known as 'Through Reds'

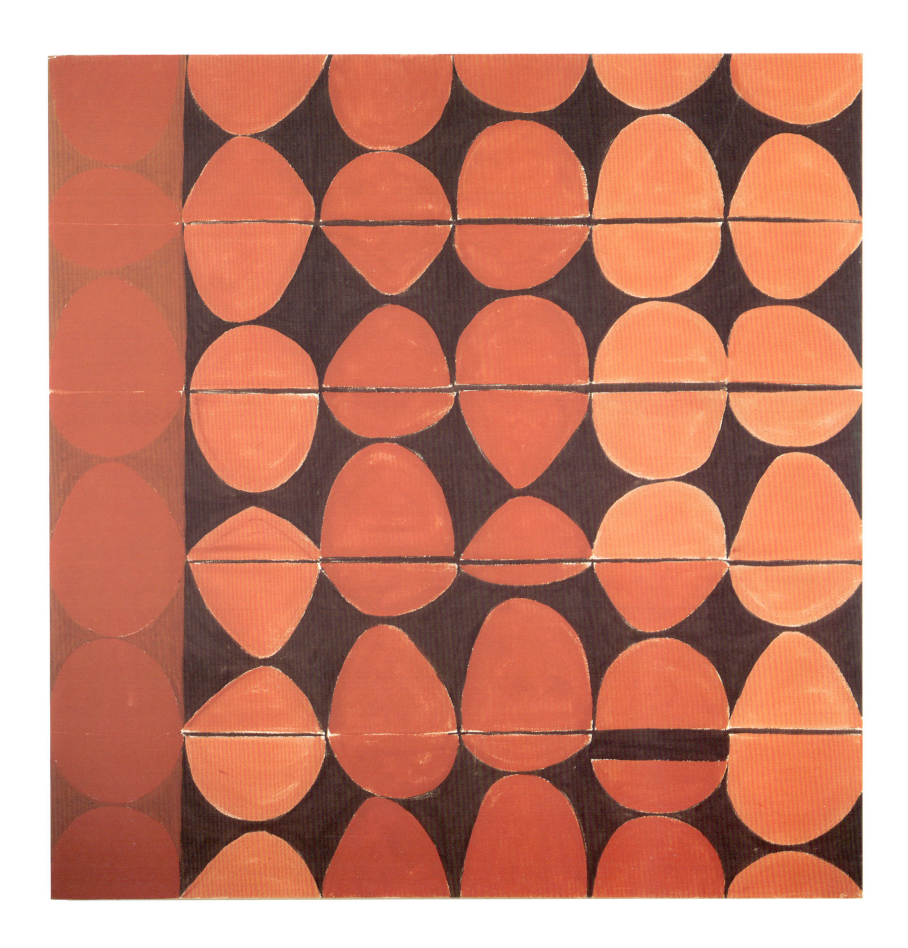

Photograph of an iris by Tom Barrett, who had given Terry Frost the Gertrude Jekyll and Lord Herbert texts on black. Three photographs by Terry Frost: doorway in the St Peter and Paul Fortress, St Petersburg, 1981; arcade in the Casa Grande cactus museum on the Apache Trail in Arizona, 1990; painted wall in Toronto. Photograph of a carnival dancer from a postcard.

△ *Black Study*
c.1969
gouache and collage,
11 × 8 in, 28 × 20.3 cm
(the artist)

◁ *Black Study*
1969
ink,
11 × 8 in, 27.8 × 20.3 cm
(the artist)

◁ *Black Study*
c.1958–59
ink,
8 × 10 in, 20.3 × 25.4 cm
(the artist)

W S GRAHAM MADRON   A SOBER GREY DAY WITH THE MIST IN FROM THE WEST   25 2 77

Dear (Tall man mad on colour) Terry,

I got your letter about Alan. I dearly hope he is not
as seriously ill as you conclude. Maybe his good greed-
iness to overpower us all with talk will help his glands
and organs to get over this wee bit. Your letter gave
me a shock and made me realise how I would miss him not
around in the great Betting Yard of the world. I know
the younger Alan better. In the recent years you are
nearer to him.

I understand what you mean about 'the deadly drink' and
not eating. Even although some of us feel we have to
take in the toxins (to maybe cushion us off &&&& from
the fact that our values are moving away from the normal)
I would not like to hasten myself down into the burny-burny.
I dreamt I dwelt in Alo Halls.   "Mama Mama, the red
wine burns like fire." (Translation of the first line of an
aria from a Sicilian opera.)   TTBB.   Pour me a double.

Alco

I have written Alan from my heart and what is left of my
soul.   I pray to the Invisible he will get through.

I hope you are proceeding with eyes which dont see over-
brown (hot) or over-blue (&&&).

cold

Love,

Sydney

Black Suspended Forms
1971
pencil and watercolour,
$16\frac{5}{8} \times 14\frac{7}{8}$ in, 42.2 × 37.7 cm
(the artist)

Letter from W. S. Graham, February 1977; the
'Alan' referred to is Alan Lowndes.

Constructions and sculpture

Working for Barbara Hepworth, I knocked ten tons of Connemara blue marble about and made those big holes through. It was hard work but the thing is that it taught me about form in a way which I had never understood before. I tried carving as a result – it stopped me painting for about nine months, then one day I decided it wasn't for me and I went back to painting. But I made constructions and they were very important for me. I had seen Gabo constructions and the way Peter Lanyon was using them. Also, there were Anthony Hill, Adrian Heath, Victor Pasmore, the Martins . . . and even Roger Hilton made constructions on paper at the time of the 'This is Tomorrow' show . . .[1]

Throughout his working life since the early 1950s, Terry Frost has made constructions in wood or cardboard, painted in bright colours. Some are wall reliefs, some appendages to paintings and some are free-standing sculpture. Others are mobiles, turning and changing as they hang or made to rock to and fro like a boat on a lazy swell. These constructions are closely linked to Terry's use of collage, in that they often play a series of variations upon a given repertoire of shapes.

In 1964 I made constructions from a bag of old off-cuts which Anthony, who was then a school-boy, found outside a piano-factory on his way home from school. In the bag were quadrants, and so many shapes, and I made a whole series of reliefs.

I make constructions regularly; it is not an occasional art form for me. I make them from wood, cardboard, paper, shoe-laces, string . . . Some are large, four or five feet high, some are very small, but all of them have colour. Even my Christmas cards are constructions.[2] Without thinking about it too much I was probably influenced to begin with, in 1951, by Ben Nicholson and Peter Lanyon. Making constructions now is what I'd call pure abstraction, just like those paintings where I am most rigorous and pure, like the 'Through Greys' or the 'Canada Whites'.[3] They clean the system. After doing them for a while I can see things in a new way. The stage is set for new images.[4]

Construction
1951–52
painted card and wood,
(destroyed)

1. From a talk given at Plymouth City Art Gallery, November 1976; Terry Frost worked for Hepworth in 1951–52, see pages 54–55. The 'This is Tomorrow' exhibition was a collaboration by teams of artists and architects, shown at the Whitechapel Art Gallery in 1956 (Hilton withdrew from the project before the show)

2. See page 205

3. See pages 189–191 for 'Through' paintings and page 135 for 'Canada Whites'

4. From an interview with David Lewis, October 1993, see page 238

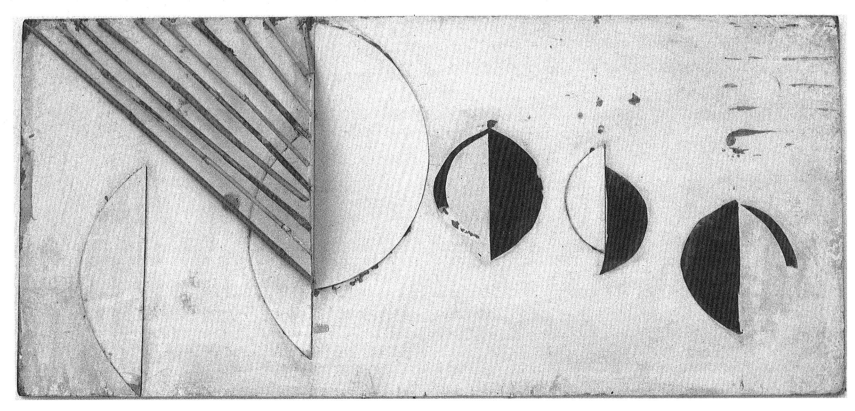

Construction, Leeds
1954
painted wood, metal and board,
$7\frac{1}{2} \times 10\frac{1}{2} \times 3\frac{1}{2}$ in deep, $19 \times 26.7 \times 8.9$ cm deep
(whereabouts unknown)
The D-shapes turn on swivels to show their colour
in the reflective surface behind.

Construction
1964
painted canvas and wood,
$12\frac{1}{4} \times 15\frac{3}{8} \times 1\frac{1}{2}$ in deep, $31 \times 39 \times 3.8$ cm deep
(private collection)

▷ *Construction*
c.1990
painted wood,
40×41 in, 101.6×104 cm
(the artist)

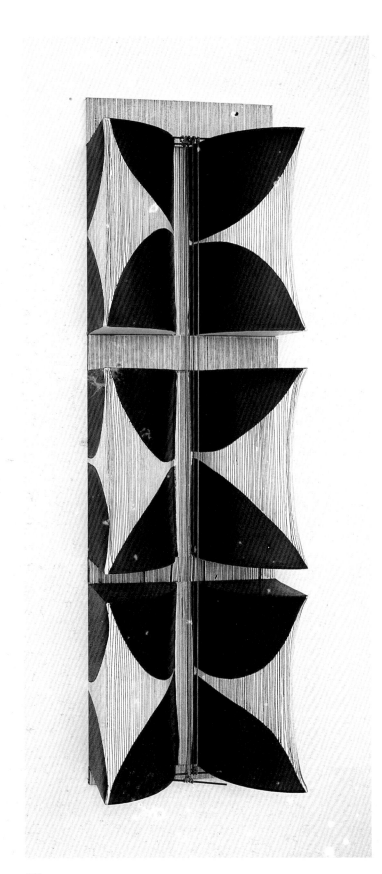

Construction
1966
painted canvas over wood,
66 × 19⅜ × 9½ in deep, 167.6 × 49.2 × 24 cm deep
(the artist)

Recent sculpture including
Rocker
c.1988
painted wood,
34 × 68 × 30 in deep, 86.4 × 172.7 × 76.2 cm deep
(the artist)

Bundle of Sunsets
1970
painted and filled canvas
(the artist)
An extension of the 'Suspended Forms', see page
123, these forms were used for other soft sculpture
including coiled and looped pieces made between
1970 and 1972

Study for Soft Sculpture
1970
gouache,
9 × 7 in, 22.8 × 17.7 cm
(the artist)

Necklace
c.1978
onyx and silver,
(Kathleen Frost)

This and other pieces were made
to Terry Frost's designs by
Michael Manzi of Penzance.

Necklace and Pendant Design
c.1976–78
collage, ink and gouache,
$7 \times 11\frac{3}{4}$ in, 17.8×29 cm
(the artist)

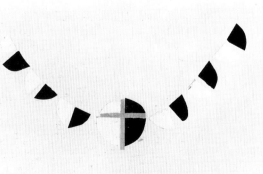

Design and decoration

Terry Frost has always been interested in decoration and has applied colours and motifs from his painting to all sorts of things, from ceramics to the icing for cakes and from watch-straps to T-shirts, with characteristic bravado. He has always made his own Christmas cards, usually card or paper collages and reflecting a current theme in his work. Over the years they have become almost a miniature retrospective collection.

In 1962–63 the Victoria and Albert Museum, in collaboration with the Goldsmiths' Company, commissioned a number of contemporary artists, Terry Frost among them, to design jewellery. Much later, in the late 1970s, Terry worked with the Penzance jeweller Manzi on designs for black, white and silver jewellery.

In the late 1970s, working with the potter Colin Haxby in Diss, Terry made designs for the decoration of production pottery commissioned for the Pier Art Gallery, Stromness. The ceramics he made in his early days at Camberwell included a tall jug, a shape he adapted for the new designs. There were mugs, regular and outsize, and a set of six large plates, all in strong red, black and white designs. At the same time Terry painted a series of large dishes and plates.

Recently, Terry has been commissioned to design silk scarves for the Tate Gallery, and watches and more ceramics for the Royal Academy. He is working on designs for a Red, Black and White ballet with music by Jimmy Coxon.

A group of Christmas cards made by Terry Frost, from about the mid-1970s, photograph by Ricky Atkinson

A group of Christmas cards in the studio, 1977

Mugs and plates designed by Terry Frost and
produced by Colin Haxby in Diss, c.1978
(the artist)

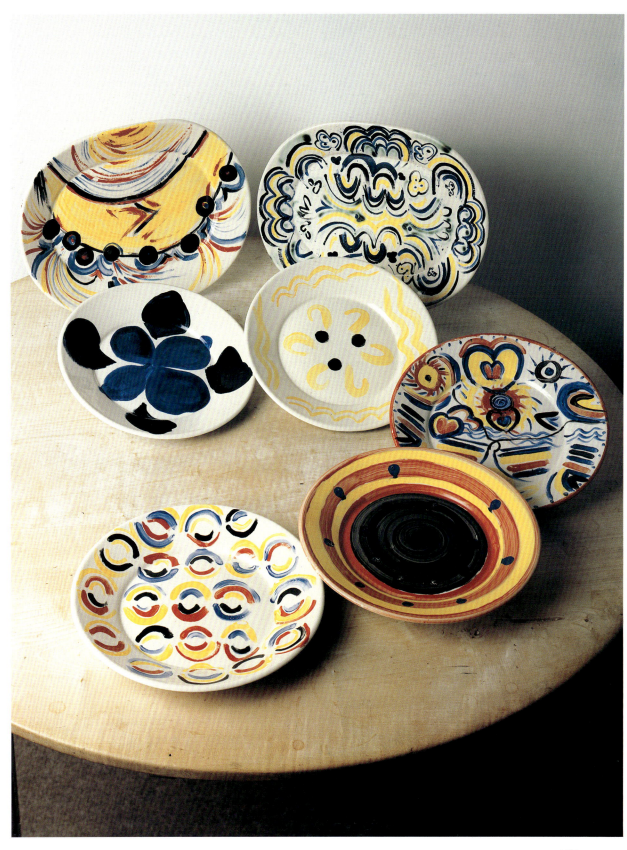

Plates and dishes painted by Terry Frost made as
unique pieces by Colin Haxby in Diss
(the artist and private collections)

Terry Frost: printmaker

David Archer

Printmaking has been an integral element in Terry Frost's creative output since his student days at Camberwell in the late 1940s. He has experimented with every discipline held within the graphic tradition and has without doubt become a master in each of the various processes. The Leeds drypoint series (1956), the Zurich lithograph suites (1968–72), the Lorca portfolio of colour etchings (1988–9) and the astounding group of monotypes produced for his 75th birthday (1990) are each, in turn, amongst the finest prints created by a British artist in the post-war period.

Terry Frost will always be associated with St Ives and its abstract tradition of painting and sculpture; if one examines the history of this group, he must be considered the most consistent and innovative printmaker in their ranks. Others such as Ben Nicholson did produce significant numbers of fine prints but tended to do so in sporadic bursts often with long gaps between prints. During his residence in Cornwall, Nicholson cut just six drypoint plates. These were the only prints in any medium he was to make in St Ives. Lanyon and Wynter were kindred spirits with Frost; all experimented widely with various techniques, linocuts, monotypes and lithographs. The approach of those younger St Ives artists was one of exploration mixed with the excitement of possibility. Often when studying formative paintings in their development one finds that they were preceded by a printed image which suggested to them a new direction to follow.

However, to think of Terry Frost purely in the context of his role in the St Ives movement is much too narrow and restrictive. He has been making graphics continually for the last 45 years, and with the exception of Victor Pasmore no other abstract artist can claim such a contribution to the art of British printmaking.

When Frost began his student period at Camberwell in 1947 it was during a time of post-war shortage and utility. This was reflected in the forms of printmaking available to the students, and led to the popular use of the monotype, strongly encouraged at Camberwell by its then Principal William Johnstone. The monotype required very basic materials and no printing press. The image was drawn onto a sheet of glass or a lithographic stone using oil paints or printing inks and a range of textures could be achieved by wiping the surface or applying fabric; a sheet of paper was then placed on top of the ink and the image transferred using gentle pressure. Each print was thus unique.

Frost's Camberwell monotypes chart his development, under the tutelage of Victor Pasmore and Kenneth Martin,

towards abstraction. 'Miss Humphries – Camberwell' and 'Standing Nude Seen From Behind' (both c.1948) show the gradual simplification of the human form. After the print was pulled from the glass an ink pen was used to help give clarity to these images. Within two years all obvious references to figuration had disappeared; a group of monotypes based on the Golden Section were made c.1950–51, the very formal arrangement of shapes softened by subtle shading and texture. The 'hands on' approach inherent in the making of monotypes has remained with Terry Frost ever since, as has the concept of a unique printed image. For him the potential of each print is unlimited, the image can be recreated time after time through the application of collage and hand colouring.

Having settled in St Ives in 1950, Frost faced the same difficulty as other local aspiring printmakers. Access to printing presses and technical advice were severely limited. Bryan Wynter was almost alone in owning a small studio press. Anyone wishing to create intaglio prints under proper studio conditions had the option of seeking the assistance of the etcher E. Bouverie Hoyton, head of Penzance School of Art. John Wells and Peter Lanyon both printed engravings at the School. Frost attempted small scale drypoints in his own studio. Printed using manual pressure and with inexperienced paper selection, the results were disappointing. 'Penzance' (1949) was re-editioned to better effect some years later at Corsham and showed the artist was well aware of the medium's capabilities.

Later in 1951 Frost began to concentrate on the linocut, a method more suited to his preferred way of working in his own studio surroundings. Concurrently he had started to create his 'Walk Along the Quay' paintings. The spontaneity of linocuts such as 'Walk Along the Quay' (1951) and 'Double Quay' (1952) printed in colours with deliberate variation in the blocks' registration, produced a harmony and rhythm that would resurface in the 'Movement' paintings.

In 1952 Frost began to teach life drawing at Bath Academy of Art at Corsham; although he had the opportunity to use its printmaking facilities his relationship with Henry Cliffe, the head of the department, was not good. This may have been responsible for the rather small number of prints produced by the artist on the site; but those actually printed included 'Blue Moon' (1952) a highly successful combination of lithography and linocut on a much larger scale than those images printed in his studio. The following year the artist created his first ever screenprint; the technique had been pioneered in St Ives by Peter Lanyon in the late 1940s; Denis Mitchell then set up the necessary facilities in his studio and encouraged artists to use them. The resulting print was a beautiful 'Walk Along the Quay' image with a certain 'homespun' character. It is one of the first

Blue Moon
1952
lithograph,
$14 \times 10\frac{3}{4}$ in, 35.5×27.3 cm

artist's screenprints in Britain – at this stage screenprinting was mainly being used for commercial jobbing printing.

Frost moved to Leeds in 1954, having been awarded a two-year fellowship funded by E. C. Gregory. He was confronted by a change of environment: landlocked in the bleak surroundings of the Yorkshire Dales, the effect on his graphics was quite marked. What are now referred to collectively as the 'Leeds' drypoints are assured, wonderfully crafted images stripped by the artist to the bare essential of line. The compositional strength of works such as 'Yorkshire Landscape' and 'Ridge, Yorkshire' (both 1956) show the hand of a natural printmaker, and it is regrettable that they were never editioned and exist only in small quantities.

Likewise two lithographs from 1957, 'Verticals and Sun' and 'Orange and Brown Sun' were only proofed in small sets.

Robert Erskine had opened the St George's Gallery in London in 1954 to specialise in graphic art and three years later he gave Frost a number of commissions to create limited edition lithographs. Almost for the first time the artist had a fully trained technician at his disposal. 'Composition in Red and Black' (1957) was printed by John Watson at the Central School of Arts and Crafts. 'Red and Grey Spiral' and 'Brown Figure' (both 1957) were printed in Edinburgh by Johnston Douglas. These works showed the growing emergence of figuration – groups of vertical lines and spirals became motifs for arms and legs. The prints were exhibited widely, including at the 'Fifth International Biennial of Contemporary Colour Lithography', Cincinnati Art Museum in 1958.

In the early 1960s the artist became more involved in teaching, holding a succession of posts at Coventry, Newcastle and Reading. He was still using a range of techniques and continued his interest in lithography and drypoint: applied collage and hand colouring on the prints had become regular features. As the female form evolved in his paintings, likewise in his prints certain references recurred. There is a strong erotic nature in some works; they contain leather laces to suggest a corset, colour shapes imply breasts and buttocks and chevrons penetration.

Most graphics from the early and mid 1960s exist only in proof form; working without the assistance of a publisher meant that editioning a print was too time-consuming and costly. Frost had been exhibiting his paintings in London at the Waddington Galleries; other younger artists shown by the gallery included Richard Hamilton, Peter Blake and Patrick Caulfield – all active printmakers. To accommodate the growing collectability of prints Waddington Graphics was established to publish works by the gallery's exhibiting artists. Frost was again in a position where he could work with professional studio printers; between 1967 and 1972 Waddington Graphics published several groups of large

Double Quay
1952
linocut
$5 \times 5\frac{1}{2}$ in, 13×14 cm (AD7 and 8)
There are proofed variations of this image but it was not editioned.

The AD numbers given in the captions here refer to the Austin/Desmond Gallery's catalogue of Terry Frost's prints 1948–1990, 1990

coloured prints by the artist. In 1967 a set of lithographs was produced at the famous Curwen Studio, and the following year Frost worked with the printer Chris Prater at the Kelpra Studio on a set of four screenprints. The quality of printing on both occasions was superb, large segments and quadrants of vibrant floating colour set against delicate backgrounds.

Frost then travelled to Zurich to work with Mathieu, a specialist in colour lithography. The depth of technical advice he received astounded the artist. What particularly impressed was Mathieu's ability to reproduce an exact colour from a small sample painted by the artist on paper. To do this in the quantity required for editioning a large print is an artform in itself. Frost insists that in one particular print 'Orange Dusk' (1970)[1] there is a combination of colours that he has never been able to duplicate. The Zurich lithographs are amibitious in their size and in the range of surface finishes; together with the Curwen lithographs and the Kelpra screenprints they represent a major body of work.

It was to be some time before Frost published any more work through a commercial gallery, preferring instead to develop new ideas in his own studio and in the print departments at Reading, Umea in Sweden where he taught summer schools, and the R C A. He had started to study translations of poetry by Federico Garcia Lorca, enthralled by the poet's emotional interpretation of colour and the mystery surrounding his early death. In 1974 'Variations' a screenprint was proofed, based on the Lorca poem of the same title, and the same screens were used to print the image in a variety of colours. 'Far Away and Alone' (1976) included a passage of text drawn onto the screen by Frost using pen and brush; the calligraphy became dominant in the illustration of certain poems.

Alongside these first Lorca images there was a regular flow of other graphics ranging from very formal abstract frameworks to updated versions of moored boats. A group of etched self-portraits appeared in the early 1980s, as did a pair of ambiguous aquatints in which for the first time the prow of a Newlyn fishing boat doubled as the horn of a bull.

In 1988 Frost screenprinted more Lorca-based images and this was the first time a uniform group centred on the poems had been produced and in effect it was the beginning of the Lorca portfolio.[2] The flat surface finishes of these prints did not, however, capture the energy and depth of the artist's preliminary work. By now, Frost had obtained the copyright for English translations to eleven Lorca poems and permission for the original Spanish. At this stage Gordon House, much admired both as a painter and graphic designer, took the project under his wing. He produced a mock-up boxed set of folders, each printed with a text and loosely holding an image. House then introduced Frost to Hugh Stoneman who operated a print studio in Islington; Stoneman had

Untitled (Yorkshire)
1956
drypoint,
$4\frac{1}{2} \times 6\frac{1}{4}$ in, 11.5 × 15.8 cm (AD13)

1. Reproduced on the cover of the Austin/Desmond catalogue (AD34)

2. See also page 216

Red and Grey Spirals
1957
lithograph,
$18\frac{1}{2} \times 29\frac{1}{2}$ in, 47×75 cm (AD16)

studied painting at Camberwell before travelling to Paris to train under S. W. Hayter at Atelier 17. Frost had realised that a colour intaglio process would give him greater freedom to incorporate hand-colouring and embossing, each essential in his interpretation of individual poems. Stoneman and Frost undertook trial proofing of two images 'Variations' and 'Thamar and Amnon'; Having seen these, Austin/Desmond Fine Art agreed to publish the boxed set.

The publication took seven months at the Print Centre to complete. Many printing devices were employed on the eleven etchings, 'Lament for Ignacio Sanchez Mejias' and 'Saint Raphael (Cordoba)' both used a combination of separate colour plates, hand applied colouring and pencil, as well as embossing. For 'Thamar and Amnon' a turps resist was used to gain background brushstrokes, 'Pause of the Clock' included the glaice transferré process. The text was screenprinted onto the folders in both English and Spanish. The artists' pen and brush calligraphy was used in the design of the frontispiece and the solander box. It was finally published in October 1989.

All the images, despite their abstract nature, retain a narrative quality, an expressive use of colour and form helping to suggest objects and events. These prints are perhaps as important as any translation of the poet's work. There was no other publication printed in a British studio during the 1980s that can compare in its vision, printing or presentation to this set.

The following year a suite of linocuts including 'Trewellard Suns' was published by the Paragon Press. Besides the editioned prints, which themselves included a certain amount of hand-colouring, these linocuts formed the basis of a strong group of hand-painted works on paper between 1989 and 1992.

In 1990 Frost was commissioned by Austin/Desmond to create an exhibition of monotypes in celebration of his 75th birthday. These were undertaken at the Print Centre, with Hugh Stoneman and Alan Cox acting as printers. At his Sky Editions imprint Cox had worked on monotypes with many artists. Prunella Clough, Robyn Denny, Jim Dine, and John Hoyland among others had used his technical expertise. The scale of any printed image is related to the dimensions of the press it is printed on, and at the Print Centre Frost was working for two weeks on a 5×13 ft flat bed press. Working in a very direct and painterly fashion the artist used brushes to apply printing inks onto large sheets of perspex, and these were then sent through the press. Although printing inks take a long time to dry out, each image was executed within 45 minutes regardless of its size. Several of the prints measured 4×8 ft, possibly the largest monotypes ever printed in England. Frost was reluctant to rework a sheet and overprint the same image, preferring instead to hand colour those which hadn't 'hit it off' in his Newlyn studio.

Black, Purple and Blue
1969
lithograph,
$22\frac{7}{8} \times 19\frac{1}{4}$ in, 58×48.8 cm (AD29)

The artist mixed his own inks and on several prints used a transparent oil-based tinted glaze to intensify or reduce the action of some colours. In these monotypes Frost took advantage of the situation and revisited themes from the previous forty years. There were images related to the 'Walk Along the Quay' and 'Movement' series, Irish landscapes reminiscent of the 'Leeds' period, laced images, Lorca prints and groups of spirals (inspired by flowering cacti). In a relatively short creative burst Frost excelled, in part by going back to the essence of his printmaking, producing some of his finest ever graphic work.

Given the depth of graphic material produced by Terry Frost over the past four decades it is unaccountable that it has not received more recognition. In the important exhibition 'Avant Garde British Printmakers 1914–60' held at the British Museum in 1990, Frost was one of only three artists represented in four print mediums. It was after the period covered by the exhibition that he went on to create many of his most important prints. A catalogue raisonné of his work would be virtually impossible, so many images have been produced in small numbers and then hand worked, making them hard to distinguish from paintings. For Frost painting and printmaking are inseparably wed, ideas generated from one leading to new discoveries in the other. His is a singular vision and a unique talent.

Trewellard Sun
1990
linocut with hand-colouring,
25 × 25 in, 63.5 × 63.5 cm

Squeeze
1990
monotype,
48 × 96 in, 122 × 243.8 cm
(private collection)

Lorca

Poetry comes to me when I'm alone, maybe in a foreign country sitting at a dining table alone or riding on a train. Lorca awakened something in me. I love black and Lorca and the Duende and black envelop me. Images wrestle with me when I read Lorca. He probes the distance between each emotion.

I've been in love with Lorca's poetry for fifteen years. For ten years I've been making paintings, collages, prints, all given to me by Lorca. It has given me some of the best years of my life and at last some of my ideas are coming together in a book.

With Lorca I travel on a ride to no-man's-land. There I am; my emotions take on a new distance and the extent between life and death becomes forever. Black and Red become a symbol for death and life, lust, passion, tenderness, fear, love. The black and white of the words on paper become gods like the sun and the moon.

Rider's Song
1989
etching from the Lorca Portfolio,
$22\frac{1}{4} \times 15\frac{1}{8}$ in, 56.5 × 38.4 cm

Notes on the Lorca project, 1989

Frost and the Duende

Linda Saunders

'*Manuel Torre . . . pronounced this splendid sentence on hearing Falla play his own* Nocturno del Generalife *: 'All that has black sounds has duende*' . . .

These black sounds are the mystery, the roots in the mire that we all know and all ignore, the mire that gives us the substance of art . . .

The great artists of the south of Spain . . . whether they sing, dance or play, know that no emotion is possible unless the duende comes'.[1]

'*I* saw *the duende when I was in Spain*', *said Terry Frost, 'in a fish market. My god, I thought, what are they all doing in black? I thought people would wear white for the heat – it was a terribly hot day. Then they slithered a great silver fish in front of me! Then they began to carve it up. What with the sound of the Spanish, which was beautiful to me, and then this silver fish – it was a magic moment.*'

'*Will you paint that?*'

No – but he would use it : such experiences get into the work, priming his need to make discoveries. It was the same in Cyprus, when he saw a vast orange sun and full blue moon in the same dawn sky. 'I was between two gods.' Such things blind you ; you must leave them alone, maybe for years. It's not enough to represent *them in paint : 'I want to do more than that . . . You've got to find your way there. There's no true answer to it.'*

> *When the moon rises*
> *the bells hang silent*
> *and impenetrable footpaths*
> *appear*[2]

Lorca said of the ballads of cante jondo *(deep song) : 'At the bottom of all these poems there is a terrible question that has no answer'. His own poetry is haunted by this question, while his images and colours call to the painter in everyone :*

> *Green flesh, hair of green,*
> *with eyes of gold and silver.*

But it means more *than green, Frost insists – 'So how the hell do you paint Lorca?'*

In his etching for the poem 'Arbole arbole' ('Tree tree'), he seems to have found just such an essential green, vivid yet soulful, achieved in its relations to white and black – for it is both translucent and laden with darkness ; it's intrinsic

also to the shapes and directions of the design, which catch the poem's movement, deriving from the wind that alone encircles the girl's waist and from the erotic thoughts of would-be lovers who pass by in their 'suits of azure and green' ; and it suggests the girl's heedlessness, her thoughts directed elsewhere, to some green moon, her identity untouched as the tree's, 'dry and green' – 'seco y verdé'. A flight of chevrons (Frostian signs, arrows of desire) wings towards an outer planetary ring (Frostian loops, satellite discs) ; there's a transcendent sexuality, an urgent but dreamy aspiration.

'*You've got to find your own freedom to make something of it*', *says Frost, his aim always to make something of the 'kicks' or 'jolts' he receives from the visible world. Music and poetry, too, direct arrows to the heart. 'Deep song shoots its arrows of gold right into our heart' : Lorca does not soft pedal his enthusiasms. Neither does Frost, who keeps himself open, purposefully, to such experience. And a work of art must give this kind of shock to jaded, safe and practical ways of looking. Frost asked once, like an evangelist, 'Are you prepared to have your pre-conceived ideas upset by really seeing unprejudiced for once, or for one moment of truth?'*

> *When the moon rises,*
> *the sea covers the land*
> *and the heart feels*
> *like and island in infinity.*[3]

I asked him whether it had extended the emotional range of his 'vocabulary', his search for painterly, abstract equivalents for felt experience, to test it against such poetry. 'Although I am a coward, I like danger', he replied. 'It is dangerous to try and find out anything. That's why I like painting, because you don't know. Like trying to climb Everest and not being a climber. I haven't got a bloody clue.' He has often complained that people 'cannot see for know-ing' ; if they are artists, they resist the danger of discovery, merely exploiting their own facility. So he has sought out the danger, the edge, of not knowing what you can do about something as marvellous as – that music, this poem.

His portfolio of eleven colour etchings each folded between one of Lorca's poems, the Spanish printed alongside the English translation, is the flowering of fifteen years of trying in paintings, collages and many prints to do something about such lines as

> *When the moon rises*
> *moon of a hundred equal faces,*
> *the silver coinage*
> *sobs in the pocket.*[4]

The poems are full of yearning, lost or unattainable love, death, knives and, above all, Andalusian pain – peña, which the poet once described as 'the struggle of the loving

This is a revised and expanded version of an essay published in *The Green Book*, vol.III no.3, 1989

1. Federico Garcia Lorca in 'Play and Theory of the Duende', a talk that 'showed the poet at his most Andalusian', first given in 1933, see Ian Gibson, *Federico Garcia Lorca*, Faber & Faber, London, 1989, p.367

2. From 'La Luna Asoma', 'The Moon Rising'

3. Ibid

4. Ibid

intelligence with the incomprehensible mystery that sur-
rounds it' (indeed, the artist's struggle with the duende). Did
Terry Frost, knocking his mid-seventies, protégé and friend
of Adrian Heath, Victor Pasmore, Ben Nicholson, Peter
Lanyon, have an affinity with the Andalusian personality?
No. He didn't know enough about it, didn't know Spain
well, was after all only working from translations. But –
along with his afficion for black –

   '*I have passions*', *he said.*

   '"*An Andalusian either shouts at the stars, or kisses the*
red dust of the road"?'

   Oh yes, Frost of the north he might be, no Latin blood,
but he recognised that. He has something of the earthiness,
that's clear, and thrills to the emotional intensity, and as
many northerners do, while saying they don't understand it,
to the dark blood of the southern Spaniard and his obsession
with death. Quite natural to him besides is Lorca's stricture
that '*You must not read Goncora [the Spanish poet], you*
must love him'. *Frost's reading and rereading is closer to love*
than study; by love he avoids the trap of illustration, by not
knowing *what will come from this passionate steeping in the*
colour of poems. ('Colour is the eye's music', Lorca said.)
He may be swept off his feet, perhaps, by one moment, one
phrase. 'Black olives in my saddle-bag', he misquotes,
revealingly, from 'Rider's Song' – transposing the 'black'
from the rider's pony. 'Well that was enough for me. I'm
a great black olive fan – and in my saddle bag*! I had to*
do it.' And so black olives nudge into being black moons –
relations of Frost's recurrent black suns – and the relish in
the mouth sharpens the romance and danger of riding alone,
with its hint of fatality (that red crescent!) Lorca's premon-
ition: 'before I reach Cordoba' . . .

   The box to contain etchings and poems – a Solander box
which opens like a book – was to be black, he had insisted,
against contrary opinion: because of the duende. It is
emblazoned with a white circle on which a widened red
chevron holds a segment of black to suggest the hour at which
Ignacio Sanchez Mejias, the bullfighter, died in the ring,
and where Lorca stopped the clock, tolling the words 'Five
in the afternoon' through his great lament for his friend.
Frost has given a motif already redolent with his own per-
sonal as well as elemental associations the impact of a precise
meaning for the book. Elsewhere, inside, the reader will come
across the conjunction of recognisably Frostian signs with a
potent emotional bearing on the poems – a potency that's
dependent on 'getting it true'. As the poet instinctively seeks
complementary or warring sounds, a certain echo just here,
a stop or rasp there, so the artist uses colour and shape, dis-
tance and edge; the elements in his design must be as keenly
and resonantly tuned as are the poet's music and imagery.
Like the poet, and the singer of cante jondo, *he must also*
be able to 'break all the sweet geometry' he has learnt – to

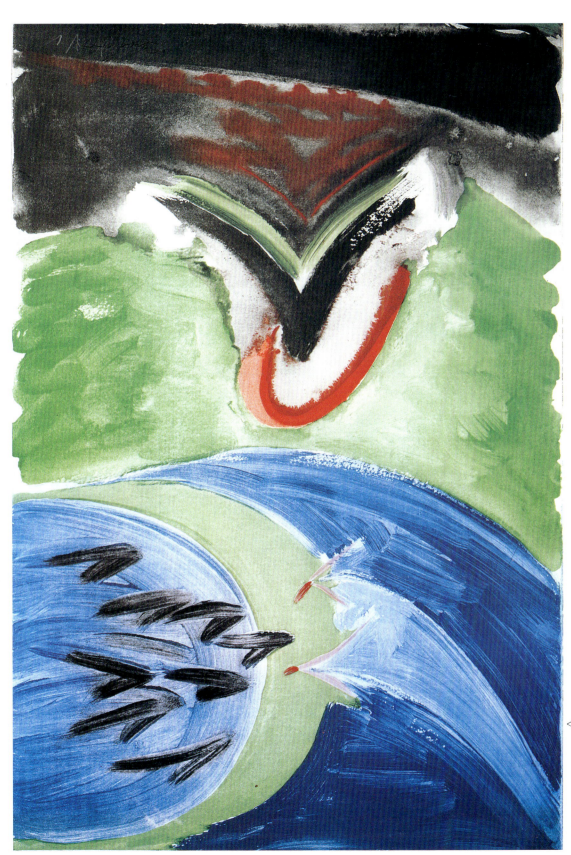

◁ *Lament for Ignacio Sanchez Mejias*
1989
etching from the Lorca Portfolio,
$22\frac{1}{4} \times 15\frac{1}{8}$ in, 56.5×38.4 cm

Thamar and Amnon
1989
etching from the Lorca Portfolio,
$22\frac{1}{4} \times 15\frac{1}{8}$ in, 56.5×38.4 cm

let in the duende. A tall order in this case, but one that Terry Frost has practised for and grown from.

He discovered poetry in a prisoner of war camp where he also started painting. Milton and Keats were more plentiful than bread, apparently, and the heightening of vision that near-starvation can cause left the doors of his perception permanently on the latch. (Nor would life be easy later on for an abstract artist on the westerly toe of Britain.)

At Camberwell in the late 1940s Frost came in on Synthetic and Analytical Cubism and the geometrical analysis of Old Masters according to the Golden Section, restrictive disciplines for someone who describes himself as an instinctual primitive, but a training which has given his work structure, a 'sweet geometry' he can use now or break with the same unthinking certainty with which a tree knits together its cells yet with which it can always surprise with new forms (Frost tends to use such organic images to describe his way of working: D'Arcy Thompson's On Growth and Form *was a seminal work for many English abstract painters at that time). For artists of 'The St Ives Years' (a quarter century ending around 1964, as defined by the Tate's 1985 exhibition) such ideas, along with Constructivist ideals, came together with an almost numinous sense of place and a search to express not just the mood of the landscape but of being a feeling part of it, or of moving through it as through time. Adrian Heath in perceiving Frost as a Romantic to whom emotion was more important than reason must also have remarked this area of affinity with other St Ives artists. Roger Hilton's idea of the abstract artist 'swinging out into the void, his only props his colours and his space-creating powers' seems pertinent to Frost, who wrote in the early 1950s that his 'idea' usually starts from 'an experience of nature or rather the experience of one human being wandering, observing, questioning, worrying, trying to see the truth, trying to penetrate the mystery of life . . .'. John Wells, also, argued for abstraction as a means of painting something 'more': the mystery that attends natural events – 'the journey of a beetle across a rock . . .' – provoking 'thoughts of one's own whence and whither?'*

But Frost needs his mysteries to be felt 'on the pulses' (as Keats had it), not involving philosophical/spiritual teasers. Sun and moon are primordial mysteries, gods enough for him; the elements 'are true', not a tricky question of faith. They are particularly tangible in Cornwall – out alone on the moors at night, 'when you're leaning against a wind that is making noises, it [the duende of the Cornish landscape?] comes right up to your feet'. Songs with duende 'consult the wind', wrote Lorca, 'the sea, the moon and things as simple as a violet'.

In his 'Duende' lecture, Lorca struggled to express an eternal artistic problem: a simultaneous respect for form and the attraction of chaos – of the unknown and all that escapes

Far Away and Alone
1976
screenprint,
20 × 30 in, 51 × 76.2 cm
One of the earliest prints inspired by Lorca

Five in the Afternoon
c.1989
etching proof with trial layout,
approx. $22\frac{1}{4} \times 30\frac{1}{4}$ in, 56.5×76.8 cm
(the artist)

human art. As soon as you make an image, you 'clip the wings of the imagination' – Frost quotes Bachelard – or even a mark. Perhaps this is the thought behind Frost's rather delphic assertion that 'the medium destroys the image'? For he holds by reverie, 'the capital concept', as he calls it, 'where all the imagery goes on,' before the medium, before the first mark.

In reverie, Lorca led him on and on. 'You make all kinds of images, you make them up, from reading those few lines.'

'In your case, it's visual reverie?', I asked.

'I don't know that you can say it's visual – it's a total feeling.'

But something finite must be made of the 'total feeling'. Somewhere between order and chaos, form and dissolution, flies the danger and the duende of art? – 'the subtle bridge that unites the five senses with the raw wound', as Lorca put it, his own exquisite bridge thrown sometimes quite lightly, gaily, across the storm winds of death.

Frost's own characteristic, abstract vocabulary refers to the hulls of sailing boats, keels, masts, the tug or slack of ropes, the sun (almost visionary encounters in later works), reflections in moving water, the buoyant rhythms of harbour life. Yet he is dealing in mysteries rather than phenomena – with the space around things, the poise of the moment in time, contrary and elemental forces in landscape, sex and the dance of creation. To see without knowing is to cut loose from your moorings in facts, narratives, explanations. Abstract art casts the eye adrift, insists on sensation, the elation or anxiety geared to certain configurations of form and line and colour, nameless recognitions. Echoes from the world of things-with-names have the poignant 'lightness-of-being' of an elusive memory. Lorca couldn't bear logical poetry. 'Mystery is what makes us live', he wrote, 'only mystery.'

Mysteries of colour Frost will expound at length – of black especially, his 'magic' colour that absorbs all the others. Everyone – as he has proved from teaching experiments – will mix a different black from red, yellow and blue, and see it as 'true' black. He himself started with black, times being lean, learning from the uncompromising decisions it exacted in contrast with white. When he added red, he had his favourite trinity of colours. They are so positive, you cannot afford to muff the shapes they define.

Starting with the 'Lament for Ignacio Sanchez Mejias', the long and soul-rending elegy which must be Lorca's finest and most mature poem, Frost risks all on the opening throw. The range and richness of imagery face the artist with a daunting reductive task. He might take clues from the simplicity that Lorca celebrated in deep song: 'simple, genuine mystery, without gloomy forests and rudderless ships'. The poet himself, for all the complexity and length of the 'Lament', has taken lessons from the starkness of ballad, from say, 'The moon has a halo/My love is dead'.

And Frost takes the primary force of his image from the bold colour of three of Lorca's lines:

> *Oh, white wall of Spain!*
> *Oh, black bull of sorrow!*
> *Oh, hard blood of Ignacio!*

The image could have been an outrageous cliché, featuring as it does black horn, red splash of blood and merciless, acid-yellow sun – but is not. I think he has 'got it true' – as must a matador: the art of the close shave! The horn is more wedge than sickle, an echo from that hull shape that is part of Frost's familiar vocabulary, but whose dipped angle is ominous here, an axe rather, or – 'the infinite corner of the shade, terrible projected corner' in the bull-ring that Lorca described in his prose fragment 'Sun and Shade'. In 'Sun and Shade', the poet wrote that 'Bullfighters die in the ring because of these antagonistic halves', and 'between the yellow and the black there is a dangerous play of distances': Frost has a strong intuition for such things, whether or not he has read a particular work – not through reading but through love. There is more in the etching than drama and fatality: a pale half-halo behind the sun, an embossed bow of subtle unwhiteness beneath it, hint at 'the sweat of the snow', at 'arsenic bells and smoke'.

What Lorca willed repeatedly in the 'Lament' not to see – the reader must feel this – was not just the death of the matador, but by extension the fate of Spain in the Civil War, even his own death, at the age of thirty-eight before a Fascist firing squad in 1936. Hindsight makes some lines unbearably prophetic:

> *. . . a pure shape which had nightingales*
> *and we see it being filled with depthless holes.*

In this poem, Lorca is tossing his own heart over the bull's horns. Distances speak of the absence of the dead:

> *Now the moss and the grass*
> *open with sure fingers*
> *the flower of his skull.*

Is it strange to find Terry Frost, with his celebratory eye for the robust swing of life, taking on such themes? Perhaps not: look again now at such pictures as 'Black Sun' (1982). What Frost intuits from the Spanish duende is the power of death which is not separable from the power of life. 'A dead man in Spain is more alive as a dead man in any place else in the world', wrote Lorca; Spain is a country 'open to death', 'a country of ancient music where the duende squeezes the lemons of dawn'. From Frost's brush with the duende, perhaps, comes the fierce brilliance of some of his more recent suns, the understanding that they are cauldrons of creation and extinction both.

The etching for the 'Lament' is the strongest of the series,

Lament for Lorca
1989
oil, acrylic and collage on canvas,
$66\frac{3}{4} \times 41\frac{1}{4}$ in, 169.5 × 104.8 cm
(the artist)

I think, as it has to be. But others too are instinct with distances, seem to draw on Lorca's great well of longing for other worlds, of the past or of love. Certainly Frost was inspired by 'Rider's Song'; the yearning 'o's of Cordoba, alone (sola), moon (luna), are echoed by the artist's circular forms, and just how 'far away and alone' is measured by the blue-grey of the aquatint (an unusually muted colour for Frost), given piercing emphasis by the one crimson crescent low in the picture.

Each unfolded image is utterly surprising after the last, but with its own inevitability. This rightness overrides what might seem to the literal-minded to be representational lapses. To complain that while Lorca set 'Thamar and Amnon' in a waterless landscape of 'tiger and flame' and 'frizzled air' Frost has made his lyrically fluent image largely from intense watery blues and lush greens would be to miss not only the inner *atmosphere of the poem but also how appropriate the picture's sensuality and ravishing beauty is to the ballad subject matter. Indeed, the poem tells the story of an incestuous ravishing, Amnon tempted beyond endurance by his sister's nakedness under the moon of a hot night. I asked Frost what he felt about his image in relation to the poem. 'It's got the wind in it, it's got the terribleness. There's a bit of turbulence in the brushstrokes – I'm usually much cooler than that.' It is the most sensual of his Lorcan etchings, full of urgency and contrary winds, 'the raw wound', vulnerability and irrepressible blood. 'It's a shattering thing', said Frost, of the poem – 'Your kisses in my shoulder are wasps . . .'.*

Perhaps Terry Frost has most fellow feeling for 'The Old Lizard', whose 'burnt-out eyes' still watch the sun.

> *You watch the setting sun*
> *and your eyes shine,*
> *Oh, dragon of the frogs,*
> *with a human radiance.*

This last image in the portfolio is equal to the first (if I must choose, these are the best), though very different in mood. Its drama is, paradoxically, in its composure – the intensity of the red sun contained in the background blue, held in the elipses of its own darker echo and the slightly paler blue half-halo of the moon emerging behind. For Frost put the moon in too 'for good measure', as the image derives from those awesome Mediterranean skies he described to me. 'The Old Lizard' reflects another phenomenon he'd wondered at: '. . . the sun has changed to red and it's going to slip behind the mountain, but it leaves that semicircle in front, though you know damn well it's gone behind – I don't know the scientific reasons for that . . .'. Only knows that 'I drowned in sunset once', coming out of Hemingway's bar in Ronda, standing on the bridge there.

The book is – literally – inspired, a homage, a work of love. Yet it is a beginning as well as a summation. Terry Frost now feels free to take his affair with Lorca further, into large paintings. Already the yearning, interplanetary blue he used in the etching for 'It is True' ('Es Verdad') has changed in a seven foot painting to searing yellows and oranges, the painting's éclat also utterly different in mood from the blue etching. The image begins to merge with that of the 'two gods' – sun and moon – which dominate Frost's recent work. He has drawn the words into the painting to remind himself, 'It is true'. The lyrical play of heart shapes is a reminder too, and he can risk such symbolism with the licence of Lorca's own exquisitely light touch:

> *For love of you*
> *my heart*
> *and my hat hurt me.*

Spirals

Terry Frost has said 'spirals are forever' and indeed they
have run like a thread through all his work. He has seen
them in many sources, from Arizona to the Alhambra and
from whirling sheeps' tails in a high wind to eddies in the
receding tide. They appear in a relief of 1951–52, see
page 17, in a linocut of 1952 where they are doubled and
in lithographs from the late 1950s. They underlie a number of the soft suspended forms of the late 1960s and their
movement seems to be behind the flat geometry of the
'Newlyn Rhythms'. They resurface in powerful and
heraldic form in the 'Arizona' triptych of 1990 and in a
quiet, subtle way the Lorca etchings of 1989. In 1991
Terry began to make paintings of large spirals painted in
a single sustained stroke. When he was commissioned to
produce a piece for a tall narrow site on the staircase in
the new Tate St Ives building, he painted spirals for the
seasons ranged vertically on a loose canvas banner.

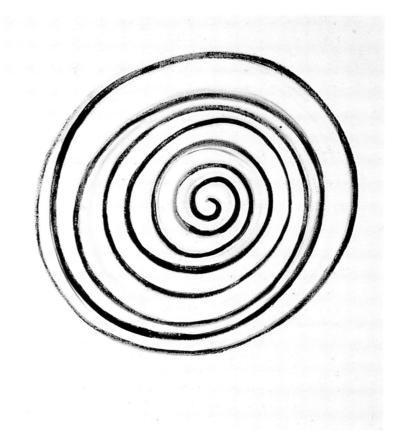

Two Spirals
1991
acrylic on canvas,
40 × 80 in, 101.6 × 203.2 cm
(the artist)

Spirals
1991
acrylic and collage on thirty canvases
each 25 in, 63.5 cm square;
Terry Frost proposes two or three different possible
configurations and is considering adding a 75 in,
190.5 cm square spiral in the centre.

Arizona Spirals
1990
triptych, acrylic on canvas,
72 × 144 in, 182.9 × 365.8 cm
(the artist)

Tate St Ives banner, 1993;
photograph by Anna Bailey

Conclusion

It is perhaps ironic that in a century of so many movements in art, and so much revolution in visual language, the gap between art and the public has narrowed rather than widened. Public art galleries have become national and regional treasuries. Cities advertise their orchestras and their museums as well as their football teams. People in thousands travel hundreds of miles for shows like the big Picasso, Matisse, Van Gogh and Miró retrospectives. On any given day the Tate in London and MOMA in New York are crowded.

One reason is the media. Documentaries on television have brought artists making art into our living rooms. This is a new experience. Painting as object suddenly becomes painting, present participle – an unfolding language to communicate between an artist and ourselves. We see painters and sculptors in their own environments as human beings, speaking about their uncertainties and about the things in life that turn them on. They talk directly to us, their eyes looking into our eyes. We witness the creative act itself with the sound track running.

In the case of Terry Frost there is something rather comforting about it. His exuberance, his warmth, and his laughter are catching. He is an ideal subject. He is one of us. As a result several documentaries have been filmed in his studio. There he is, walking around Newlyn harbour, talking about the boats, the ropes, the water, and the nets. There he is on the top of the hill, in Gernick Fields, talking about the clouds, the sun, and the everywhere-presence of the sea. And there he is, in his studio, at that big ramshackle table with its profusion of coloured papers and paintings and collages in process, talking in one breath about memories of Camberwell, or Yorkshire, and in the next about Cyprus twenty-five years later and the hot orange sun setting over the Mediterranean down a long dry valley, and then about Lorca; and while he is talking he begins scratching around for brushes and colours because words have become inadequate, and the camera closes in on his hands as he begins to paint, exploring visually, not for us but *with* us, what words cannot say.

He has a way of drawing us into the experience of making an abstract painting as though we were doing it ourselves. He weaves what he sees and what he remembers in ways that are totally credible, and that also make us understand his art.

I had an old blue Bedford van, which was the first vehicle I had. You must have had that feeling when you go out in the morning to start the damn thing, cold winter's morning, sharp, beautiful, very cold. Not a spark of life from the battery, and I had to wind and wind; you know, you get as sick as hell; and as I looked up I saw that beautiful sun – because I was making a circle I suppose as I was winding. I never thought of that at the time. There was that beautiful sun absolutely clear, the air was so cold, and then I had to go and see if I could get a battery from somewhere, so I had to walk through the grounds of Tetley Hall; and in walking through the grounds the sun sort of got behind the trees, and I had to go through a wall which had some undergrowth and stuff around it, and so I had to get down, and in getting down I experienced the movement of going through, and of coming through the other side to the sun again, spinning behind the trees . . .

Imagination is what I believe in, it's all right having a good painting in your head, but it's another matter to make a black mark and red mark which will actually communicate to other people something about the idea, the feelings and the emotions that you're after, that you've been excited about, to make a communication through that is another matter . . .[1]

The description is deceptively simple. It's an experience most of us can share. But for him it's the starting-point of a painting. One way it might be used to make a static representation of the scene would be to make a traditional landscape painting. But a static representation can't reflect what Frost had experienced. There is that circular winding of the crankshaft on a cold morning, and suddenly seeing the circle of the sun. There is the coldness – 'sharp, beautiful, very cold'. There is the 'linear' experience of bending down and passing through a darkness, and suddenly seeing the sun again, 'spinning through the trees'. The result is a beginning of visual voyages of discovery through painting. But not on the scene, *sur le motif* as he would say. He carries the experience back with him to his studio. The sun is a circle or possibly, since it 'spins', it's a spiral. There are lines of movement. A painting begins. We are in Frost's studio. We are surrounded by his brushes, pots, canvases. The moment a brushmark hits the empty surface it has a quality of its own: colour, texture, edge, wetness, dryness, opacity, transparency. Another brushmark, and then another. The canvas develops a life of its own. It develops a life that actually never ends: up to a certain point it has been an intense part of Frost's life; now it's an intense part of our's.

1. From the soundtrack of the film 'Colour Positive', made for BBC tv's Omnibus 1977, produced by Barry Gavin and directed by John Hooper.

◁ *Spiral (Red)*
1991
acrylic on canvas,
75 × 75 in, 190.5 × 190.5 cm
(Tate Gallery)

There is another aspect of the description that is worth mentioning, and that's its air of confidence. Most of us would have been thoroughly put out by the old Bedford truck and its dead battery. Not Terry. He saw the sun, and together they went dancing. He makes the process of painting seem effortlessly lyrical and upbeat. There is an endearing innocence and directness about him that is far from naïve. It is a way of life: and it lies at the essence of his art.

Terry came to painting when colours were dark, when Europe was rubble, when countless thousands of men and women returned from the war to broken economies and factories, when every family grieved for relations and friends, when his own city had been devastated and food and clothing were scarce, and all were reflected in dark colours, deep greens, maroons, blacks and browns. Forty-five years afterwards we realise that this man has transformed English art. He has brought joy and radiance. The sun and the moon shine together. The ocean dances with light. So do his canvases and collages. None of us will ever be the same again.

Time is crossed out
Moments in abeyance
Dreaming of quality
Dreaming of concern,
The safety net of dreams by the day.

Time is crossed out
The body goes on, but the spirit sails
On a time escape to real thoughts
Of blue sky and so blue
Of gold carpets of desire
Of letters beautifully written
So truthful, so necessary,
Then, crash.

Time is with us
And the act of defence closes its visor.
No letters, act your part,
Parcel your dreams up for a time.
Look forward to the pleasure
Of complete abeyance and unwrapping
The parcel of dreams.

Untitled poem by Terry Frost, early 1970s

Orange and Black, Leeds
1957
oil on canvas,
56 × 80 in, 142.2 × 203.2 cm
(Maak Gallery)

This painting was made after the episode with the
Bedford van and the sun in the trees.

To Terry Frost

A Northern man, found or lost,
Athletic, artist Terry Frost.
With extraverting laugh & slap
He hits the poet on the back.

Ho Ho, Ho Ho, the poet says
To put the extravert at his ease.
But while the words fly far about
Two lonlier men wave & shout.

— W S Graham

Postscript

Things I like that stick in my imagination library : for instance I've never made a work relating to crocodiles on the River Nile, or grenades hitting the branch of a tree and rebounding, of jays and the poem 'Judging the Distance' by Henry Read, of the couple by the farmhouse and the apple blossom – yes . . .

Manuscript by W. S. Graham, 1968

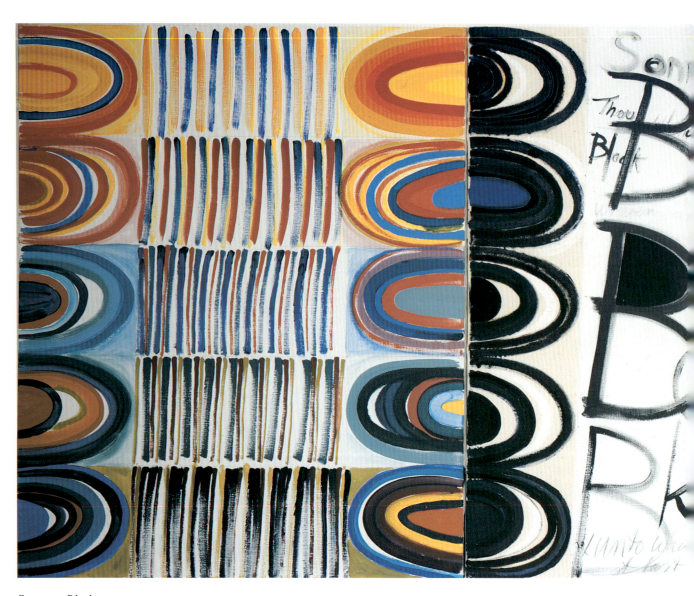

Sonnet to Black
1994
triptych, oil and acrylic on canvas
72 × 180 in, 183 × 457 cm
(the artist)

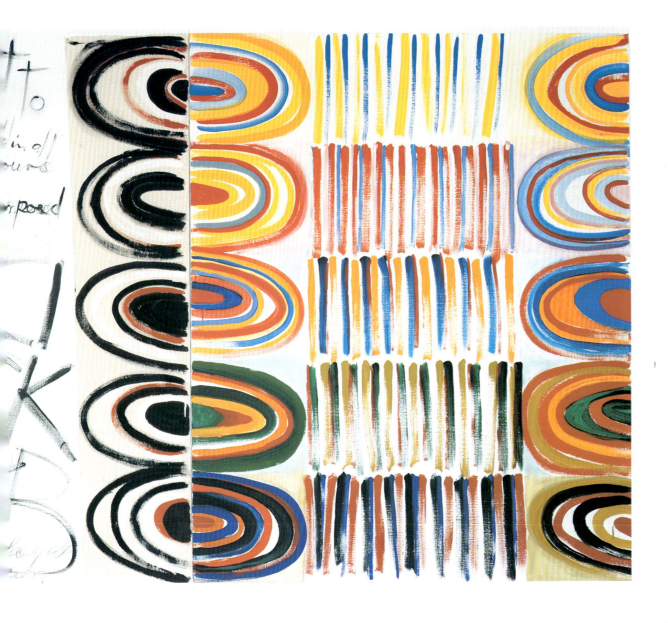

Exhibitions

ONE-PERSON EXHIBITIONS

(important shows including retrospectives marked *)

1944	Leamington Spa Library
1947	Downing's Bookshop, St Ives
1952	*Leicester Galleries
and 1956, 1958	
1957	Austen Hayes Gallery, York (shared)
1960	*Bertha Schaeffer Gallery, New York
1961	*Waddington Galleries
and 1963, 1966, 1969, 1971, 1974, 1978	
1964	*Galerie Charles Lienhard, Zurich
	*Laing Art Gallery, Newcastle-upon-Tyne and tour to York, Hull and Bradford
	California Palace of the Legion of Honor, San Francisco and tour to Santa Barbara and San José State College
1965	Arnolfini, Bristol
and 1971	
1967	Queens Square Gallery, Leeds
	Lincolnshire Association Arts Centre, Lincoln
1968	Bear Lane Gallery, Oxford
and 1970	
1968	Waddington Prints
	Gallery 5, Reading
1969	*Museum of Modern Art, Oxford
1970	*Plymouth City Art Gallery
and 1986	
1971	Institute of Contemporary Arts
	Peterloo Gallery, Manchester
	Dartington Hall, Devon and tour to Arnolfini, Bristol (see above)
1973	Leeds Playhouse
1974	Oxford Gallery, Oxford
and 1978	
1976	*Arts Council and South West Arts retrospective, tour: Plymouth City Art Gallery; Royal West of England Academy, Bristol; Serpentine Gallery; Chester Arts Centre; Laing Art Gallery, Newcastle; Leeds City Art Gallery; and Birmingham City Art Gallery. Smaller version, further tour from 1977 including Newlyn Art Gallery
1977	Le Balcon des Arts, Paris (shared)
1978	Compass Gallery, Glasgow
1980	Frans Wynans Gallery, Vancouver
and 1982	
1980	New Art Centre
and 1983	
1982	Rufford Craft Centre, Nottingham

	London, Ontario Regional Art Gallery
	Thielsen Galleries, Ontario
	Gloria Gallery, Nicosia (shared)
1986	*University of Reading and Newlyn Art Gallery, and tour to Plymouth (see above)
1987	Angela Flowers Gallery
1988	Gillian Jason Gallery
1989	Belgrave Gallery
	Austin/Desmond Gallery, works on paper
	*Mayor Gallery (catalogue contains biography, exhibitions list and bibliography)
1990	Austin/Desmond Fine Art, prints
	Austin/Desmond at Huxham, Exeter, prints
1993	Austin/Desmond Fine Art
	Tate Gallery, photographs
	Tate Gallery St Ives
1994	Peter Scott Gallery, Lancaster University
	Mayor Gallery
	Adelson Gallery, New York
	Belgrave Gallery
	Andrew Usiskin Fine Art
	Coram Gallery

SELECTED GROUP EXHIBITIONS

1951	Artists from St Ives, Mansard Gallery, Heal's
	Abstract Art, AIA Gallery (two shows the same year)
	Festival exhibition, Porthmeor Studios, St Ives
	Danish, British and American Abstract Art, Riverside Museum, New York
	Abstract Art, Gimpel Fils
1952	CAS exhibition, Tate Gallery
	Weekend exhibition, 22 Fitzroy Street
	British Abstract Art, Galerie de France, Paris
	The Mirror and the Square, AIA at the New Burlington Galleries and tour
1953	Space in Colour, Hanover Gallery
	Weekend exhibition, 22 Fitzroy Street
	CAS exhibition, Tate Gallery
1954	Abstract, Cubist, Formalist, Surrealist, Redfern Gallery
	Romantic Abstraction, Symon Quinn Gallery, Huddersfield
1955	Nine Abstract Artists, Redfern Gallery
	Pittsburgh International, Carnegie Institute
	50 Years of British Art, British Council tour
	6 Painters from Cornwall, British Council tour
1956	Recent Abstract Painting, Whitworth Art Gallery, Manchester
	Critic's Choice (Herbert Read), Arthur Tooth + Sons

	Six Painters from Britain, Canada tour
1957	Statements, ICA
	Metavisual, Tachiste, Abstract, Redfern Gallery
	Dimensions: British Abstract Art 1948–57, O'Hana Gallery
	British Art, Galerie Creuze, Paris
	Lissone International painting prize
	Tokyo International
	New Trends in British Art, Rome, New York
	John Moores Liverpool 1, Walker Art Gallery
1958	Pittsburgh Bicentennial, Carnegie Institute
	Guggenheim International, New York
	Gregory Fellowship exhibition, Bradford City Art Gallery
	Seven British Painters of Today, Welsh Arts Council tour
1959	Heron, Frost, Wynter, Hilton, Waddington Galleries
	Pittsburgh International, Carnegie Institute
	Guggenheim International, New York
	Recent Paintings by 7 British Artists, British Council tour to Australia and later, 1960–61, South America and Africa
	Seven British Painters of Today, Welsh Arts Council tour
	John Moores Liverpool 2, Walker Art Gallery
	The Developing Process, ICA
1960	British Painting 1720–1960, British Council tour to Russia
	Gregory Memorial exhibition, Leeds City Art Gallery
	Aspects, works on paper, Waddington Galleries
	Art Alive, Northampton Art Gallery
	The Penwith Society 10th Anniversary exhibition, Arts Council tour
1961	21st International Watercolour exhibition, Brooklyn Museum, New York
	Pittsburgh International, Carnegie Institute
	John Moores Liverpool 3, Walker Art Gallery
1962	Kompass II, Stedelijk Van Abbe Museum, Eindhoven
	British Art of the 20th Century, Gulbenkian Foundation, Lisbon and tour
	6 Painters, Waddington Galleries
	Howard Wise Collection, Walker Art Center, Minneapolis
	West Country Artists, Hanover Gallery
	British Art Today, San Francisco Museum of Art and tour
1963	British Painting in the Sixties, CAS at the Tate and Whitechapel Galleries

Some Aspects of Contemporary British
Painting, British Council tour to Canada
John Moores Liverpool 4, Walker Art
Gallery
The Dyer Bequest, Bristol City Art Gallery

1964 Contemporary British Painting and
Sculpture, Albright-Knox Art Gallery,
Buffalo
1954–1964: Painting and Sculpture of a
Decade, Gulbenkian Foundation
collection, Tate Gallery
New Painting 1961–64, Arts Council tour
Young British Painters, North Carolina
Museum of Art, Raleigh
British Contemporary Artists, New
Metropole Gallery, Folkestone
The Gregory Fellows, Arts Council tour
The Gregory Fellows, Queens Square
Gallery, Leeds

1965 John Moores Liverpool 5, Walker Art
Gallery
Corsham Painters and Sculptors, Arts
Council, Bath Festival and tour
Four Painters and Two Sculptors, Bangor
Art Gallery
Frost, Heron, Hilton, Wynter, Waddington
Galleries
Peter Stuyvesant Foundation collection
purchases, Whitechapel Art Gallery

1966 Blow, Frink and Frost, Prestons Art
Gallery, Bolton
Richard Demarco Gallery Inaugural
exhibition, Edinburgh
3rd Open painting exhibition, Ulster
Museum, Belfast
Metamorphosis, Sir Alfred Herbert
centenary exhibition, Herbert Art
Gallery, Coventry

1967 Recent British Painting, Stuyvesant
Collection exhibition, Tate Gallery
The Open One Hundred, David Hume
Tower, Edinburgh

1968 4th Open painting exhibition, Arts Council
of Northern Ireland, Belfast
Twelve Artists, Reading Museum and Art
Gallery
British Art Today, Hamburg Kunstverein

1969 John Moores Liverpool 7, Walker Art
Gallery
On Paper, graphics, Manchester College of
Further Education and the Ikon Gallery,
Birmingham

1970 British Painting 1960–1970, British
Council, National Gallery of Art,
Washington
AIA Retrospective 1930–1970, AIA Gallery

1972 More Love than Money: Ronnie Duncan
Collection, Park Square Gallery, Leeds
John Moores Liverpool 8, Walker Art
Gallery

1973 Brown, Christopher, Frost, Bath Festival
exhibition

1974 British Painting 1974, Arts Council,
Hayward Gallery
(from 1974 to about 1990, Terry Frost has
occasionally shown at Newlyn Art
Gallery)

1976 Clough, Frost, Heath, works on paper, JPL
Fine Arts
Colour, Southern Arts tour

1977 British Painting 1952–1977, Royal Academy
Cornwall 1945–77, New Art Centre
Artists at Curwen, Tate Gallery
Cyprus Summer School Staff exhibition,
Gallery Zygos, Nicosia
Pier Art Gallery exhibition, Tate Gallery

1979 Frost, Hilton, Nicholson and Pearce, Theo
Waddington
British Drawing Since 1945, Whitworth Art
Gallery, Manchester
Nicholson, Frost, Hilton, Waddington
Galleries

1980 St Ives Summer Festival Exhibition,
Penwith Galleries, St Ives
Hayward Annual, Arts Council, Hayward
Gallery
Pictures for an Exhibition, Whitechapel Art
Gallery

1982 Three Degrees of Frost, Prescote Gallery,
Banbury
Art from Cornwall, Galerie Artica,
Cuxhaven

1983 Printmakers exhibition, Royal College of
Art

1984 Landscape in Britain, Arts Council,
Hayward Gallery
English Contrasts, Artcurial, Paris
Homage to Herbert Read, Canterbury
College of Art
Frost, Paraskos, Charalambides, Gloria
Gallery, Nicosia

1985 St Ives 1939–64, Tate Gallery
One City a Patron, Southampton Art
Gallery collection exhibition, Scottish
Arts Council tour

1986 British Prints of the Post-War Years,
Redfern Gallery

1987 Looking West, Newlyn Art Gallery and the
Royal College of Art

1988 Camberwell Artists of the 1940s and 50s,
Belgrave Gallery

1988 Some of the Moderns, Belgrave Gallery
and 1989, 1990

1989 St Ives 1939–63, tour to Japan
The Presence of Painting, South Bank
Centre (formerly Arts Council), Mappin
Art Gallery, Sheffield and tour
Frost, Mitchell, O'Malley, Berkeley Square
Gallery
Painting the Visible World, Austin/
Desmond Fine Art
Corsham 1946–72, Michael Parkin Fine Art
and tour
Post-War British Art, Austin/Desmond

1991 20th century British painting and sculpture,
Belgrave Gallery

1992 Adelson Gallery, New York
British abstract artists of the 50s and 60s,
Belgrave Gallery
Realism to Abstraction, Bury St Edmunds
Art Gallery

1993 Royal Academy Summer Exhibition
Austin/Desmond Fine Art
Tate Gallery, collection and acquisitions

1994 Here and Now, Serpentine Gallery
Painters' Prints, Curwen Gallery
British Abstract Painting, Flowers East

Interviews

A LIST OF THE INTERVIEWS GIVEN BY
TERRY FROST THAT HAVE BEEN USED IN
THE PREPARATION OF THIS BOOK

(When an interview is in the Tate Archive it is noted as TGA
and a reference no. is given)

Tapes made in the course of collaborative preliminary
research for the Tate Gallery and the Carnegie
Institute, Pittsburgh, for what later became the Tate
Gallery's 'St Ives' exhibition, 1985:

David Lewis, Sarah Fox-Pitt, in Newlyn
(TGA: TAV 368 A,B) 10 April 1981

David Lewis, Sarah Fox-Pitt, in Newlyn
(TGA: TAV 370 A,B) 6 June 1981

David Lewis, Sarah Fox-Pitt, in Newlyn
(TGA: TAV 369 A,B) 17 April 1984

Tapes made by David Lewis for his own research:

Newlyn, 2 and 10 April 1979
Newlyn, December 1989
Newlyn, 16 December 1991
Newlyn, 23 July 1993
Pennsylvania, 15 October 1993

Tape made for 'Artists in Conflict' by the Department
of Sound Records at the Imperial War Museum:
(accession no. 000961/03) August 1977

Soundtrack for the film 'Colour Positive' made by
Barry Gavin for BBC tv's Omnibus
(TGA: TAV 273 A) November 1977

Tape made by Elizabeth Knowles for Newlyn Art
Gallery, interview conducted by Anthony Frost,
in Newlyn, March 1987

Tape made for the sound-track of a film on Terry
Frost made by Michael Milburn-Foster, interview
conducted by Adrian Heath and John Hoskin,
July 1987

Tape made by Mike von Joel for *Artline* magazine,
in Newlyn, 1989

Tape made by Sarah Fox-Pitt in preparation for an
archive display at the Tate:
(TGA: TAV 1217 A,B) May 1993

Tape made by Dave Lee of *Art Review* magazine,
in Newlyn, 1993

Index of works reproduced

In this list, all works are paintings unless otherwise stated

Note: the double spread on pages 154–155, the end-papers and the jacket design were all created in 1994 specially for this book.